NATIVE AMERICANS of CALIFORNIA

and NEVADA   by Jack D. Forbes

Illustration of Pomo Indian Dancer
on cover by Douglas Andrews

Paper Edition ISBN 0-911010-32-7
Cloth Edition ISBN 0-911010-33-5

Naturegraph Publishers, Healdsburg, California 95448

ii

JACK D. FORBES is the author of APACHE, NAVAHO AND SPANIARD (1960), THE INDIAN IN AMERICA'S PAST (1964), WARRIORS OF THE COLORADO: THE YUMAS OF THE QUECHAN NATION AND THEIR NEIGHBORS (1965), MEXICAN-AMERICANS: A HANDBOOK (1967), AFRO-AMERICANS IN THE FAR WEST: A HANDBOOK (1967), NEVADA INDIANS SPEAK (1967), and EDUCATION OF THE CULTURALLY DIFFERENT: A MULTI-CULTURAL APPROACH (1968). He is also the author of numerous articles on minority group history and culture and is himself of Powhatan Indian descent. Dr. Forbes has taught at the University of Southern California, Citrus College, San Fernando Valley State College, and the University of Nevada, and has held research fellowships from the Social Science Research Council and the John Simon Guggenheim Memorial Foundation.

THE FAR WEST LABORATORY FOR EDUCATIONAL RESEARCH AND DEVELOPMENT is a regional educational laboratory, established through a Joint Powers Agreement in February, 1966. Present signatories include the Regents of the University of California, the California State Board of Education, the Trustees of the California State Colleges, the County Superintendent of Schools of the County of Monterey, the Board of Education of the San Francisco Unified School District, the Regents of the University of Nevada, and the Nevada State Board of Education.

Portions of work reported herein were performed pursuant to a contract with the U. S. Department of Health, Education and Welfare, Office of Education.

PREFACE

Leaders in the field of Indian education and Indian affairs in California and Nevada have frequently asserted that they are in great need of an introductory synthesis dealing with the history and socio-cultural evolution of native groups living in the region, especially as this subject is relevant to contemporary issues in education and community development.

This handbook is primarily designed to provide an introduction to the evolution of Native American peoples in the Far West (with strong emphasis upon California-Nevada), especially in relation to those historical-cultural experiences likely to have contributed to the present-day conditions of native communities and individuals. Secondarily, it is designed to provide an introduction to basic concepts relating to Indian studies (for those who wish to delve deeper or construct curricular units) and to the multi-cultural, community relevant approach to Indian education.

This handbook is not completely comprehensive, especially as regards detailed descriptions of native cultures at the time of initial European contact. Excellent sources, such as A. L. Kroeber's Handbook of the Indians of California and R. F. Heizer and M. A. Whipple's California Indians: A Source Book are available to fill the need for that kind of information.

Every effort has been made to utilize native groups' own names for themselves in order to avoid a kind of colonialism in nomenclature. Unfortunately, many groups still have not made their own choices clear. Thus the reader should not regard the names utilized herein as the "last word" on the subject but should rather check with local Indian organizations as to their current preferences.

Needless to state, the viewpoint presented herein is that of the writer and not necessarily that of the various organizations making the publication of the handbook possible.

Finally, the author wishes to acknowledge the assistance of many individuals including especially the research assistance of Tina Bergquist and the typing of Theo Campbell.

Jack D. Forbes
Berkeley, California
September 1968

A Special Note for the Non-Indian
Reader

It is regrettable but true that most non-Indians in the United
States have received a "mis-education" as regards the story of the
Indian experience in North America. This "mis-education" is largely
the result of the ignoring of factual Indian history in the schools,
thereby allowing romantic mythology and stereotypical mass media to
fill the vacuum so created. The tragic result of all of this is that
while most non-Indians have a vague idea that Indians were "wronged"
at some remote time period they have no accurate notion of what actually took place or of the continuing reality of Indian life in this
country up to the present date.

The Indian experience in California since 1769 has been an especially ugly one. The author has made no effort in the pages which
follow to "tone-down" or soften the often harsh realities of native
history in the region being dealt with. Some non-Indians, who are
unfamiliar with this reality, may be offended by the approach pursued but it is believed that corrective steps to alter the problems
apparent in contemporary Indian conditions must be based upon an ab-
solutely frank understanding of the real world which has surrounded
native life. It would be unfair to the educator or worker in Indian-
related projects to do otherwise.

Finally, the author wishes to state that he does not assign any
kink of "collective guilt" to the white population as regards what
has happened in the past. The future, though, is a different matter,
for we all have a responsibility which cannot be brushed aside. The
kind of society which is now being brought into existence is our collective challenge.

J. D. F.

TABLE OF CONTENTS

FRONTISPIECE

David Risling, Hoopa president of the California Indian Education Association, 1969. Photograph by Dennis Galloway.

INTRODUCTION: THE SIGNIFICANCE

OF THE NATIVE PEOPLE AND

HERITAGE

The Biological Legacy

It is estimated that there are more than thirty million Americans speaking native Indian languages living in the Americas today, while perhaps as many as one hundred million Americans possess some degree of native ancestry. The native genetic heritage is clearly the dominant strain in Paraguay, Bolivia, Peru, Ecuador, Mexico, Greenland, and most of Central America, while indigenous ancestry is one of the important elements in the racially-mixed populations of Chile, Colombia, Venezuela, Brazil, and Panama. Elsewhere in the Americas, as in the United States, Canada, the West Indies, Uruguay and Argentina, the Indian racial heritage has been important in certain regions or provinces but has tended to be absorbed within a dominantly African or European population. Nonetheless, "Indians" and tribal groups survive in every mainland American republic (except in Uruguay where a rural mestizo or mixed-blood population alone survives) and even on a few Caribbean islands.

It is difficult to estimate the number of persons of native descent currently residing in the United States because the census has never sought to enumerate all such persons and because much mixture took place during the colonial period. There are, however, at least five million individuals with a significant degree of Indian ancestry, including some 600,000 members of tribal organizations and the bulk of the Mexican-Americans, Afro-Americans, Puerto Ricans, French Canadians, and other persons possess varying degrees of native descent. Black Americans, in particular, share in the Indian genetic legacy. One survey indicates that about one-third of the Afro-Americans sampled know of an Indian ancestor. Historical records indicate extensive African-Indian inter-mingling in the West Indies and the southern United States during the colonial period. Entire tribal groups were absorbed into the black population in the South and the West Indies and that process continues in some areas to the present day.

Therefore, it is quite obvious that the genetic legacy of the Native American is great indeed, especially as one considers the whole of the Americas. It is also apparent from population statistics that the Indian and part-Indian peoples of the Americas are increasing

in number at a rapid rate, particularly as compared with predominantly middle-class European-derived groups. In the United States,
as well as in Latin America, the Indian-part Indian population
possesses a very high birth rate and the proportion of persons of
native descent in the total population will doubtless steadily
increase in the future.

It may well be that as many as 30 million (maximum estimate)
or 10 million (minimum estimate) United States citizens possess
some degree of indigenous American ancestry. For the majority of
these people, of course, the amount of Indian "blood" is propor-
tionally slight but the fact of a firm genetic connection with
America's ancient past is a reality nonetheless. For example, a
person whose last pure Indian ancestor was born in approximately
1800 could be descended from as many as 2,000 Indians who were
living when Christopher Columbus first landed in the Bahamas. Interestingly, because Indian "marriage circles" in the United States
(the group from which marriage partners were normally obtained)
seldom numbered more than 3,000 persons, a person of 1/64 Indian
descent today, whose last pure Indian ancestor was born in ca.
1800 can statistically possess as many Indian ancestors living in
1400-1440 as a person of "full-blood" Indian ancestry living today.
Thus a person with a small proportion of native ancestry nonetheless has a significant connection with the history of the given
group of Native American people to which he is related, supposing,
of course, that he is aware of the connection and its ramifica-
tions, and supposing also that he is inclined to identify in any
way with distant ancestors and/or relatives.

Should intermarriage rates between persons of part-Indian
and non-Indian descent continue to climb it is theoretically
possible that by the period 2050 - 2100 the majority of United States
citizens could be of part-Indian descent, although the knowledge
of any Indian ancestor will be nonexistent for most individuals.
At the same time, however, the population of many tribal groups
(such as the Navajo) should be significantly larger than today.

In summary, the biological or genetic legacy of the Native
American is of considerable significance, especially from Mexico
to Paraguay. In the United States, it would seem clear that the
modern North American people have collective roots which extend
not only to Europe, Africa, and Asia but also back into the
ancient American past.*

---

*See Jack D. Forbes, The Indian in America's Past (1964), for
further information on race mixture.

The Historical and Cultural Legacy

The way of life of the dominant population in the United States is often referred to as "Western European" or simply as "Western" (i.e., a part of "Western Civilization"). In point of fact, however, much that is basic to this way of life originated in the Middle East and North Africa (the wheel, monumental architecture, supra-tribal political organizations, horticulture, Christianity, Judaism, et cetera). The culture of the dominant North American population is thus a very mixed or heterogeneous heritage.

This mixed heritage, which has become the common legacy of all North American people, also derives a significant part of its character from contributions made by Native American groups. To a considerable degree all who reside in the United States have become "Indianized" while at the same time, of course, Indians have become "Europeanized." Unfortunately, this process of borrowing from the native population has been largely overlooked by students of so-called "American Civilization" and is, therefore, not well understood by the average citizen.

The various European groups which invaded North America several centuries ago were all proud and ethnocentric peoples. They ordinarily considered themselves to be superior to other, culturally different populations and even, in some instances, held themselves to be divinely-ordained conquerors or "civilizers." This supremely egotistical viewpoint led the English and the Spanish, in particular, to minimize the native influence upon the styles of living which gradually evolved in the conquered portions of North America. That the English of Virginia and New England were, for example, economically dependent upon native inventions (tobacco, maize, hominy, squash, pumpkins, maple syrup, et cetera) did not lead to more favorable attitudes towards the Indians nor did this dependence lead to any early intellectual recognition of the presence of a modified culture.

Tragically, the ethnocentric insularity of Anglo-Americans (English-speaking persons) did not diminish with time. Even as the English way of life was being modified by forest warfare tactics, the fur trade, the Indian slave trade, dressed deerskin clothing, the canoe, the toboggan, the political influence of the Iroquois confederation, thousands of native place names, hundreds of Indian words, and numerous other items, the Anglo-American persisted in obscuring the origin of these changes. The way of life and style of dress of Daniel Boone, for example, was highly Indianized but Boone was not, and is not, regarded as an Indianized person. Rather, his type of deerskin clothing has been regarded

simply as a "pioneer" style variant of Anglo-American culture.
Each trait borrowed from the native was emotionally "assimilated"
and thereby became, in the popular mind, a non-Indian trait.

In the same manner, of course, the Anglo-American has taken
over Afro-American musical contributions and made them emotionally
his own.

The significance of this circumstance consists in the fact
that while the European has indeed become Americanized (Indianized)
and Africanized, this process has not served to materially diminish
the Anglo's ethnocentric conviction of cultural superiority. The
latter is sustained, in great measure, by sheer ignorance as regard
the origin of much of what the Anglo regards as "his own."

Contributing to this ignorance has been the fact that Anglo-
American scholars who write about North American history have
tended to be products of their own particular ethnic past. That
is, they have ordinarily seen historical events through the eyes
of Anglo-American "pioneers" and "empire-builders." Thus most
general histories of the United States are not histories of North
America as a region nor are they histories of all of the many
peoples who have resided in and contributed to the evolution of
the United States. On the contrary, most such works are essentially
chronicles of the Anglo-European conquest and of the development of
the English-speaking white people during the succeeding four centuries. One test of any work which purports to be a general history
of America is whether it commences with the 20,000 year story of
the Native Americans or whether it dismisses the "aborigines" as a
part of the "environment" and focuses its initial attention upon
the "Old World" heritage of the colonists.

As this writer stated some years ago:

If the history of America is properly only the Anglo-
European conquest, then the history of England would be only
the Germanic conquest and subsequent events, which would
obviously be absurd. English history begins with the earliest period that English historians can discover and then
deals with the various Celtic groups, the Roman occupation,
the later Celtic states, and finally the Germanic conquest.
To leave out the pre-Germanic period would be to leave out
an important part of the history of England, and in the
same way the leaving out of the story of the Native American
has rendered American history incomplete. (See Jack D. Forbes,
"The Historian and the Indian: Racial Bias in American History,"
The Americas, April 1963. pp. 349 - 362).

It is clear that Anglo-American ethnocentrism, whether displayed by scholars or laymen, has contributed to the obscuring of
the actual extent to which modern United States culture is of non-
European origin. In addition, this ethnocentrism has often prevented European-Americans from becoming a real part of the region
in which they reside. Fostered in great measure by public school
curricula, a process has developed wherein Anglo-Americans largely
ignore the rich past of the region in which they live in order to
focus attention upon increasingly tenuous connections with the
Atlantic Seaboard colonial period and even more tenuous connections
with "Old England."

California public school pupils, for example, learn a great
deal about Plymouth Colony and the Mayflower but very little about
the native pioneers of the "Golden West." They are, all too often,
cut off from meaningful contact with the history of the hills and
valleys in which they actually live because educators (following
the lead of the historians referred to above) tend to still be
engaged in an essentially ethnocentric approach to curricula, which
approach is of necessity focused upon the Anglo-American past, and
that past is, of course, largely alien to the history of the hills
and valleys of a region such as California.

1. Indian feather headdress. n. Decorative basketry tubes. 3. Pomo feather
basket. Old drawings of G. Langsdorf . Courtesy Bancroft Library, Berkeley.

The Indian People

The significance of the Native American legacy does not consist solely in the biological or cultural contributions made to
society at large. It also consists in a rapidly growing population of modern Indian people who will continue to make a rich
contribution to American life and who, in many areas, will comprise the dominant population. In that region of the Americas
sometimes referred to as Indo-America (the region from Mexico to
Paraguay), Indian and part-Indian people comprise the majority of
the population. It may very well be that the Guarani, Quechua,
Maya, and other native-speaking peoples of Indo-America will, in
the not too distant future, acquire the political and social dominance in their respective homelands which their numbers warrant.

In the United States and Canada, the 850,000 members of tribal
organizations or native communities constitute a small minority of
the total population, but their significance is all out of proportion to their total numbers. In part, this is because native
people tend to be highly concentrated in certain regions, such as
the Southwest, Oklahoma, the Dakotas and the Alaskan-Canadian
arctic, as well as in certain counties or districts within other
areas.

The contemporary significance of the Native American is also
derived from his importance as a continuous contributor to our
socio-cultural life. And here one must go beyond such items as
ceramics, basketry, painting, sculpture, folk-lore and music to the
even more significant realm of religion, world-view, and inter-
personal relations. In religion, for instance, modern theologians
(as well as "Hippies") seem to be arriving at world-views strik-
ingly like that of many ancient Native American religions. It is
to be suspected that these modern thinkers and experimenters have
a great deal to learn from Indian religion and philosophy which,
after all, arrived at similar viewpoints centuries ago. Many
might agree, for example, that the Indian concepts of Manitou (the
all-pervading "divine" power or spirit) and Wakan-Tanka (the
Great Mystery or Great Spirit) represent very appropriate ways of
referring to the ultimate spiritual foundation of life.

Of great importance is the fact that American Indian religions,
like all great traditions, focus upon the development of moral men
possessing a deep awareness of their relationship with the total
universe. The Sioux religious leader Black Elk (Hehaka Sapa) has
stated:

peace...comes within the souls of men when they
realize their relationship, their oneness, with
the universe and all its powers, and when they
realize that at the center of the Universe dwells
Wakan-Tanka, and that this center is really everywhere, it is within each of us.

John Epes Brown, who studied under Black Elk, points out
that

such knowledge cannot be realized unless there
be perfect humility, unless man humbles himself
before the entire creation, before each smallest
ant, realizing his own nothingness. Only in being
nothing may man become everything, and only then
does he realize his essential brotherhood with all
forms of life. His centre, or his Life, is the
same centre or Life of all that is. (John Epes
Brown, "The Spiritual Legacy of the American Indian,"
Tomorrow, Autumn 1964, pp. 297-307).

The socio-political implications of the Native American
approach to life could, indeed, be profound in several dimensions.
This writer has suggested that:

In this age of "mass" culture and revolutionary
social change, in this era of large-scale alienation
and personal anonymity, it is especially important
that the small folk society be provided with the means
of survival and development.

Modern nations have, with little thought, allowed the
development of industrialized mass society to proceed
in such a way as to destroy many of the social and
cultural relationships which give meaning to human life.
The results speak for themselves: crime, juvenile de-
linquency, high suicide rates, widespread mental ill-
ness, escapist activities of all kinds, and an often
cheap commercialized way of life which affords no real
satisfaction for the average person. Loneliness in
the midst of crowds and nothing meaningful to do in
the midst of hyper-activity typifies the modern mass
culture...

Mankind has at least one hope, however, and that is
that the numerous tribal and folk societies which
still survive in almost every part of the world can

be provided with the means for self-protection
and self-realization... Tribes and folk societies can and do provide their people with a
way of life which is usually much more psychologically healthy and meaningful than do mass
cultures, and...we must allow the smaller societies to preserve themselves in order to provide
mankind with a continuing alternative to the
super-culture and super-society. (Jack D. Forbes,
"Tribes and Masses: the Self-Development of Folk
Societies," unpublished ms.).

John Collier, Commissioner of Indian Affairs from 1933 to
1945, felt that the world at large had a great deal to learn
from the socio-religious orientation of still-functioning native
societies:

They had what the world has lost. They have it
now. What the world has lost, the world must have
again lest it die. Not many years are left to
have or have not, to recapture the lost ingredient...
What, in our human world, is this power to live?
It is the ancient, lost reverence and passion for
human personality, joined with the ancient, lost
reverence and passion for the earth and its web of
life.

This indivisible reverence and passion is what the
American Indians almost universally had; and
representative groups of them have it still.

If our modern world should be able to recapture
this power, the earth's natural resources and
web of life would not be irrevocably wasted
within the twentieth century, which is the prospect now. True democracy, founded in neighborhoods and reaching over the world, would become
the realized heaven on earth. And living peace--
not just an interlude between wars--would be born
and would last through ages... (John Collier,
Indians of the Americas, 1948 pp. 7 ff.).

Finally, the Indian people must be regarded as an extremely
significant portion of the North American population because in
their present condition and in their life-history since the 1580's
they serve as perhaps the key witness to the "true" character of
the dominant Anglo-American group. As this writer wrote in 1966:

The Indians are a looking-glass into the souls of
North Americans. If we want to dissect the Anglo
and analyze his character we must find out what he
does when no one else cares, when no one is in a
position to thwart his will--when he can do as he
pleases. And with the Indian the Anglo has done
what he pleased, with no one to care, and with the
Indian ultimately too weak to resist, except
passively...(Jack D. Forbes, "The Indian: Looking
Glass into the Souls of White Americans," Liberator,
August 1966, pp. 6-9; September 1966, pp. 14-17).

The North American native people, then, constitute a unique
"test" for the real intentions and most deeply-held values of Anglo-
Americans. The history of the North American white population, their
present beliefs, and their future behavior cannot be understood without examining very closely the treatment accorded those relatively
powerless native groups under their control and subject, ultimately,
to their will.

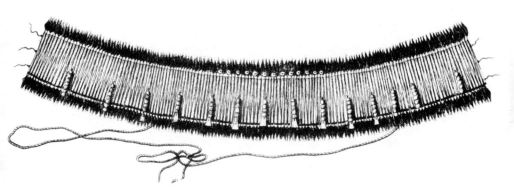

2. Pomo flicker feather band dance headress. Old drawing of G. Langsdorf.
Courtesy Bancroft Library, Berkeley, California.

II. THE EVOLUTION OF NATIVE CALIFORNIA AND NEVADA

The Origin of the First Westerners

The ancient past of the native peoples of the Americas is shrouded in mystery, and it is quite possible that this will always be so. Virtually all native groups in the Americas have regarded themselves as having been created in or at least near their own homelands, and certainly it is true that in an important psychological sense most Indians had become literally a "part" of the locality in which they lived. Native Americans ordinarily exhibited an extreme attachment to their place of birth and to their native environment, a degree of attachment hardly to be comprehended by semi-nomadic European-Americans. Thus, no matter where the ultimate geographical "home" of American Indians may have been, their spiritual "home" is located firmly in the Americas.

The European newcomers to the Americas could not believe that their holy book, the Christian Bible, had failed to take note of the history of the Native American's ancestors. The Europeans were, of course, in possession of their own origin myth, borrowed from the Hebrews (who in turn had adapted it from earlier Semitic peoples). It was doctrinally necessary that American Indians be linked to this origin tale and the most common device, first conceived by Spanish writers, was to suggest that the American natives were descended from one of the "lost tribes" of ancient Israel.

"Lost tribes" or not, subsequent European writers almost always look for Indian origins outside of the Americas, although increasingly this search took the form of pseudo-scientific or scientific scholarship. Unfortunately, this endeavor has failed to yield evidence answering any of the basic questions apt to be asked by a layman.

Certain concepts seem to be supported by growing bodies of data, such as the thesis that all present day humans belong to a single species and experienced a common ultimate origin (perhaps in Africa), and, secondly, that the ancient Americans possessed occasional contacts with Asia, Polynesia, and Europe. (These documented contacts are, however, too late in time to explain the initial peopling of the Americas, especially in the case of Polynesia and Europe). If it is correct that all peoples originated in Africa or Eurasia then, of course, it would follow that the Native Americans' ancestors must have migrated to the Americas from elsewhere. A glance at a map would suggest a route from Asia via Bering Strait to Alaska, but thus far no solid evidence has been found to document this thesis. No archaeological remains found in either Siberia or Alaska are ancient enough to shed light upon such far-off migrations, and it may well be that most of the early sites were along the coast and are now covered with water due to the post glacial rise of level of the oceans.

The physical characteristics of Native American peoples were at one time thought to link them with the so-called Mongoloid peoples of Asia, but the problem is now generally seen to be much more complex than was formerly supposed. For one thing, the American Indian peoples did not comprise a physically uniform population. Although the variations in physical type found in the Americas are not as great as those found in Eurasia or Africa, they nonetheless are great enough to suggest that perhaps several different ancestral groups mixed either before or after migration to this hemisphere.

In any event, it would be a mistake to think of Native Americans as part of a "Mongoloid" racial family since several of the more important characteristics of the so-called classic Mongoloid type are virtually absent among American Indians (such as B and AB blood types and the epicanthic eye-fold). This writer would suggest that Native Americans, by and large, comprise a population standing somewhat between the extreme Caucasoid and Mongoloid types and may represent either the end-product of the mixture of several Mongoloid and Caucasoid type groups or the survival of the type from which Mongoloid and Caucasoid are both derived. The reader should, however, be aware that such terms as Caucasoid, Mongoloid, Negroid, et cetera, are almost completely discredited as referring to "races" (groups of people who are genetically distinct) and are used herein only as simplistic illustrative devices. (See Jack D. Forbes, Afro-Americans in the Far West, 1967, for a discussion of the concept of race).

In point of fact, one must (initially at least) deal with each Indian people as a separate descent group (usually coupled with its immediate neighbors), with physical characteristics which are somewhat unique. We may collectively use such terms as "Americanoid" or American Indian, but we do not know that such different peoples as the heavily bearded natives of San Francisco Bay, the light-skinned delicately featured natives of central Panama, and the sharp-featured Indians of the central-eastern United States do, in fact, possess the same genetic history. In all likelihood, they possess both common and divergent ancestries.

In summary, the current stage of knowledge in relation to Native American origins is such that the prudent student should refrain from accepting sweeping theories and should wish to maintain a skeptical attitude. We simply do not possess any certain answers and it is best to frankly acknowledge this fact.

The Earliest Americans

Throughout the Americas archaeologists have been studying sites which may indicate that man has been present here for perhaps 40,000 years. These sites vary from collections of burned organic material or

animal bones to assemblages of so-called core and flake tools. Unfortunately, the dateable sites (dateable by chemical analysis) are not
always clearly of human origin while the very primitive "chopper" tool
assemblages are usually not found in association with anything which
can be dated to everyone's satisfaction.

Nonetheless a number of archaeologists are coming to accept the
existence of an American way of life which preceded the development of
projectile points (stone heads for spears and knives) and which is almost
solely represented by crude percussion - produced pebble tools and
"hearths" (places where portions of animals were burned, presumably as
a part of a cooking process). If such a way of life did indeed exist
(and many archaeologists are still doubtful), it came to an end about
13,000 b.p. (b.p. = before the present) in the central United States and
perhaps 9,000 b.p. in the west.

Although positive evidence for the existence of a pre-13,000 b.p.
pre-projectile point stage is still inconclusive, certain indirect arguments suggest at least the possibility that perhaps a few humans may
have been in the Americas for a long period of time. First, it would
seem likely that the post-13,000 cultures (which produced excellent
spear-points) were preceded by more primitive stone-workers; and,
second, the last glaciation of the Pleistocene period (the "Ice Age")
is thought to have covered virtually all of Canada and the northern
United States with ice sheets similar to those which still survive on
Greenland. This vast barrier to passage from Siberia-Alaska is thought
to have endured from 40,000 to 11,000 b.p. (or perhaps 13,500 b.p. in
the Pacific Northwest). If men were south of the ice in 15,000 - 13,000
(which seems highly likely) it is possible to argue that they would have
had to pass to the south from Siberia-Alaska before 40,000 b.p. because
otherwise the ice would have forced them to remain in the latter area
until ca. 11,000 b.p. (Siberia and Alaska were only partially glaciated
during the ice age and were connected by a wide land bridge).

The evidence at hand, though, only allows us to assert with confi-
dence that by 13,000 - 10,000 b.p. early Americans were hunting now-extinct big game animals in various parts of the Americas south of Canada,
using unique kinds of spear-points and knives not found anywhere else in
the world. Farther north, in Alaska and northeastern Siberia, nothing,
so far as we now can prove, was happening at all (since no really early
sites have turned up in northeastern Siberia and the oldest sites in
Alaska and northern Canada are of doubtful antiquity).

Quite obviously, we can say little with certainty about the earliest
Americans, except that they may have lived here as early as 40,000 years
ago, that they may have produced crude pebble tools, that they may have
burned portions of now-extinct animals in large pits or hearths, and
that they may have wandered in from Siberia between ice ages, (but leaving no certain trace of their passage behind). Above all, we can say
nothing about what they looked like, since so few skeletal remains
definitely older than 10,000 b.p. have been located in the Americas

and very little has been found dating from the 9,000 - 5,000 b.p. period. (It should be noted that very recently a human skull found at Laguna Beach, California, has been dated at 17,000 b.p. by the radiocarbon method).

Ancient American Cultures

Beginning about 13,000 years ago ancient Americans began to produce spear points and knives which represent, especially by 11,000 b.p., an impressive command of point making technology. Little is known about the material culture of these people, aside from their "points" and unlined hearths, and almost nothing is known of their non-material culture or physical appearance. It does seem almost certain though, that they were big game hunters, moving about in pursuit of large mammals (such as the now extinct large bison, the mammoth, and the mastodon) and that they may have been in great part responsible for the killing off, largely by 9,000 b.p., of the old Pleistocene herd animals.

Interestingly, projectile points of a basically similar nature are found in southern-most South America as early as 11,000 b.p., thus indicating that the Americas as a whole were going through an ancient "technological revolution" virtually simultaneously. Also quite significant is the fact that the projectile point tradition developed in the Americas was unlike that of interior Asia, was apparently an independent development, and later spread to northeastern Asia from America. It should also be noted that the big game hunting complex described above was apparently not very significantly developed in the California-Nevada region, although points of this early type are found in the Far West on occasion.

Perhaps as early as 12,000 - 10,000 b.p. vegetable food-grinding tools appear in the southwestern United States at one site and this represents an important event, for between 10,000 and 9,000 years ago the big game hunters were forced to alter their style of life due to the gradual disappearance of the large herd mammals although the Mammoth may have survived to 8,000 - 7,000 in southern Arizona. The "economic revolution" which ensued in both Americas is typified by the appearance of food-grinding tools (such as manos, milling stones, and, later, mortars and pestles), new kinds of spear and atlatl (spear-thrower)points, and the presence of human burials.

This stage of development in most of the far west and southwest is called the "Desert Culture" stage, because the area was becoming progressively drier. This tradition, which endured for thousands of years, was typified by the importance of tools useful in vegetable food consumption and the relative unimportance of tools designed for hunting, except in certain localities. In the intermountain west, the Desert Culture stage also featured the use of caves or rock-shelters for housing, bark or grass beds, twined basketry, netting, matting, fur cloth, sandals (moccasins rare), the atlatl, relatively small projectile points, flat milling stones, scrapers and choppers, digging sticks, fire drills and hearths, wooden clubs, tubular smoking pipes, sea shell ornaments, deer-hoof rattles, medicine bags or pouches, bird-bone whistles, and other items.

It is quite clear, thanks to the preservation of wooden and fiber materials in dry caves, that the American westerners of 9,000 - 8,000 years ago possessed a rich inventory of utensils and that they were resourceful and inventive people. (It is likely that many of these traits evolved during the preceding Big Game Hunting period but the open camp sites of that era would not have allowed for the preservation of perishable materials).

Farther west, in the southern California deserts, a series of sites reveal what some writers have termed a "Western Hunting Culture" because food-grinding tools are largely absent. Between 9,000 and 7,000 years ago, the natives of this area produced heavy projectile points (for the atlatl probably) and a small number of other stone tools, but these assemblages are largely found around the high shore lines of now dry lakes (such as Lake Mohave) or in other unprotected sites, so that wooden or fibre materials could not be expected to survive. A very similar culture, or series of cultures, also existed along the Pacific Coast, modified to some degree by the gathering of shell-fish (California coastal seashells were being traded into the Great Basin as early as 9,000 years ago).

About 7,000 b.p. the Desert and Western Hunting traditions began to experience changes in southern Arizona, where the Cochise Culture developed, and in California, where the Milling Stone Horizon appeared. The Cochise tradition gradually moved into a pre-horticultural phase which placed great emphasis upon wild vegetable foods and then, after coming under Mexican influence, into a horticultural period which ultimately evolved into the advanced cultures of Arizona and New Mexico.

In the coastal regions of southern California (and into the San Joaquin Valley) about 7,000 b.p. (or perhaps later) the Milling Stone Horizon featured a way of life emphasizing vegetable plant gathering, shell-fish collecting, and some minimal hunting. Projectile point technology appears to have declined in this period, probably because the hunting of large game was no longer important. Sites are characterized by deep-basined metates, manos, scrapers, choppers, hammerstones, some bone tools, and burials (with the body flexed, extended flat, or subsequently reburied).

Local variations are apparent among the coastal peoples, as along the Santa Barbara coast where shell-fish were apparently not being utilized (indicating perhaps an occupation by interior-dwellers who were new to a coastal environment). In the interior desert areas, in the meantime, the "Western Hunting" tradition apparently endured with little change until about 5,000 b.p. when the Pinto spear point (used on the atlatl) appears along with some milling stones. Thus the Southern California desert peoples would appear to have been moving in the direction of the Desert Culture stage (with vegetable food utilization) but the hunting of game apparently remained of greater importance than in areas farther east and north. Post holes found near Little Lake, California would seem to be the first evidence of houses found in this portion of the west.

On the whole, the California desert, from Owens Valley to the Mexican boundary, remained a conservative area, changing but little until about 2,000 b.p. Coastal southern California also changed slowly, although in the Santa Barbara region a number of new traits appear, including the basket-hopper mortar (perhaps indicating the perfection of the important acorn-leaching process), the mortar and pestle, heavy projectile points (with an emphasis upon hunting and shell-fish), massive bone and shell-beads, and flexed burials with the grave materials covered with red ocher coloring.

In northern Nevada the Desert Culture tradition underwent a series of changes after 4,000 b.p. as a part of an adjustment to life along the shores of a number of large lakes which existed at that time. Duck decoys, nets, fishhooks, feather robes, cordage, snares, twined bags, and twined and coiled baskets were made by these early Nevadans, along with many stone, bone, and wood tools. By 2,000 b.p. some early traits, such as the use of the atlatl, were dropping away (to be replaced by the bow and arrow) but a large number of characteristics continue onward into more recent times as a part of the way of life of the Northern Paiute and adjacent peoples. As Jesse D. Jennings has stated: "the facts are that one can argue for a cultural continuum, with increasingly marked regional variation in technological details, in the Great Basin up until historic times " (Jennings and Norbeck, eds., Prehistoric Man in the New World, 1964, p. 161).

At about the same time as northern Nevadans were adjusting to a lakeshore environment, in the 4,000's b.p., central Californians were entering what is known as the Early Horizon. In this, the first well-known culture for the northern two-thirds of California, the Native Americans exhibited a considerable interest in the after-life and religion by rigidly disposing of the dead in a face-downward, fully extended manner with extensive grave offerings. The material existence of the people included the use of large, heavy projectile points, shell ornaments, slab metates, mortars, fiber-tempered baked clay balls and twined basketry. The atlatl was the principal weapon and warfare would appear to have been uncommon (due to the absence of skeletons exhibiting signs of violent death).

By 3,500 b.p. the central Californian way of life was altered some-what by the introduction of flexed burials, some cremating, coiled bas-ketry, the wooden mortar, barbed harpoons, and the bow and arrow (used in addition to the atlatl). Village sites were larger, indicating a more extensive population, signs of warfare are common in burials, and grave goods are uncommon except in connection with cremations. This latter

may indicate an increasing emphasis upon wealth-display (and accumula-
tion by certain individuals), a characteristic typical of northwestern
California at a much later date.

During the 3,000's (at the latest) people began to live in villages
along the shores of San Francisco Bay, where their dependence upon shell
fish gradually led to the building up of large "shellmounds." Farther
south, natives began inhabiting the bulk of the Channel Islands (Santa
Rosa Island may have been inhabited earlier), thus indicating the evolution of a strongly maritime-oriented way of life.

Cultural Elaboration and Variation in the Far West

Important changes began to take place throughout the Southwest and
Far West shortly before the time of Christ, stimulated in great measure
by the existence of advanced cultures in Mexico. As early as 5,000 -
6,000 b.p. a crude variety of maize horticulture had apparently spread
from Mexico to southern New Mexico. During the period 3,000 - 2,000 b.p.
new crops (beans, squash, and better varieties of maize) were acquired
by border-area Southwesterners and a new stage, that of Horticultural
Desert Culture, ensued. By 2,300 b.p. pottery was borrowed from Mexico
and a line of cultural evolution commenced (known as Mogollon) which
contributes in many ways to the development of the Anasazi (Pueblo
Indian) heritage farther north.

At about 2,000 b.p. another significant tradition appears in the
Gila River area of Southern Arizona, a tradition now thought to be
ancestral to the later Ootam (Pima-Papago) way of life. This tradition
included such traits as horticulture (not very advanced), cremation,
pottery, and the carving of fine bowls and utensils from stone. These
traits are significant because they appear to spread into California
gradually. For example, southern Arizona type horticulture reached the
Colorado River between 1000 - 1200 A.D.and still later spread westward
as far as the southern California desert areas and to near the coast
in northern Baja California. Southern Arizona type pottery spread to
the Colorado River in the 1000 - 1200 A.D. period also, and later spread
towards the coast, reaching the latter in the San Luis Rey area only
about 1500 - 1700 A.D. Carving bowls and utensils of soft stone spread
more rapidly (apparently) to the Pacific Coast, perhaps reaching the
Channel Islands region by 500 - 1000 A.D. (or earlier). (Interestingly
this steatite [soap-stone] industry comes to dominate the Santa Barbara-
Los Angeles region to such an extent that the spread of pottery is
apparently greatly slowed down). Whether or not cremation spread solely
from southern Arizona or originated independently in central California
is not clear, but it seems highly likely that the cremation practiced
in southern California after 500 - 1000 A.D. was largely or wholly
derived from the southeast.

By 2,000 b.p. the Horticultural Desert stage appears also in the San Juan River drainage area of Utah and Arizona where it is known, somewhat erroneously, as "Basketmaker." We shall refer to it as Pre-Anasazi, since it leads directly into the later development of Anasazi cultures. Between 2000 and 1600 b.p. the San Juan-area natives developed a way of life which was transitional between the Desert Culture (described earlier) and the Anasazi, and which resembled the Horticultural Desert stage in southeastern Arizona-New Mexico and the much later cultures of such desert groups as the Yavapai, Hualpai, Havasupai, and Southern Paiute. This stage lacked pottery (present in later Horticultural Desert cultures) but possessed a poor variety of maize, squash, slab-lined cists, cave-storage areas where baskets, bags, sandals, nets and cords have been found, and, rarely, houses of wood enclosed in mud mortar. The atlatl served as the principal weapon.

Interestingly, the crops planted by the Pre-Anasazi (and by the later Anasazi as well) were not derived from the Mogollon or Pre-Ootam cultures but apparently came from Mexico via the Texas-Plains area.

About 1600 b.p. (400 A.D.) the Pre-Anasazi Americans came heavily under the influence of natives to the south and east, acquiring traits such as semi-subterranean houses lined with stone slabs, pottery, beans and new varieties of maize. The bow and arrow appeared later, perhaps near 600 - 700 A.D., probably coming in from the north. (Interestingly, the bow and arrow appeared in the Desert Culture of northern Nevada before 2,000 b.p. and in the Middle Horizon of central California, before 300 A.D.).

Anasazi cultures, as such, appear after 700 A.D. in the "Developmental Pueblo" period (also called Pueblo I and Pueblo II). At this time great experimentation occurred in housing, with both semi-subterranean and surface structures and rectangular and round plans. The houses were often constructed with many rooms and were made of either stone slabs, adobe bricks, or wattle and daub. Kivas (underground ceremonial or storage chambers) also were in use, pottery greatly improved in quality, cotton fabrics appeared (doubtless a Mexican influence), and a heavy emphasis upon sedentary horticulture was apparent. This early "Pueblo Indian" way of life proved to be very popular among peoples previously influenced by the Horticultural Desert stages and between 700 and 1100 A.D. it spread over most of Utah and southeastern Nevada, with Anasazi pottery of this period also appearing in the Mohave Desert of southern California probably as a trade item. (It is also possible that Anasazi miners worked turquoise deposits in the California desert during this general era).

Between 1100 and 1300 the central Anasazi area entered into a period of great cultural elaboration while the Utah-southeastern Nevada-northwestern Arizona regions continued to preserve the Developmental Pueblo style of life to some degree, although the limits of Anasazi style occupation tended to become more circumscribed than before 1100 (except in the Flagstaff-Verde Valley area of Arizona where Anasazi

influence is strengthened between 1100 and 1300). After 1300 Anasazi
cultures retreat to roughly the modern Pueblo Indian areas of Arizona and
New Mexico, but the natives of southern Utah, southern Nevada, and northwestern Arizona preserved, in essence, a style of life reminiscent of
Horticultural Desert, Pre-Anasazi times (with pottery, some horticulture
where feasible, and other features of the Desert Culture tradition
referred to earlier).

    Farther to the south, in the Phoenix-Tucson region of south central
Arizona, other events took place during this general period which are
of significance in understanding later southern California culture. At
about 1000 A.D. (according to recent thinking) a culture referred to as
the Hohokam spread from Mexico into the Gila-Salt basin. The Hohokam
culture featured a number of new traits, including the construction of
great irrigation systems, Mexican-Mayan style ball-game courts, pyrite
mirrors, curvilinear art, red on buff pottery, intensive horticulture,
an emphasis upon trade, the development of an intensive pottery-manu-
facturing center at Snaketown, Arizona,and, perhaps, Mexican-style
emphases on military activities.

    By 1070 a Hohokam "colony" existed near Flagstaff while Hohokam
pottery was being utilized on the Colorado River (between 1000 -
1200 A.D.) and was traded into the San Fernando Valley of southern
California. Between 1250 and 1300 the Hohokam way of life was largely
replaced in south-central Arizona by a modified Ootam-like culture and
an Anasazi-like multi-story pueblo-building complex derived either from
northern Mexico or central and eastern Arizona. Similar types of
pueblos were also constructed on the Colorado River, prior to the 1530's
and probably before 1400. (See Jack D. Forbes, Warriors of the Colorado,
1965).

    The Hohokam way of life, with some Pre-Ootam elements, did not dis-
appear completely after 1250, however. By 1150 - 1250 the ancestors of
the Hamakhava (Mohave), Halchidhoma, Quechan (Yuma), and other Yuman-
speaking Colorado River peoples were developing their European-contact
period cultures, utilizing many Hohokam traits (including a style of
pottery which remained very similar to Hohokam,cremation, similar
houses of a semi-subterranean type, clay figurines reminiscent of Hohokam
work, Hohokam-type horticultural crops, and a military orientation which
may have been derived, in part, from Hohokam behavior). Some Hohokam
traits also survived in southern Arizona, among the Maricopa and Ootam
peoples.

    The developments described above for the Anasazi, Hohokam, and
other southwestern traditions, occurring after 2,000 b.p., were paralleled
in general by trends towards cultural elaboration and differentiation
apparently taking place throughout California and the Great Basin.
(Although it should be borne in mind that the richness and diversity of
more recent cultures may sometimes be more apparent than real, being due
to the greater likelihood of complete assemblages of goods being preserved

in more recent archaeological sites). In general, archaeologists are able
to distinguish cultures in the 300 - 1000 A.D. period which they believe
are directly ancestral to those of Native American cultures contacted by
Europeans.

In central California what is known as the Late Horizon commenced
about 300 - 500 A.D. and endured with relatively little change, so far
as material traits are concerned, until the period of European invasion.
Archaeological traits which characterize this era include cremation,
grave-offerings, wide-ranging trade, elaboration of ornaments, small
obsidian arrow-points, large stone mortars, and tubular steatite smoking
pipes. In general, the Late Horizon is based upon the Middle Horizon
and there is no evidence of sharp cultural discontinuity in Central California for a period of at least 4,000 years.

During the Late Horizon Anasazi influence reached central California,
not so much in terms of material goods (although Anasazi-influenced Great
Basin pottery does spread into the southern Sierra Nevada area) but rather
in terms of ceremonial-religious behavior. In particular, the Kuksu
religious system, found among natives of the Central Valley of California
in the nineteenth century, would appear to be closely related to Anasazi
ceremonial patterns. As Robert F. Heizer has stated:

> Based on both archaeological and ethnographical evidence,
> central California seems to have come under fairly strong
> influence from the Southwest over the last millennium.
> (Heizer, "The Western Coast of North America" p. 128 in
> Jennings & Norbeck, Prehistoric Man In The New World).

The development of advanced cultures in northwestern California is
not well understood, primarily because early archaeological sites are
lacking generally in the coastal region from northern California through
southern Alaska. Shell-mound sites in the former area reveal that by
500 - 1000 A.D. a way of life had evolved which was essentially the same
as that of the eighteenth century, in so far as material goods are concerned. On the other hand, the earliest levels at Humboldt Bay featured
burials with a lavish burning of goods in a pit, with the corpse placed
on top of the still-burning embers, while upper levels revealed the
development of the later practice of using extended burials with no
burned goods. This change is perhaps quite significant since it would
seem to indicate that these Californians shifted their value system from
one emphasizing wealth-destruction (so as to facilitate the well-being
of a departed person in the after-life, as well as perhaps to prevent
wealth-accumulation by individuals) to one emphasizing wealth-accumulation
and display (typical of later Northwest Coast cultures). Gradually, therefore, the stratified society of northwestern California, with certain
families dominant because of their possession of wealth, evolved during
the past 1,000 years.

The development of the pre-European culture in northwestern California was closely connected with the general development of maritime-

oriented, complex cultures all along the coast of northwest North America. In turn, it is now thought by some scholars that this maritime stage was closely related to early Eskimo developments and, in fact, it has been suggested that the cultures of the coast of Canada and southern Alaska developed from an "Eskimoid" base (as early as 2500 - 2400 b.p.). Unfortunately, little time-depth exists in most coastal sites in this general region. (But it should be pointed out that a Columbia River site near the Dalles, with a date of 8,000 b.p., shows the beginnings of a river-maritime orientation which is earlier than any Eskimo developments).

     The Eskimo-type sea-hunting culture of the Bering Sea region appears to have developed around 3000 b.p. on the Asiatic side of the Bering Strait. It is now generally believed that this maritime culture was largely derived from the coastal and island maritime heritages of East Asia's Pacific rim and certainly not from interior Siberia or the Siberian Arctic coast. On the basis of this approach we might suggest that Asiatic maritime influences gradually spread north to the Bering Sea region by 3,000 years ago and then subsequently were diffused to southern Alaska and down the coast as far as north-western California. Still further, it is possible to suggest that certain traits found along the Northwest Coast were spread in some manner to the Santa Barbara region of southern California, bypassing the central California coast.*

     One possible mechanism for the diffusion of maritime cultural elements may well have been Asiatic travelers drifting or sailing from East Asia by means of the Japanese Current. This Current, which flows from the Philippine Sea to the Californias by way of the Gulf of Alaska, comprises the only easy, natural sea-route to America from Asia. It was utilized continuously between 1565 and 1821 by Spanish galleons and by perhaps as many as sixty drifting Asiatic crafts in the century after 1770. Japanese junks, with living survivors, are known to have reached Santa Barbara and Sitka during the early 1800's, and Asiatic ceramics have been found in Indian sites from the western Canadian coast to the central California coast (although some of these ceramics may have been carried by European vessels). It has also been suggested that there is evidence of much earlier Asiatic contact with the Americas in connection with the appearance of Japanese-like pottery in Ecuador (dated several thou-sand years ago) and the existence of certain Oriental-like traits in

---

* It should be noted, however, that it may be difficult to argue for a diffusion of maritime cultures from the Bering Sea area to the Northwest Coast if the currently known time difference is only 500 years (3,000 b.p. in the Bering region and 2500 b.p. in the Fraser River delta of British Columbia), since the uncertainty of archaeological knowledge in this area renders such dates highly problematic. Further, the early Columbia River riverine-maritime adaptation could indicate an independent origin in North America.

the Mayan-Mexican region. Significantly, Chinese records mention the voyage of a group of Buddhist monks to what must have been some part of North America, and a return voyage to China, in the fifth century A.D.

It is very unlikely that maritime influences could have been derived from Polynesia, both because of the recency of the occupation of Hawaii and because there are no favorable currents to carry visitors from the South Pacific to the Americas. On the other hand, Polynesian-South American contact, initiated primarily from South America, seems well-established (see, for example, Thor Heyerdahl, "Feasible Ocean Routes To and From the Americas in Pre-Columbian Times," American Antiq-uity, v. 28, no. 4, 1963).

Southern California cultural development entered into the late pre-European period at about 500 - 1000 A.D. During this era the ways of life first seen by Europeans evolved, with several centers of development. The most distinctive cultural tradition was a rather complex, maritime-oriented way of life developed along the coast from Point Conception to, perhaps, Orange County with its center in the Santa Barbara-Goleta area. Another interesting development consisted in the appearance of certain Anasazi-like traits (such as ground-paintings comparable to Anasazi sand-paintings) in the Vitam (Shoshonean) speaking sections of central Southern California.

The exact process whereby different Anasazi-like traits reached separate zones in southern and central California is not known, but several possible avenues can be indicated. For one, the Anasazi-influenced people residing in southeastern Nevada, northwestern Arizona, and Utah prior to 1100 - 1300 A.D. might well have maintained direct trade relations with California, as is suggested by the diffusion of pottery, possible turquoise mining in the Mohave Desert, and California sea-shells found far in the interior. (It is remotely possible that central California Indians, who later possessed the Kuksu religion, visited Anasazi communities. This would help to explain how Anasazi proctices came to have a counterpart far to the northwest.) Secondly, middlemen may have helped to diffuse specific items both before and after 1100 - 1300. It is known, for example, that the Hamakhava of the Colorado River visited both the Hopi, in the east, and the San Joaquin Valley, Los Angeles area, and Ventura in the west during the eighteenth century (or earlier). It is also known that the Halchidhoma served as middlemen between the Riverside area and Arizona, and that the Quechan and other Colorado River Yumans traveled to the Pacific Coast in the west and Zuni in the east as early as the 1540's.

A third possible source for the diffusion of Anasazi elements into southern California were the pueblos, mentioned earlier, which existed on the lower Colorado before the 1500's. Unfortunately it is not known whether or not these people possessed such Anasazi traits as ground-paintings.

Finally, it has been suggested that several Vitam groups (the Tongva, Maringayam, Iviatim, et cetera) were newcomers, from the northeast, arriving in Southern California in ca. 1150. If this theory is correct, then it may be that these people were living in those Great Basin areas directly involved in Anasazi culture of the Developmental Pueblo stage, and later carried certain aspects of that heritage into Southern California. Unfortunately, their failure to maintain the horticultural aspects of the Anasazi tradition argues against such a process.

In summary, it is quite clear that California and the Great Basin were not completely isolated from developments taking place elsewhere. Influences from Mexico and the Southwest and from the Northwest Coast are especially apparent during the period after 500 A.D. but earlier ages also reveal evidence of trade and cultural interchange. On the other hand, the natives of much of the California-Great Basin area tended to be rather conservative in terms of the basic characteristics of their cultures and archaeology tends to reveal processes of very slow and gradual culture change rather than sharp shifts. On the whole, it is difficult to see much evidence for any widespread migrations in the pre-European contact period, and if such migrations did take place they apparently took the form of extremely slow changes which failed to introduce cultural schisms. Where changes in language occurred, as they doubtless did, it is very likely that the process was similar to that which took place in the Kupa (Warner's Valley) area after 1769 in which Kamia-speaking villages absorbed Iviatim-speaking newcomers to such an extent that the valley people gradually became Iviatim in language although continuing to trace their ancestry to both groups. (The best general sources for information on the archaeological period include the chapters by R. F. Heizer, Jesse D. Jennings, and Alex D. Krieger in Jennings and Norbeck, eds., Prehistoric Man in the New World, 1964; and R. F. Heizer and M. A. Whipple, eds., The California Indians: A Source Book, 1951).

4. Indian ground shell necklace. 10. Storage basket. 6 and 7. Strings of ground shell money. Courtesy Bancroft Library, Berkeley, California.

Prelude To Invasion

For two or three centuries, from the 1530's through the 1760's (or later, depending upon the region in question) natives of the California-Great Basin region were on the periphery of European expansion, exposed to occasional raids or exploratory forays but not confronted by any permanent attempts at conquest. Points of direct contact with Europeans were limited to the following: 1) Spanish, English, and Dutch vessels along the coast; 2) Spanish land and sea expeditions to the Colorado River; 3) contacts with Spaniards at the Hopi villages and pueblos of northern New Mexico; and 4) little known contacts with Spanish traders in the Ute territory of Colorado.

Direct contact with Europeans commenced when Hernando de Alarcón sailed up the Colorado River to the Yuma area in 1540. A few months later Melchior Díaz traveled from Sonora to the Colorado River by land, hoping to meet Alarcón and thus open up a maritime source of supplies for the Vásquez de Coronado expedition, then invading New Mexico. The Díaz party, of some interest because it was the first European group to definitely enter the present state of California, assumed in practice the form of a raid, largely because the Spaniards precipitated hostilities on the Colorado River by seizing and torturing Indians as a "preventive" device. (Early Spanish groups tended to use extremely harsh procedures on occasion, in order to frighten natives into prompt submission).

Subsequently, the Colorado River area was visited by the Juan de Oñate expedition in 1604-1605 (coming from New Mexico), by several groups led by Father Eusebio Kino during 1699 - 1702 (from Sonora) and by groups led by Father Jacobo Sedelmayr in 1744 -1750 (from Sonora). In addition, frequent Spanish activity in the Hopi-Verde Valley region and in northern Sonora-Arizona had an impact upon the Yumans of the Colorado.,

Various coastal areas of California were visited by Juan Rodríguez de Cabrillo (1542-1543), Sir Francisco Drake (1579), Pedro de Unamuno (1587). Sebastian Rodríguez Cermeño (1595), Sebastian Vizcaíno (1602-1603), by unrecorded landings of the Spaniards' Manila galleon (sailing each year after 1565), probably by Dutch and/or English "pirates," and perhaps by occasional Oriental craft. Dutch and English buccaneers frequented the Baja California coast after 1587 and could have visited Southern California waters. The evidence for Asian contacts is less convincing, but consists in a second-hand story of two small stange-looking vessels with golden pelicans as figureheads in the Gulf of California in 1540,* eight strange(non-Spanish) vessels seen off the coast of Colima, Mexico in 1573,

---

* Whose sailors had both "Negroid" and straight hair and said that they came from across the Pacific Ocean.

Indian accounts of a ship carrying non-Indians wrecked near San Luis Obispo in ca. 1747, non-Spanish nautical debris seen near Monterey Bay in 1774, and metal goods (pieces of swords, a new "machete" and copper rings) in the possession of northwest coast natives in 1775 which the Indians said always came from the north. These instances can, however, be explained in part by possible unrecorded European voyages as well as by Asian visitors.

The natives of the interior Great Basin area were probably not visited directly by Europeans before the 1770's but they may well have contacted Spaniards among the Hamakhava (1604 - 1605) or among the Utes of Colorado (1600 - 1680 and after 1695). It is certain that Southern Paiutes often traded at Hopi during this entire period but it is not known if any were from north of the Colorado River. In any case, indirect knowledge of the Spaniards presence in the Southwest is certainly to be suggested.

Virtually all of the contacts described above were of a friendly or at least non-hostile nature, although it is to be suspected that occasional vessels visiting the coast created difficulties perhaps through the actions of sailors seizing native women. Some such explanation is likely for the native attack upon Unamuno's crewmen near San Luis Obispo in 1587 (where one of the Filipinos with the expedition was killed along with some of the attacking natives).* In 1595 Cermeño's vessel was wrecked at the same bay on the Marin County coast visited by Drake twenty years previously. At first the natives were friendly, as they had been with Drake, but fighting commenced after a time, perhaps due to the Spaniard's gathering of Indian food supplies.

The brief contacts with Europeans prior to 1769 had little direct effect upon Indian cultural patterns but certain influences need to be noted. European trade goods, Chinese silk, et cetera, were acquired but not enough to alter the native material cultures except perhaps in northwestern California where a demand for iron led to some metal-reworking. Horses began to be used by Indians in northwestern Sonora as early as the 1690's but their diffusion towards the Colorado River was quite slow. The Ootam of southern Arizona received a few horses by 1700, the Halchidhoma of the Colorado were trading for them in 1744 and by the early 1770's the Quechans possessed numerous mounts. Horses had perhaps begun to spread into desert Southern California by 1774-1776 but they were not very numerous and basically the Colorado River was the "frontier" for horses at that date. To the east, horses began to be acquired by the Pueblo Indians, Apaches, and Navajos during the seventeenth-century and thereafter spread northwards to the Utes and Shoshone-Comanches (who were living adjacent to each other in the Wyoming region during the seventeenth and early eighteenth centuries). It is not known when the Great Basin Numic-speaking groups began to acquire horses

---

* Interestingly, the Spaniards referred to their Filipino crewmen as "Yndios Luzones," i.e., "Luzon Indians."

but it would seem likely that they were commencing to receive them by the 1770's, at least in the Utah area. (The Lewis and Clark expedition found the Shoshones of Idaho well-mounted).

Wheat was introduced on the Colorado River in 1702 and by the 1770's the Hamakhava were raising it, in addition to their native crops. Later this wheat spread to southern Utah and was subsequently introduced into New Mexico as "Paiute Wheat." By 1823 the Cahuillas of Coachella Valley were raising wheat, perhaps derived (along with their other crops) from the Colorado natives.

It would appear that another effect of Spanish contact was the spread of disease. It seems quite likely that the coastal population was reduced after 1542 by this means and it is probable that a similar decline took place along the Colorado River. The Quechan, for example, would appear to have dropped from 4,000 or more in the 1700 - 1750 period to 3,000 by the 1770's and it is probable that some reductions along the river had occurred before the 1690's. Increased warfare and slave-raiding, stimulated by the Spanish slave-trade, also took its toll in Arizona and along the Colorado River during this same general period. It is possible also that Southern Paiute captives were being seized by Utes and others for resale in New Mexico, as they were after 1800.

We know little about native cultures during the 1540 - 1769 period, other than that kind of knowledge which can be derived from archaeology, pieced together from European accounts or inferred back into this period from ethnological research. (It should be stressed here that the detailed descriptions of Western American cultures found in works such as A. L. Kroeber's monumental Handbook of the Indians of California are based primarily upon data gathered between 1900 and 1930 from Indian individual's whose personal memory rarely extended back beyond the 1840's). The archaeological evidence, as already cited, argues for continuity throughout this period in terms of the material aspects of native cultures. The evidence of European visitors does, however, suggest that changes were sometimes taking place in those characteristics not likely to be seen in archaeological sites.

The Colorado River area is the best known portion of the California-Great Basin region prior to the 1770's. In this locale it would appear from the documentary evidence that a number of important changes took place. For example, in 1540 the Spaniards found some seven or eight Indian socio-political units residing on the river below Yuma, only two of which (the Kohuana and Halyikwamai) can be equated definitely with later groups. Several of these units were bi-lingual and it seems likely that Ootam-speaking people were residing on the river along with Yumans. By 1604-1605 only five groups were residing below Yuma, in the following order: Halchidhomas, Kohuanas, A-ha-yes (perhaps the later Kaveltcadom), Halyikwamais, and Cocopas, all Yuman-speaking. Upriver from Yuma were Ootam-speaking people (at the mouth of the Gila),

Bahacachas (Quechans) and Hamakhavas. By the 1690's the Quechans had moved south to Yuma, the Halchidhoma had moved north to the Blythe area, the A-ha-yes had disappeared (perhaps going east along the Gila), and the Ootam group had retreated to the east.

Evidence exists, therefore, for considerable movement as well as for the disappearance of several small groups in the delta. It may well be that the Colorado River peoples were in the process of achieving their later stage of political unification, especially between 1540 and 1604, i.e., evolving from small single-village or band units into multi-village, multi-band "tribes" or republics.

Other changes can be discerned along the Colorado River before 1769, including perhaps a slight decline in trade relations (the trips being made to the Zuni area in 1539 - 1540 are replaced by shorter excursions into northern Sonora) although travel to the Pacific Coast remains common. It would also seem that warfare gradually increased in intensity in the Colorado River - southern Arizona area, perhaps largely as a result of the desire to acquire horses and other trade goods through the sale of captives to the Spaniards of Sonora.

The material culture of the River Yumans, in so far as it is revealed by pre-1769 diaries, is largely the same as that of later years although some differences can be noted. For example, Alarcón observed in 1540 that

> these Indians were adorned in different ways. Some had
> streaks covering their faces almost entirely. Others
> had their faces half-covered, all blackened with soot....
> Some wore masks of the same color, shaped like their
> faces. On their heads they wore a deerskin... helmet, and
> on it a small crest with some feathers.... They have their
> ears pierced with many holes in which they place beads and
> shells. All of them, both small and large, wear a multi
> colored sash about the waist; tied in the middle is a round
> bundle of feathers which hangs in the back like a tail.

In many respects this description could apply to a River Yuman of the 1800's, but the use of masks, skin helmets, sash around the waist, and feather bundle would appear to have dropped out later in favor of complete nudity for males (except for a blanket occasionally thrown over the shoulders). In 1540 the leader of the Halyikwamai "wore a garment closed in front and back and open on the sides, fastened with buttons worked in a chequered black and white. It was made of fiber or rattan." Such distinctive dress for leading men also disappeared in later years. These examples may indicate a decline in the complexity of Colorado River material cultures after 1540.

The European accounts relating to those few California coastal Indians actually visited reveal few differences from later years. The Hukueko people of Marin County apparently changed but little between the visits of Drake and Cermeño (1579, 1595) and the 1800's.

Likewise, the major characteristics of the advanced maritime cultures of the Santa Barbara - Catalina Island area are in evidence by 1542 and 1602. Many village names recorded by Rodríguez Cabrillo were still in use in the late eighteenth century, such as Misopsno (Carpinteria).

During this two-century period the Indians of California, with the partial exception of the Colorado River natives, failed to prepare politically and militarily for the Spanish invasion, as is rather understandable. They had had no previous experience at interacting with aggressive Europeans, a people long at ease in the context of imperialism and machiavellianism. They had no reason to expect an invasion, nor did they, at first, understand that the democratic, non-unified nature of their societies would inhibit effective resistance. (See Jack D. Forbes, Warriors of the Colorado, 1965, and Apache, Navajo and Spaniard, 1960 for discussion of the advance of the Spanish Empire into northern Mexico and the Southwest).

The Spanish Invasion and Native Response

The Spanish-speaking persons who invaded California in 1769, although of American Indian and African as well as Spanish descent, were participants in a cultural legacy very different from that of the unconquered Native Americans. Basically, these Hispanos (Spanish subjects of whatever race) were citizens of an authoritarian state, members of a mass (i.e., populous, complex, and widespread) society, and participants in a legacy of religious intolerance and conformity, a legacy of centuries of almost constant warfare involving conquest, a legacy of messianic fanaticism (stressing both "Hispanidad" - Spanish culture in general and Catholicism in particular), and a legacy of machiavellianism (i.e., the willingness to use duplicity on a large-scale in order to achieve goals not revealed to the people being dealt with). Hispanic culture also possessed certain morally positive characteristics, such as a relative lack of racial prejudice; however, it is the above traits which appear to be crucially important in explaining the initial success of Spanish imperialism in the various sections of the Americas.

The Native Americans of much of California possessed almost an exactly opposite way of life, featuring as it did the almost total absence of warfare in the European sense (local feuds, involving few casualties, were the natives' almost only adventures in warfare), a total absence of the concept of conquering or exploiting other peoples (except in the case of debt slavery in the northwest and other, but rare, forms of individual exploitation), a relative absence of the machiavellian type of mentality (Indians tended to be direct in their approach to achieving goals rather than developing complex, devious strategies utilizing opposite-appearing tactics), and a general tolerance of differing approaches to religion and purely individual behavior. Still further, most California Indians functioned within very small political units of fifty to five hundred persons whose leaders seldom possessed more than ceremonial authority.

Given these differences it is not at all surprising that a few hundred Hispanos, equipped with guns, steel-tipped lances, swords, leather-jackets and pants, horses and, especially, with years of agressive military experience, were able to initially overcome in a short space of time many thousands of ill-equipped natives. (The latter not only fought in small groups, and on foot, but possessed no body armour and few missiles capable of penetrating the invaders' leather clothing). More significantly, the Hispanos possessed the very great psychological advantage of knowing full well the ultimate purposes of their initial intrusion, while the natives, except in the extreme south, could only suppose that the newcomers intended to leave after a time, or that they merely intended to befriend the natives, as Spanish propaganda asserted.

In 1769, when Spanish garrisons were established at San Diego and Monterey, a long-time interest in northwesterly expansion by the Spanish Empire was realized. The motives for this advance were varied and included the ambitions of a senior official in Mexico (José de Gálvez, was personally responsible for the move), the desire for the exploitation of the reputed wealth of the region, a desire to control the Colorado River and thereby pacify hostile Indians in Arizona, and anxiety over the possibility that the Russians or British might seize the harbor at Monterey (San Francisco bay was not known to the Spanish until later in 1769). Missionary motives were also present but should not be overemphasized since thousands of natives farther south had not yet been Christianized.

Between 1769 and 1800 the coastal zone as far north as San Francisco and southern Alameda County was brought under Hispanic control with the establishment of forts (presidios) at San Diego, Santa Barbara, Monterey, and San Francisco, smaller garrisons of soldiers at each of some two-score missions, and irregular militia units at three civilian towns (Los Angeles, San Jose, and Branciforte - Santa Cruz). In addition, between 1780 and 1781 two "military colonies" existed on the Colorado River at Yuma and in the 1790's artillery companies were stationed at the major ports. Although seldom exceeding 500 men, the Spanish military force was highly mobile and was capable of rapidly congregating at points of danger, an important consideration in view of the fact that they had to control or deal with up to 70,000 Indians in the coastal zone.

California, during the Spanish era, was essentially a military colony with no civilian government except at the lowest levels. However, the military officers in control of the province shared authority with the Franciscan missionaries (who were also salaried employees of the King of Spain although doctrinally subject to the Pope in Rome). The missions of California were indeed royal-governmental institutions, erected on land belonging (according to the Spanish viewpoint) ultimately to the Crown although reserved to the natives with the missionaries as trustees. The purposes of the missions were several, but "Indian control" can be identified as the most important initial purpose. Subsequent purposes included the assimilation of the natives into Hispanic society, the development of a means of economic support for the military and clerical establishments, and the conversion of the Indians to Spanish Catholicism.

The kind of mission implemented in California was of the reducción or congregación (reduction or congregation) type, a variant of missionary activity developed in northcentral Mexico in the 1570's and utilized throughout Coahuila, Texas, Chihuahua, northwestern Sonora and Baja California. This type of mission was not erected in an already existing pueblo with sufficient population to support a church but was utilized as a device for gathering together (congregating) natives who were dispersed in small villages and for "reducing" them from their "free, undisciplined" way of life to that of a disciplined subject of Spain. It should be clear, then, that the missions of California were not solely religious institutions. They were, on the contrary, instruments designed to bring about a total change in culture in a brief period of time.

The California missions were also authoritarian, coercive institutions (totalitarian best describes their comprehensive nature). One cannot comprehend the effect of the missions upon Native Californians unless one realizes that Indians inducted into a mission were not free to leave (except for brief periods under license) and were constantly subject to the absolute control of the Franciscan missionaries, overseers, and soldiers. Physical force was used to keep the natives from leaving as well as to maintain discipline, including such punishments as whipping with a barbed lash (for both men and women), use of the stocks and hobbles, solitary confinement, and, on occasion, mutilation, branding, and even execution.

We do not know, in every case, exactly how Indians were initially recruited into the missions but it is clear that few came voluntarily for religious reasons. In the early years natives were ordinarily recruited by the offer of "free" meals and gifts (not realizing that they would soon be working harder for their food and clothing than they ever had before). Subsequently, a standard device was to baptize young children in their home villages and then to require them, as "converts", to enter the mission at ages 5 to 7. Normally, the child's mother followed to be with the child and the father followed to be with his wife. By the 1790's, however, the reputation of the missions as places where Indians were unfree and as death-traps made it necessary for the missionaries to resort to outright force, beginning especially in the San Francisco Bay area. Spanish military expeditions ordinarily brought back gentiles (unconverted Indians) as well as cimarrones (runaways). Another common variant was to bribe or frighten a village leader into supplying quotas of converts, as in the following incident:

[In January 1804 a Franciscan from San Miguel Mission] went with a soldier to Cholan [Cholame] rancheria*

---

* Rancheria refers to a small village, not large enough to·be considered a pueblo.

fourteen leagues away and asked Guchapa, chief of
all the rancherias in that region, to let him have
some of his young men to make Christians of them.
Guchapa refused and repulsed the friar and his
escort with threats, declaring that he had no fear
of the soldiers since he knew perfectly well that
they died like other men. It was important to
modify this chieftain's views, and [Captain] Guerra
despatched a sergeant with thirteen men to arrest
Guchapa, which was effected after a brave resistance;
and as a captive the chief, being duly rewarded with
beads, agreed to bring in all the Christian fugitives
in his jurisdiction, and left his son as a hostage
for the fulfillment of his contract. (H.H. Bancroft
History of California, v.II, p.150).
Within the missions, the Franciscans and their soldier escorts exercised
complete control over the neophytes (as the converts were called), this
control even extending to regulation of sexual behavior, splitting off
children from parents (e.g., locking up all unmarried girls above the age
of seven in a "nunnery" each night and the males in another building),
forbidding native marriage and divorce practices, and, of course, attempting to suppress all aspects of Indian religion and curing practice
(Indian doctors or curers were flogged whenever apprehended).

From several viewpoints the missions were an immense
success. The natives of the coastal zone were indeed congregated in a
few places when they could be more easily controlled, their threatening
numbers were reduced by the extremely high death-rate in the missions
from 70,000 to about 15,000 by the 1830's, tens of thousands were baptized
(and buried) as at least nominal Catholics, and, perhaps most importantly
of all, an economic base was provided for the Hispano ruling classes.
By about 1800 the neophytes were providing much of the support for the
Spanish clergy and army, including especially food, while after 1811 they
literally provided the entire support for the province. The gente de
razon ("people of reason" or Spanish-speaking persons) were entirely
dependent upon the products produced by the neophytes for both food and
other supplies (the latter either being manufactured directly by the neophytes or obtained through the sale of neophyte-produced goods).

From the native viewpoint the missions were a catastrophe of indescrib-
able proportions, since the coastal population was largely eliminated by
sickness induced by concentration in unhealthy mission compounds, new foods,
new styles of labor, probably an insufficient diet (often with little meat),
and, perhaps most important of all, a state of psychological depression.
It is indeed disheartening to read diaries of pre-mission travelers com-
menting upon the vigor and enterprise of the natives and then to read the
accounts of later visitors who almost invariably note the apathy,
lethargy, and depression exhibited by long-term neophytes. Although the
missionaries did attempt to mitigate the "slave-labor camp" character of

the missions with Catholic religious pageantry, musical groups, and rarer educational programs, the net effect of the experience was apparently still quite devastating for the average Indian. For those few who cooperated openly with the conquerors or who were enthusiastic converts life was perhaps a little better, but for the masses it was apparently tragic indeed.*

The mission was not the only instrument of conquest introduced by the Spaniard. Three others need also to be mentioned briefly: the presidio, the pueblo, and the rancho. The presidios or forts not only served as centers for military control but also were places where Indian labor was exploited. The presidios (and almost everything else in Spanish California) were erected by Indian labor, unpaid in the case of neophytes or prisoners, or poorly paid in the case of gentiles. All of the soldier families acquired native servants and thus, as time passed by, each presidio became a town composed of a gente de razón ruling class and native laborers. The pueblos (civilian towns), such as Los Angeles and San José, developed in a similar manner, with the settlers (most of whom were retired soldiers) utilizing Indian labor on a share-crop or board and room basis. It would appear that a number of coastal natives preferred to become laborers in the towns rather than neophytes in the missions (and the Franciscans often protested that natives were becoming ladino, i.e., Hispanicized, without being missionized). The settlers and soldiers, needing cheap labor, were not averse to this process.

The rancho** provided another means whereby Indian labor was integrated into the Hispano economy. Beginning in the 1780's soldiers and settlers were allowed to graze stock and raise crops in the countryside, using Indian labor entirely. Gradually, these grants of land became more formal but several things should be noted: title to the land always was retained by the Crown, Indian village rights were never quieted by a rancho grant, and the ranch owner almost always lived most of the year in town, leaving his stock and crops in the hands of Indians working on a share-crop basis. Gradually (after the 1830's especially) the Indians became serfs and an economy similar to that of the Deep South (of the late nineteenth century) developed.

The Spanish Empire was able to expand successfully with a relatively small number of fighting men in large measure because the Spaniards understood very well the process of conquest and colonialization. Thus, terror was the basis for control (rebellion was usually dealt with severely) but this was supplemented, as in the case of Guchapa, with bribes and privileges.

---

* Indian leaders in the missions, appointed by the missionaries, were required, for example, to lash their fellow-Indians in minor disciplinary cases.

** Rancho literally meant a hut in the country off by itself.

The Spaniards often attempted to recruit the Indian leadership into the imperial system by means of favors which ranged from uniforms, staffs of office, titles, and other gifts to annual salaries and the right to exploit Indian labor (these latter privileges were found primarily in Mexico and farther south). In addition, enthusiastic converts to Catholicism, frightened individuals, and native women intermarried with Hispanos often served imperial purposes. Thus when a native rebellion was being planned the Spaniards ordinarily had informers available who would warn them in advance. Very few Indian revolts (and they were frequent) took the Spaniards by surprise!

Intermarriage between Spanish-speaking persons and California Indians was quite common and was officially encouraged by the Crown as a device for facilitating the control and hispanicization of the native population, as well as a means for meeting the needs of the numerous unmarried soldiers sent to California. Unfortunately, intermarriage failed to improve the position of the Indian masses because the Indian partner in the marriage and the children were ordinarily absorbed, socially and psychologically, into Hispanic society. That is, every effort was made to maintain a social and cultural wall between Spanish-speaking persons (who were often Indians from Mexico) and California Indian neophytes or gentiles. It might have been militarily disastrous for the empire to have allowed gente de razón of Indian blood to have developed a feeling of unity with the native masses.

During the period under discussion, 1769 to 1821, native groups in the interior were very much affected by the Spanish invasion. Partly this was due to continued efforts at expansion of the empire (as with the abortive effort along the Colorado River in 1780 - 1781 and the successful expansions to San Rafael in 1817 and in the San Bernardino - San Diego back country between 1818 and 1823), but in great measure it was due to other types of activity. The natives of the Marin - Sonoma - Solano and Sacramento to Bakersfield areas of California were very much affected by raids for converts and by the 1830's several thousands, from as far away as the Sierra Nevada foothills, had become neophytes along the coast. The Southern Paiutes of Utah and southern Nevada were affected by slave-raids conducted by New Mexicans, and Utes (and, perhaps, Navahos) designed to supply the servant needs of northern Mexico.

Numerous Spanish expeditions were sent out between 1769 and 1821, reaching north along the coast as far as Alaska, the interior of California (except east of the Sierra Nevada), virtually all of Southern California, and much of Utah. It is possible that irregular parties of Hispanic fur-traders and slave-raiders also crossed Nevada since the Indians of central California were certain that they had been visited by, or told of, Europeans coming from the east who had crossed or approached the Sierra Nevadas. All of these exploring parties, and especially the raids, had a considerable impact upon native society. Diseases were undoubtedly introduced, the ethnic boundaries were probably altered to some degree, and part-European children were doubtless left behind. Other direct and indirect influences will be mentioned below.

In almost every instance the Native Californians responded in a friendly, albeit sometimes shy, manner towards the Spanish intruders. The natives tended to believe the Hispano assertions of friendship and usually aided in the process of erecting temporary buildings as well as supplying the food which made the Spanish intrusion possible. Not many months or even weeks had passed, however, before the raping and seizure of Indian women and the appropriation of native property began to alter the situation. Incidents soon took place as at San Gabriel where Indian heads were mounted at the entrance to the mission because an outraged husband had dared try to avenge an assault upon his wife. More serious incidents often occurred as well, as at San Diego, where the Kamia actually destroyed the infant mission in 1775, and succeeded in killing three Hispanos. The coastal Kamias were not pacified until late in 1776.

At San Francisco the Indians at first fled across the bay (allegedly due to an attack by the Indians of San Mateo) and then returned in December 1776 to attack the Spaniards, with little success however. Elsewhere the same pattern tended to be followed during the 1770's, with the Indians occasionally becoming irritated enough to fire off a few arrows but with the Spaniards easily thwarting their efforts.

During the 1780's and 1790's Indian resistance stiffened somewhat along the coast and reached major proportions along the Colorado River. The latter area had long been an important objective of Spanish imperialism because it was seen as a key point on the land route to California and as a means for outflanking the rebel Ootams and hostile Yavapais and Apaches of Arizona. The Quechan people at Yuma were persuaded to allow the Spaniards to establish posts in their territory after their kwoxot (leader), Olleyquotequiebe (Salvador Palma) had been regaled in Mexico City and after they had been promised many gifts, clothing, et cetera. In 1780 two military colonies, composed of soldier-settlers, were established across from Yuma and at Xuksil (Algodones), and it was expected that the Quechan would be Christianized and settled in these colonies. Unfortunately, the soldier-settlers, priests, and officers offended the Quechan at every turn, whipping the leading men, damaging native food supplies, and behaving in a generally exploitative manner.

On July 17 - 18, 1781 the Quechan, with some allies, and under the leadership of Salvador Palma, Ygnacio Palma (his brother), Francisco Xavier (a Halyikwamai raised in Sonora) and others, staged a well-planned revolt which totally destroyed the Spanish establishment. Fifty-five to ninety-five Hispanos were killed, seventh-six or more were captured, and the Quechan were free again. During the balance of 1781 and 1782 the Spaniards repeatedly launched large-scale military assaults upon the Quechans but the latter, with extreme bravery and fortitude, threw back every assault. The Quechan liberation struggle was ultimately successful and the Spaniards were forced to admit defeat in 1783. Thereafter the Colorado River was completely under Native American control and the provinces of Sonora and California were cut off from each other. (See Forbes, Warriors of the Colorado for the full story of the Quechan war for independence).

Perhaps as a result of the Quechan example other Indians became more troublesome to the invaders during the 1780's. In October 1785, led by the Hapchi-vitam and by a female religious leader, Toypurina, the Tongva attempted to destroy San Gabriel Mission.* This rebellion was discovered and thwarted by Spanish vigilance as was one in July 1786 in which the Hapchi-vitam again planned a revolt, in alliance with the Indians of Atongaibit (Victorville) and the Colorado River. In 1794 Indians were arrested at San Luis Obispo and Purisima for planning a revolt.

In the San Francisco Bay area northern California's first hero known by name appears on the scene when, in February 1793, Charquín (Charkeen) fled from San Francisco Mission and begin struggling against all those who favored the missionaries' objectives. Serious resistance to the invaders was soon provided by the Saklán of Contra Costa county and their allies, the Cuchillones ("Little Knives") of the Karkin Strait area. During 1795 - 1797 these native groups defeated parties of San Francisco neophytes sent to recover runaways from the mission. In July 1797 the Spaniards attacked the Saklán and Cuchillones (who had dug pits to prevent the soldiers from using their horses effectively). The invaders captured nine gentiles and eighty-three runaway neophytes. The Saklán put up a brave resistance, wounding two soldiers and losing seven of their own men. The establishment of San Jose Mission at that time on the east shore of the bay greatly irritated the Saklán and several incidents occurred, including a raid by the Spaniards in 1800 (killing a chief and capturing twenty runaways). Thereafter, the Saklan disappear from the record, but their neighbors to the north and east continued sporadic fighting through 1810. In one battle at Sespesuya, on the north shore of Karkín Strait (Estrecho de los Carquines), the natives preferred to perish in their burning houses (set aflame by the soldiers) rather than surrender.

Considerable sporadic resistance also occurred at San Juan Bautista (where the Ansayanes stubbornly fought), Mission Santa Clara and elsewhere during the 1790's and early 1800's, but it was generally put down with ease. More serious, because difficult to combat, were neophyte efforts at poisoning or murdering the Franciscans. In 1801 four or five priests became ill from alleged poisoning at San Miguel and San Antonio and in 1812 the priest at Santa Cruz was killed by some of the neophytes of that mission. Other plots were frequently reported.

Between 1800 and 1820 most of the coastal natives' will to fight was broken and, except as runaways, they offered little resistance.** In the interior, however, great changes were taking place during these two decades, changes which were to produce greater resistance in later years. Perhaps most important of all was the continued spread of horses from the Colorado River into Southern California during the 1780's and 1790's. Also, by the latter period, natives near the coast were acquiring horses either by serving as cowboys for the Hispanos or by theft. As early as 1783 Indians

---

* Toypurina was captured and deported to the north where she later married an Hispano.

** Although in 1810-1811 the neophytes of San Gabriel, in alliance with Mohave River natives and the Hamakhava and Quechan planned an abortive rebellion.

ran off horses in the San Jose area while in later years horses became
so numerous along the coast that it was no problem acquiring them. By
1818 a Spaniard was expressing great fear because of the growing habit
of using horses on the part of San Joaquin Valley natives.

At the same time as they were acquiring horses, the Indians of the
Central Valley were also becoming more knowledgeable about Spanish fighting tactics and more aware of what Spanish conquest would mean. Hundreds
of runaways were among them and they knew full well what the missions
were like. Thus from San Diego to Sacramento and Clear Lake, along the
whole frontier, mounted Indians were preparing themselves for increased
warfare during the period from the 1820's through the 1840's. This process, perhaps more than anything else, was to prevent Hispano-Mexican expansion into the interior of California.

The Native Californians also offered various other forms of resistance of a more passive nature, the most obvious of which was flight to
the interior. Indians ordinarily ran away singly or in small groups,
but, on occasion, mass flights took place as when 200 natives fled from
San Francisco in 1795 or when, in 1803, the entire Kamia population of
Santo Tomás Mission (in northern Baja California) fled to the Colorado
River. The exploits of many of the individual cimarrones are rather
interesting. In 1812, for example, one Salvador fled from San Juan Capistrano all the way to Sonora but was shipped back in 1819. Much earlier, a Baja California Indian forced to serve in California, Sebastian
Taraval, fled from San Gabriel to the Colorado River, being the first
Christian to use the land route between California and Sonora.

Runaways became so numerous in the early 1800's that large sweeps
were made on occasion by troops through the Central Valley looking for
them, while smaller squads of soldiers were constantly out. In 1818 a
Franciscan reported that the refugees and gentiles had set up "a republic of hell and a diabolical union of apostates" in the tulare marshes
of the San Joaquin Valley. Other refugees fled to the Colorado River,
where some were met by Jedidiah Smith in 1826.

This form of resistance was not only effective in keeping the Spaniards busy, but also contributed to the diffusion of horticulture, horse-
back riding, and other Hispano-Mexican traits to the interior. By the
late 1820's crops were being grown by refugees in the Kern County area
while horticulture was even more widespread in the Central Valley in the
1830's and 1840's. By 1823 the Cahuillas were also growing crops, but
theirs may well have been derived from the Colorado River. (See Jack
D. Forbes, "Indian Horticulture West and Northwest of the Colorado River,"
Journal of the West, January 1963).

Religious resistance was also offered to the invaders. In general,
the natives did their best to secretly preserve their ancient religion
in the missions, although it became increasingly difficult to do so. Native
revivals are known to have occurred as in the Santa Barbara area in 1801.

At that time (after a destructive epidemic) the deity Chupu (Ashoop) appeared in a neophyte's vision. Chupu revealed that all who were baptized as Christians would die unless they were washed clean again and made offerings to their old deity. It would appear that virtually all of the region's Indians dedicated themselves to Chupu without the priests being aware of the movement until much later. In 1810 a priest reported that the same Indians were still worshiping Chupu but that he was making progress against the practice.

It seems clear that the missionized Indians seldom if ever become completely Christianized, partly because few lived very long in the missions and partly because new gentiles were constantly being brought in. Many pre-Spanish religious beliefs were retained by the coastal Indians, albeit in a garbled form, after the missions had been abolished.

Self-willed Death may have also been another form of passive resistance, although it is not clear that any Indian intentionally induced psychosomatic depression. On the other hand, it does seem clear that large-scale abortion was sometimes practiced to prevent the birth of children in the missions. (However, it should be noted that in many cases what appeared to be abortion might have actually been the result of syphilis, introduced by 1775, or measles). Apathetic work habits may also be cited as a form of passive resistance.

During this era other Europeans also appeared in the Far West, including Russians, Britons, and Anglo-Americans. The Russians and Anglo-Americans together had the greatest impact, being largely responsible (along with the missionaries) for the depopulation of the islands on the Southern California coast between 1800 and the 1820's. Russian and Yankee ships frequently hunted sea otter and seals along the shores of the islands and the crewmen and Aleut and Kodiak Eskimo hunters reportedly slaughtered many natives. The balance were carried off to the missions on the mainland.

Spanish, Russian, British, and Yankee ships also stopped in northwestern California after the 1770's, usually at Trinidad Bay. Although the Spaniards in 1775 found the Yurok people of Trinidad friendly, contacts with later visitors soon led to hostility. In 1805 a Yankee ship, the O'Cain, with 100 Aleut hunters, four Russian overseers, and fifty bidarkas (skin boats) hunted in the area, but the Yurok were unfriendly and one native was killed. That this incident occurred is not surprising since the intruders were catching fish and animals belonging, from the native viewpoint, to the Yurok.

Beginning in early 1809 the Russians commenced visiting Bodega Bay, establishing close contacts with the natives of the area north of San Francisco. Aleut hunters actually carried their bidarkas overland from Bodega in order to hunt in San Francisco Bay. Sporadic contacts continued until 1811 when the Russians and Aleuts explored the Bodega and San Francisco Bay areas and ventured up the Shabaikai (Russian) River for fifty miles. In 1812 ninety-five Russians and part-Russians and eighty Aleuts or Kodiak Eskimos founded Fort Ross at Mad-shui-nui on the Pomo Coast. Every effort was made to befriend the Kashia Pomo and Hukueko. In general, the natives north of San Francisco were happy to have allies against the Spaniards (who were frequently recruiting neophytes north of the bay), however, it is reported that the warlike Sotoyomes (a Pomo-speaking group living near Healdsburg) at first tested the Russians mettle in a battle (later they became allies). Very few Russians remained at Mad-shui-nui but those that did, along with the Aleuts and Eskimos, would appear to have intermarried with the nearby Indians and to have been consistently friendly.

Anglo-Americans, Britons, French Canadians, and New Mexican Hispanos were also entering the interior Far West in this period but, with the exception of the latter, none are known to have definitely reached as far as the Great Basin. Certainly by 1800 - 1820, New Mexicans were traveling to the Utah Lake - Great Salt Lake area to trade for furs and slaves and rumors reached the coast which can be taken to indicate that some penetrated as far as the Nevada and Colorado River areas. Anglo-Americans and French-Canadians traveled along the Snake River after 1810 and it is possible that Nevada Indians made contact with certain of these parties.

Quite obviously the years from 1769 to 1821 were of vast signifi-cance for the Native Americans of the Far West. By the later year vir-tually all of the coastal natives were living in the missions or on near-by ranchos and virtually all of the ancient villages were depopulated. In 1818 Governor Vicente de Sola could report that 64,000 Indians had been baptized and that of these, 41,000 were dead. In fifty years the coastal population had been reduced from perhaps 70,000 to slightly more than 20,000.*

The interior population had also been vitally affected, with losses in numbers undoubtedly taking place through raids for neophytes, slave-raids in Utah, and the spread of disease. On the other hand, the interior natives were becoming more warlike, were mounted, and were better prepared to resist future agression.

It seems also likely that certain movements of people were taking place due ultimately to European intrusion. It is possible, for example, that there was a general southerly and southwesterly migration of Shoshones and Northern Paiutes caused by the Crow, Blackfoot, and Cheyenne occupation of former Shoshone lands in Montana and Wyoming. Likewise, the Southern Paiutes may have commenced a westward-south westward movement to escape from New Mexican, Ute, and Navaho slave-raids. These movements may, in turn, have partially displaced groups such as the Washo although the South-ern Paiute were able to occupy territory in the Mohave Desert vacant due to Spanish missionization. Nearer to the coast it seems possible to sug-gest that certain areas depopulated by the missionaries were occupied by new groups, but this is less clear for the period before 1821.

The European had arrived, this time to stay, and the Far West was never to be placid again.

---

*It should be noted that the Spaniards were well aware that mission Indian death-rates were high prior to the invasion of California.

The Mexican-Indian Period

An independent Mexican state came into effective existence, in so
far as California was concerned, in 1822 after a dozen years of warfare
in central Mexico. Unfortunately, though, the Mexican Indian masses
who had shed their lives struggling for independence since 1810 were not
at first to benefit materially from independence for power fell into the
hands of wealthy persons of largely European descent.

The new Mexican republic (or empire, as it was briefly called) began
its existence in the midst of numerous serious contradictions, contradictions derived from the antagonistic desires of wealthy European landowners, ambitious semi-Europeanized mixed-bloods, and the predominantly
Indian peasant masses. Fundamentally, the Mexican republic before 1910
served the interests of the landowners and the ambitious, although the
constitution of 1824 guaranteed equality of citizenship to all persons,
including theoretically the conquered natives of coastal California,
southern Arizona and central New Mexico.

Between 1822 and 1825 California remained a military colony, a
colony of Mexico rather than a colony of Spain, but the rulers were essentially the same as before. After 1825 the pace of change began to
accelerate, but, by and large, the Indian masses were not to benefit
thereby. Republican ideals and political structures were introduced, but,
in essence, these served merely to allow ambitious mixed-bloods to acquire
power and property, often at the expense of Indians. By the 1840's a
feudal society had developed wherein a new class of large rancho-owners,
with military followings, vied for political power and wealth with the
Indian as only a peripheral participant. The native experienced many
changes, but much remained the same in practice.

The Mexican government was, in general, militarily weaker than that
of Spain and likewise lacked the religious and cultural fanaticism which
had led the Spaniards to seek new conquests. For these reasons, as well
as because of increased resistance, the Mexicans were unable to expand
the territory under their control appreciably, except in the Sonoma
region north of San Francisco Bay. In point of fact, the areas under
Mexican control tended often to be smaller than the areas under Spanish
control, as in the San Diego - San Bernardino back country after 1834-1840,
in northern Baja California, and elsewhere in northern Mexico and the
Southwest.

The missions in California and elsewhere were, theoretically, to be
abolished and the Indians granted equality of citizenship. This did not
happen immediately in California, however, because the Spanish-speaking
population continued to be economically dependent upon the forced labor
of the neophytes and because the Hispano-Mexicans were afraid that liber-
ated Indians would either refuse to work, would rebel, or would flee to the
interior. During the early 1820's, therefore, the missions continued to
exist exactly as before 1822 except that the Franciscans had to go
farther afield to recruit new converts. All of the coastal natives were

missionized (or living in the towns) and it was necessary to reach out into the areas north of San Francisco Bay, to the Central Valley, and to the mountain and desert areas for converts, the bulk of whom would appear to have been recruited by force.

In 1823 San Francisco Solano Mission was founded at Sonoma after a bitter struggle between the priests in charge of the old bay area missions. It would appear that the three existing missions were entirely dependent upon far-off regions, principally north of the bay, for converts and their priest-managers were afraid that a mission at Sonoma would cut off their supply. It was charged (by a San Francisco priest) that the missionaries of San Jose Mission were in the habit of raiding the Suisun region for converts, forcibly seizing gentiles and killing those who resisted.

In 1825 Lt. Col. José María Echeandía was appointed in Mexico to be governor of California and when he came north he brought with him new ideas of Mexican republicanism, equalitarianism, and mestizo upward-mobility not previously apparent in California. Echeandía possessed a democratic style of behavior, typified by his shaking hands with the African-Indian-Spanish mayor of Santa Barbara (an act which made a great impression upon the mayor, Rafael Gonzalez). He also wished to abolish the missions, not merely to liberate the Indians but also, in all probability, to break the economic power of the Franciscans and provide wealth for the ambitious Mexicans who were his supporters.

Several actions initiated by Echeandía changed the missions forever. In July 1826 and January 1831 he issued decrees to begin the process of "secularizing" the missions, that is, to turn each mission into an Indian town. These decrees did not lead to any immediate formal change, because their intent was thwarted by the Franciscans and by a new governor, Lt. Col. Manuel Victoria, but they did stir up the Indians' hopes and led to a decline in mission discipline. More significantly, in 1832 Echeandía recruited hundreds of Indians to fight with him in one of California's many armed political struggles and this act, an unprecedented one for California, set the stage for growing native unrest.

In 1834 - 1836 Governor José Figueroa, a mestizo of Aztec background, was finally forced by the Mexican government (and against his wishes) to commence the formal secularization of the missions. The plan put into effect by Figueroa and his successors was not, however, emancipation in any real sense. The absolute rule of the priest was simply replaced by that of Mexican civilian officials (administrators and mayordomos) and virtually all of the elements of physical coercion were retained. In fact, the situation may have deteriorated, for what ensued was a "sacking" of the missions by some of the more powerful Mexican families of California.

Typically, a secularized mission was to be an Indian pueblo (or, if the mission had branches, several pueblos) with one-half of the property belonging to the natives and the other half being used for support of the priests and secular officials. In fact, however, many missions were

plundered of their resources (livestock, tools, and even portions of
buildings) during the first few months, and, therefore, the Indian
pueblos began life at a considerable disadvantage.

During the era of Juan Bautista de Alvarado (1836 - 1842) and
thereafter the Indian pueblos were largely destroyed, not through any
laziness or incapacity on the part of the Indians, but rather because
the secular administrators managed to appropriate most of the mission
wealth for themselves, while they and other Mexicans (usually their
relatives) were granted the best lands formerly under mission control.
And at the same time as this official looting was occurring, the Indians
were still subject to forced labor for the support of church and state,
physical punishment, and many of the irritants of the pre-1836 mission
regime.

Understandably, the ex-neophytes tended to abandon the mission-
pueblos in favor of more favorable surroundings. Many fled en masse to
the Mexican towns, where they could at least work for themselves with
some greater degree of freedom, while others returned to the interior
or to the sites of their former villages.

In the towns the Indians tended to fall under the influence of the
worst aspects of Hispano-Mexican secular culture, including alcoholism,
excessive gambling, and sexual promiscuity. Syphilis and other diseases
took their toll, so that the Indian population tended to decline steadily,
while a portion of the people were lost in the process of Mexicaniza-
tion and intermarriage.

A somewhat similar process occurred in the rural areas of the coastal
zone where the natives came to be dominated by the Mexican rancho owners.
The typical Mexican rancho was based, economically and socially, upon the
exploitation of Indian labor, a labor which was virtually unpaid except
in the sense of possessing a certain share in crops raised and meat
slaughtered. On the other hand, native villages or settlements were able
to survive within rancho boundaries because the rancho owners needed
Indian house servants and agricultural laborers. It should also be noted
that Indians living in rural communities were able to preserve or revive
something of their pre-mission native cultures, with the rancho owners
apparently having little interest in suppressing such traits.

The Mexican-Indian period saw a marked increase in armed native
resistance to outside aggression and somewhat improved fighting ability.
In general, the entire frontier, from Sonoma to San Diego, was a "war zone"
which the Mexicans were often unable to control in spite of an increased
Spanish-speaking population along the coast. Perhaps the greatest Mexican
successes occurred north of San Francisco Bay after the establishment of
San Francisco Solano (1823) and the civilian settlement of Sonoma (1835),
but these successes occurred only after a great deal of warfare.

During the 1821-24 period the Hukueko of Marin County put up their
last resistance, under leaders such as Pomponio, Marin, and Quintin.

Pomponio was a San Rafael-area native who had been missionized at San Francisco. He later escaped and for several years raided his enemies from San Rafael to Santa Cruz. One of his associates, or perhaps Pomponio himself, once escaped from imprisonment by cutting off the heels of his feet so as to slip off the iron rings or stocks which confined him.

In 1824 Pomponio was captured at Novato and executed, but in the meantime the activities of Marin and Quintin made extended campaigns by the Mexicans necessary. Marin was forced to take refuge on an island, where he at first successfully defended himself, but he and Quintin (after whom "San" Quentin point and prison are named) were both ultimately captured.

A period of relative quiet subsequently ensued, perhaps encouraged by the fact that hired gentiles were used as laborers at Solano during the late 1820's in place, apparently, of the zealous recruitment of neophytes. An epidemic which swept through much of northern California in the early 1830's may also have affected the north bay region.

In 1834 Mariano Vallejo, an ambitious and energetic Mexican, became administrator of Solano mission and commander of the new civilian settlement at Sonoma. Thus commenced a process whereby the Vallejo family and its relations secured control over much of the Napa Valley, Sonoma, and Petaluma - Santa Rosa regions and of the wealth of Solano mission, all at the expense of the Native Californians. As a part of this process, the Vallejos constantly were in need of cheap Indian labor (which was sometimes not voluntary) and of the use of force to sustain what amounted to a vast private empire. To accomplish this the Vallejos secured an alliance with Samyetoy, a Suisun leader who came to be known as Solano, and waged warfare against the independence-loving Sotoyomes (Pomo-speaking people from Healdsburg and perhaps elsewhere), "Guapos" (Miyakama), Yolos, and others.

The details need not concern us here, but from 1834 through 1843 warfare between the Sotoyomes and Mexicans was almost constant, with the "Guapos" and Yolos also joining in, especially before 1840. The Sotoyomes were aided by the Russians to some degree, who furnished arms in exchange for furs and skins, while the Vallejos were aided by Solano and his Suisun warriors who were armed and trained by Salvador Vallejo (and on occasion by other groups, such as the Kainama). On several occasions the Mexicans reached as far north as Clear Lake, as for example in 1837 when they captured Zampay, a Yolo leader, and forced Succara, a Sotoyome leader, to agree to a temporary peace treaty.

The Vallejo policy of using Indian auxiliaries is an excellent example of colonialist strategy, taking advantage of native divisions and rewarding leaders (such as Solano) who were willing to become instruments of the invader's policy. Unfortunately for the Suisunes and others who aided the Mexicans, disenchantment usually set in but often after native strength had declined. In April 1840 Vallejo's Indian infantry attempted to rebel but they were crushed, with many killed and nine leaders executed. In spite of this, many Indians continued to fight for the Vallejos and their service was crucial in insuring Mexican control over the Sonoma region.

In March 1843 the Vallejos, with 270 men, raided the Clear Lake region for servants, forcing the Sotoyomes, Tuleyomes and others to take refuge on an island. In his usually bloody style, Salvador Vallejo slaughtered 170 Indians and a Negro fugitive from the United States who had taken refuge with the natives. This cruel campaign appears to have ended major resistance in the north bay area, although other factors were also at work: the abandonment of Fort Ross by the Russians, the decimation of the native population by disease (several epidemics are reported for the 1830's*), and the increasing Mexican population in the area south of Santa Rosa.

What fighting remained north of the bay was primarily the result of Mexican raiding. For example, in 1845 a group of Mexicans from Sonoma raided the peaceful Kashia Pomo in the Ross area to secure captives. Some Indian men were killed, two women were raped, and 150 servants were obtained. Anglo-Americans took up this practice of capturing Indian laborers in the late 1840's and 1850's as will be discussed below.

Northern California generally was very much affected by European intrusion during this period, although data is often scanty. From the south the natives of the Sacramento Valley were subject to raids for converts and laborers by the Mexicans and later by the intrusion of John Sutter and Anglo settlers. From the north the Indians were subject to visits and raids by Oregon Indians and those who were trading with natives and Europeans along the Columbia River. It is not known when Oregon Country natives began to visit California, but such visits probably commenced with the 1800-1810 period when the former acquired horses. A Spokane woman is reported to have been in California before 1814 and a Walla Walla band as early as the 1800-1810 period. In 1814 trappers in the Willamette Valley met traveling Shasta, Walla Walla, and Cayuse who invited traders to come among them (and it would appear that some did visit the Shasta and upper Sacramento later that year). The John Work expedition of the summer of 1832 found the natives of the Cow Creek - Upper Sacramento River area very much afraid of horses and subject to slave-raids by the Shasta. The Shasta not only held slaves themselves but actively traded them north to the Columbia River, as did the Walla Walla and other groups. At the Dalles an annual fair was held where "the southern tribes brought Modoc, Pitt River, Chasty and California Indians - prisoners - to sell as slaves." A similar fair was held at Yainax, east of Klamath Lake, where came

     Klamaths, Modocs, Summer Lake Snakes to
     the east; Warm Springs people from the
     north; Shastas and Pitt Rivers from
     Northern California; all those fraternized,
     and each October, when the earth had yielded

---

* A smallpox epidemic spread from Ross to Sonoma in 1838 and raged throughout the north, killing 70,000 Indians according to Mariano Vallejo.

its fruits...they met here in grand conclave,
with Nez Perces and Cayuses, and others from
the Cascades to the Rockies; from California
to the Columbia River.... Here also was the
great slave mart of the mid-mountain region.

In 1841 some Walla Wallas and Nez Perces were reportedly planning to
journey south to the Shastas to trade for furs and horses, while in 1844,
1846, and 1847 other Walla Walla groups went as far south as Sutter's Fort
to trade for cattle and other items. (See Robert F. Heizer "Walla Walla
Indian Expeditions to the Sacramento Valley," California Historical Society
Quarterly, March 1942, pp. 1-7) and Alice B. Maloney, "Shasta Was Shatasta
in 1814," California Historical Society Quarterly, September 1945, pp. 229-
234.

Fur trappers and other non-Indians generally found the northern
California Indians friendly in the 1820's and 1830's but by 1837 the
Sacramento River and Shasta groups were often hostile towards trespassers.
Through the late 1830's and 1840's battles between travelers and natives
are frequently reported.*

The Central Valley frontier presented the Mexicans with great problems,
although the native villages to the west of the delta and San Joaquin River
were all depopulated by the 1820's.

In 1827 or 1828 a neophyte known as Estanislao (Stanislaus) escaped
from San Jose Mission and, with another ex-neophyte called Cipriano,
established a band of refugees and gentiles in the northern San Joaquin
Valley. Estanislao vigorously attacked the missions and attempted to stir
up a revolt at San Jose and Santa Clara, with considerable success.
Several campaigns were launched against Estanislao in 1828 but they were
failures. In May 1829 an expedition of forty soldiers with a swivel gun,
accompanied by militia, set out for the River of the Laquisimes (perhaps
the Stanislaus River). The natives were entrenched in a wooded area near
the river and the entire day of May 7 was devoted to a fruitless effort to
force them out. May 8 was also entirely devoted to fighting, with two
soldiers killed and eight wounded. Thereafter the siege was abandoned and
the Indian "freedom-fighters" were left victorious while the Mexicans
retreated to San Jose. This represents, therefore, a great day in northern
California history, being the first substantial victory gained by Native
Californians over the invaders.

The Mexicans could not accept permanent defeat and late in May a very
large expedition was organized, composed of perhaps 100 men including
auxiliaries. On May 30 the army confronted the Indians at the scene of the
former battle. Unable to penetrate the native defenses, the Mexicans set
fire to the wooded area but were still unable to dislodge the defenders.
On the next day the Mexicans advanced into the woods, finding pits, ditches,

---

* In 1830 - 1833 perhaps as many as one-half or more of the Sacramento Valley
Indians were wiped out by malaria introduced from the north.

and barricades but no enemies. The troops immediately followed the
Indians up the River of the Laquisimes and on the following day surrounded
a portion of the "freedom-fighters" in a thicket. The Indians declared
that they would rather die than surrender and fought doggedly behind
ditches and earthworks in spite of the brush being set on fire again.
That night many of the Indians escaped although others were killed.
The next morning at least three women were captured, and perhaps one
man, and all were apparently murdered by the soldiers.

During this same period of time the Central Valley natives were
being visited by Anglo-American, British, and French Canadian fur-trappers
(accompanied by eastern Indians, Negroes, and even an occasional Hawaiian).
These fur-trappers, coming from Utah, New Mexico, and Oregon, were generally
friendly and traded with the natives, especially for horses. The Mexican
priests at missions such as San Jose were disturbed by the presence of
these newcomers, being afraid that the Indians would be encouraged to be
even more hostile towards the Mexican regime. Such a process may well
have taken place, although the Joseph R. Walker party of 1833-1834 actually
aided the Mexicans in slaughtering a group of San Joaquin Valley Indians.
On the other hand, Canadians, Anglos, and Shawnees combined with California
Indians to raid the coast from 1837 into the 1840's.

During the early 1830's the natives of the Central Valley were struck
by a serious epidemic of malaria (or perhaps by a series of epidemics)
which greatly reduced the San Joaquin Valley population (which dropped
from 83,000 to 19,000 between 1800 and 1851, as estimated by one scholar).*
Understandably, this reduction in population made offensive warfare
against the Mexicans more difficult, and it may well have staved off a
major effort at driving the Mexicans from central California.

In 1833 several Mexican expeditions went into the Central Valley,
one in November resulting in the death of twenty-two Moquelumnes.**
Many of these expeditions were now becoming slave-raids, as was charged
in relation to the frequent fighting of 1835. The need for neophytes no
longer existed, but Indian laborers were beginning to be needed on the
ranchos and many expeditions were apparently designed in part to meet
that need.

Sometime during the early 1830's one Yoscolo staged a rebellion at
Mission Santa Clara, liberating 200 Indian girls from confinement, carry-
ing off herds of cattle, and fleeing to Estanislao in the Mariposa region.
The Mexicans were unable to defeat Yoscolo until he retired to the Santa
Cruz Mountains, after a successful raid on the missions in 1839. In the

---

*5,000 Valley Indians were also carried off to the coastal missions before
1833 but some of these returned. See S.F. Cook, "Aboriginal Population of
the San Joaquin Valley," Anthropological Records, v.16, no. 2, and "The
Epidemic of 1830 - 1833," Univ. of California Publications in American
Archaeology and Ethnology, v. 43, no. 3, pp. 303-326.

** In 1834 a total of 111 Moquelumnes and 41 Cosumnes, among others, were
baptized at San Jose Mission.

Santa Cruz area he was finally defeated after a hard battle, with his severed head subsequently being displayed on top of a pole at Santa Clara.

Little is known of the later career of Estanislao, but it would seem that he and his men were still fighting the Mexicans as late as 1838-1839. During 1838 the Moquelumnes, under Sinato, Nilo, and Crispo were very active while another leader, Ambrosio, was captured and shot. Vallejo's Suisun allies under Solano raided the Moquelumnes, in March of that year but in August fifty of the latter, under Cumuchi, sought to steal horses from Sonoma. Cumuchi was captured and executed but before he died he confessed that his people had large numbers of Mexican horses near the lower Sacramento River.

During 1839 the Mexicans staged a large campaign as far as the Kings River country of the Sierras, capturing seventy-seven Indians (chiefly women and children; men over ten were to be killed according to an 1839 decree). Later in the year, however, other Mexicans were surprised on the Rio de Estanislao, losing most of their weapons and suffering ten casualties. In general, warfare continued thusly along the frontier from the San Luis Obispo region to Contra Costa between 1840 and 1847 with much cruelty but with neither side gaining the upper hand militarily.*

The establishment of a fort at Sacramento in 1839 by John Sutter, three other Europeans, ten Hawaiians, and an Oregon Indian had a great impact upon the natives of the Central Valley. Sutter shrewdly emulated Vallejo's Indian policy by allying himself with Narciso, an ex-neophyte who headed the Ochecames of Sacramento, as well as with other nearby natives. These Indians, many of whom were ex-mission converts and knowledgable about agriculture and various crafts, were hired to con-struct the fort, raise crops, catch fish, hunt for furs, and serve as soldiers. Sutter also utilized them and his non-Indian employees to raid more distant villages for captives who were usually sold to rancho-owners near the coast, thus supplying Sutter with perhaps his most reliable "crop." The Indian made Sutter's success possible, and in turn the local Sacramento natives benefited somewhat from Sutter's protection but at an ultimately great cost.

Sutter's Fort during the 1840's became a center for arriving Anglo-Americans who were encouraged to take up land in the lower Sacramento Valley. By 1847 a number of such ranchos existed, almost all utilizing local Indian labor. After 1848, however, this Mexican-style system rapidly gave way to an "Indian removal" process more typically Anglo-American,

---

* In 1848 Governor Pio Pico contracted with Dr. John Marsh and John Gantt to rid central California of its Indian problem by private enterprise. They and their men were to receive one-half of all of the livestock ob-tained and 500 beeves while the government was to get the women and children captives. Indian men would be killed if they resisted.

and although all of the Mexican grants (including Sutter's) stipulated
that Indian property rights had to be respected Anglo-Americans almost
always ignored this fact.

The Tulareños, natives and ex-neophytes in the southern San Joaquin
Valley, constantly raided the coast from the 1830's through the 1840's
often in association with Shawnee, New Mexican, and non-Indian adventur-
ers. In 1844 John C. Frémont passed through the southern San Joaquin
Valley, meeting several "dark-skinned, but handsome and intelligent Indians." He learned that
> the Indians of the Sierra make frequent
> decents upon the settlements, which they
> keep constantly swept of horses; among
> them are many who are called Christian
> Indians, being refugees from Spanish missions.
> Several of these incursions occurred while we
> were at [Sacramento].

At Tehachapi Pass Frémont met an Indian from San Fernando who rode
into camp
> well dressed, with long spurs, and a
> sombrero, and speaking Spanish fluently...
> an Indian face, Spanish costume, jingling
> spurs, and horse equipped after the Spanish
> manner...he had obtained from the priests
> leave to spend a few days with his relatives
> in the Sierra.

This Sierra native pointed out a place, on the east slope of Tehachapi
Pass, "where a refugee Christian Indian had been killed by a party of
soldiers which had unexpectedly penetrated into the mountains." Frémont
was able to purchase a Spanish saddle, spurs, and a horse from four
other Indians, friends of the San Fernando cowboy.

Thus it is clear that the natives of the southern valley and Sierras
were in both hostile and friendly communication with the coast and that
they were becoming partially Mexicanized through this process.

The coastal region in the Santa Barbara area is of some interest
because it was here that the only large scale revolt against Mexican rule
occurred among long-missionized Indians, and this revolt had considerable
impact upon the natives of the interior. The Tsamala-Kagimuswas of
Purisima and Santa Ines and the Tsmuwich of Santa Barbara had apparently
become disturbed at their continued exploitation by the soldiers and other
Mexicans of the Santa Barbara district, and in fact they were being forced
to virtually support the entire military establishment. It would appear
that the chief architect of the revolt, Pacomio (along with Bernabé,
Benito, and Mariano), had long been planning some action, although the
immediate cause was the flogging of a Purisima neophyte. In any event,
simultaneous revolts occurred at Santa Ines and Purisima, with the latter being captured and fortified by the natives. Messages were sent
to the Yokuts-speaking villages of the San Joaquin Valley and the
Santa Barbara neophytes under Andrés seized their mission, defeated a
Mexican attack, and with their belongings, fled to the Buenavista Lake

area of the southern San Joaquin Valley. Many Tsamála rebels soon joined them, along with neophytes from San Fernando and elsewhere.

On March 16 a large Mexican force succeeded in capturing Purisima, imprisoning Pacomio and the other leaders. In April another large army attacked the refugees in the valley but failed to accomplish anything. The offer of pardons and the presence of a still larger army in June did, however, persuade many of the Santa Barbara Indians to return to their mission in June and July. Large numbers remained at liberty, though, and took up permanent settlement along the Sierra foothills, north of Kern River. In the Spring of 1834 they were visited by a party of Anglo-Americans:

> After we halted here we found that these
> people could talk the Spanish language...and on
> inquiry ascertained that they were a tribe called
> the Cancoas, which tribe some eight or ten years
> since resided in...the missionary station near St.
> Barbara, on the coast, where they rebelled..., robbed
> the church of all its golden images and candle-
> sticks, and one of the priests of several thousand
> dollars in gold and silver, when they retreated to
> the spot where we found them.... This tribe is well
> acquainted with the rules of bartering for goods
> or anything they wish to buy - much more so than any
> other tribe we met with. They make regular visits
> to such [Mexican] posts where they are unknown, and
> also make appointments with ship-traders to meet at
> some designated time and place.... These people are
> 7 or 800 strong, their houses are constructed of
> poles and covered with grass, and are tolerably well
> supplied with house-hold furniture which they
> brought with them.... They follow agricultural
> pursuits to some extent, raising very good crops of
> corn, pumpkins, melons, etc.... They are also in the
> habit of making regular visits to the settlements for
> the purpose of stealing horses, which they kill and eat.

Very little resistance continued along the coast itself after 1825, although a native known as Valerio for a few years carried on a quasi-guerrilla style of raiding near Santa Barbara until being finally killed by the Mexicans.

The Indians of the Los Angeles region, although significant as virtually the only workers during the Mexican period, failed to organize any armed resistance of any significance, although a few ex-neophytes raided from their villages on the Mohave River (two campaigns of 1845 finally and literally wiped-out these refugees including their brave leader, Joaquin, who had earlier been mutilated by a mayordomo at Rancho Chino). More serious were the frequent raids of Utes and New Mexicans, the former coming from Colorado under Walkara. Throughout the 1840's and 1850's the Utes, sometimes in combination with New Mexican traders, camped in remote areas in order to steal livestock in the Los Angeles Basin. They also contributed to raiding by Southern Paiutes, since the latter were being forced by Ute pressure to move westward into the Mohave Desert. By 1842, at least, minor Paiute raiding in Southern California had commenced.

The Hamakhava of the Colorado River also came into the Southern California coastal plain as they had in earlier years. Prior to 1800 - 1820 their visits had been friendly trading enterprises but the Spaniards had forcibly interfered and thereafter the Hamakhavas aided rebel neophytes in various hostile actions. By the 1830's and 1840's the Hamakhavas were stealing horses in the Los Angeles Basin, usually in alliance with Mohave River rebels or in connection with general periods of native unrest.

After 1826 the mission Indians of the San Juan Capistrano - San Diego region gradually became more restless, in great measure due to Echeandía's attempted reforms. A few battles with Kamias and Cahuillas occurred along the frontier in 1826 and the Mexicans also attempted, unsuccessfully, to establish a post on the Colorado River. From 1827 to 1832 the frontier was quiet in the south but by 1833 a new era of Indian warfare commenced, largely brought about by the collapse of Echeandía's reforms and by increased Mexican aggressiveness in the matter of land acquisition.

In February 1833 it was reported that the San Diego natives, together with others as far north as San Gabriel, were demanding that the missions be turned over to them. This did not occur and in the spring, Tomás Jayochi, a Kamia, organized a rebellion in alliance with the Quechan. The Mexicans learned of the plot and stopped it but the following year brought even more serious events. Santa Catalina Mission was attacked in northern Baja California by Kamias, Paipais and Cocopas, Kamias and Cahuillas were raiding farther north, and the mission Indians rebelled at San Bernardino, destroying that place with attacks in 1834 and 1835. During the latter year mission Indians largely abandoned San Juan Capis-trano and the Cahuillas were hostile, planning to converge upon San Jacinto (Hemet) for a general uprising. Between 1836 and 1842 warfare was almost continuous from San Diego to San Bernardino, with Quechans, Kamias, Cahuillas, and Hamakhavas becoming even more aggressive. San Diego was virtually captured by the natives at one point and several missions in northern Baja California were permanently destroyed. The Mexican population steadily declined in the San Diego region and numerous ranchos were either abandoned or never occupied.

Gradually, however, a state of equilibrium began to be achieved in the San Bernardino-San Diego region between Mexicans and natives. In 1839 the leaders of the Kamias of Jacumba, Cartucho and Pedro Pablo, had been planning to "recover" California "which they claimed belonged to them....they were not alone, but that there were many others throughout California and in places where they would be least expected" ready to join in their plans. In actual fact, though, most Southern California native groups, once having thrown off the yoke of the missions were quite willing to live at peace with the Mexicans if the latter would respect their local autonomy and village land rights. By the 1840's the Mexicans south and east of Los Angeles were simply forced to agree, informally, to such a live and let live relationship and when they did warfare largely ceased.

Mexican rancho owners and officials also learned to emulate the Vallejo-Sutter style of utilizing Indian allies as soldiers or auxiliaries.

By ca. 1839 a group of Cahuillas moved westward to settle near Jurupa (Riverside) and after 1842 a band of mountain Cahuillas under Juan Antonio served as an auxiliary force for the Lugo family in the Colton-San Bernardino region. In a similar manner, Cabezon, a Cahuilla leader in the Coachella Valley, became a Mexican ally and Jatiñil, a Kamia leader in northern Baja California, aided the Mexicans until becoming disillusioned after 1837. These auxiliaries proved useful in helping to capture or kill runaways and in at least diminishing thefts of livestock. No really serious warfare occurred in the San Bernardino-San Diego region between 1842 and 1851, however, with the minor exception of an attempt in 1846 by the Kupanga-kitom and their neighbors in the Warner's Valley area to obtain revenge on the Mexicans during the U. S.-Mexican War. The natives' aid was not appreciated by the invading Anglo-American army and a force of Mexicans and Cahuillas under Juan Antonio put down the rebels.

Mexican travelers and Anglo-American fur trappers were able to visit the Colorado River frequently during the 1830's and 1840's, but always at the sufferance of the still vigorously independent Yuman peoples. The latter were, in turn, engaged in rather constant inter-tribal warfare, greatly increased over earlier periods. The Quechans and their allies, the Hamakhavas, Yavapais,Kamias and others were continually at war with the Halchidhomas, Maricopas, Cocopas, and their allies, doubtless stimulated in part by the fact that the Halchidhomas and Maricopas had aided the Spaniards against the Quechans in 1781 - 82. This warfare gradually led to the decimation of the Kohuanas and Halyikwamais, who were forced to abandon their rich delta lands to flee to the Halchidhoma near Blythe. By the 1820's - 1830's the latter were forced to gradually retreat eastward to the Maricopas on the Gila, while the Kohuana and Halykwamai remnants returned to the delta. During the 1830's and 1840's the latter were further reduced in number and were forced to disperse, some joining the Cocopa, others fleeing to the eastward-retreating Maricopa, and some being absorbed by the victorious Quechans, Kamias, and Hamakhavas.

In 1848, therefore, the lower Colorado River was controlled by three groups only, the Hamakhavas, the Quechans, and the Cocopas, with some Southern Paiutes (called Chemehuevis), Kamias, Paipais, and Halyikwamai-Kohuana remnants living nearby but at the sufferance of the more powerful groups. This process is interesting if only because it illustrates two important processes: first, the continued emphasis placed by native groups upon traditional inter-Indian rivalries as opposed to unification in the face of European and Mexican aggression; and, second, the many changes in traditional boundaries occurring as a result of the indirect and direct consequences of European and Mexican influences. It is very likely that similar changes took place throughout much of the Far West, although detailed documentary evidence may often be lacking or may be still unexamined.

Reference should also be made to the extreme conservatism of the Colorado River Yumans who, in spite of three hundred years of contact with Europeans and Mexicans, chose not to significantly alter their societies or cultures. Again this is fairly typical of far western native populations.

The Great Basin region was also affected by alien influences during the period from the 1820's through the 1840's, although to a lesser degree than was California. Most affected were the Southern Paiute groups of Utah and Nevada who were continually being raided by New Mexicans, Utes, and, to a lesser extent, Anglo-Americans and Navahos. Illustrating this process is an account in the diary of an Anglo-American who joined a New Mexican caravan in 1839, traveling from Los Angeles to Taos:

> hurrying on, I discovered that our New Mexicans had surrounded a rancheria of Piutes. I saw one little Indian boy, about 12 years old with his arm nearly shot off....I began to scold the New Nexicans and called them a pack of damned brutes and cowards - and they were so.
> There was one old Indian standing with his bow and arrow - they wanted to take and kill him, but were afraid to approach near enough to come within reach of his arrow - I went up to the Indian and asked him for his bow and arrows - they had solemnly promised me not to hurt him if I succeeded in disarming him - the Indian handed them to me - and I shall never forgive myself for having taken the word of those villians, for villians they were... as soon as they saw the Indian without arms they came near and riddled him with bullets. [The author then went off on his own].
>
> I found another rancheria.... an Indian came out and by signs asked me if I had come to fight. I said no; then he asked me if I was hungry, and... he invited me to alight and partake of what he had, which was atole made of the seed of hogweed, and barbecued trout.... Whilst I was eating up came the confounded New Mexicans [under Tomás Salazar], and the Indians ran to conceal themselves in the brush - all but two succeeded in escaping - those two unfortunate Piutes were taken by the Mexicans, tied, and shot in cold blood.... [The Mexicans stated that]"it is not wrong to kill these pagan Indians." (Michael White ms., Bancroft Library C-D 173, University of California, Berkeley).

Farther north, the lives of Shoshones, Northern Paiutes, and Washos were affected by numerous parties of trappers, traders, and, after 1841, overland emigrants who seriously depleted the natural food resources of the Humboldt River watershed and often precipitated minor incidents. Nonetheless, little organized warfare occurred, in part because a Northern Paiute leader, Truckee, counseled friendship with the white strangers during the 1840's. Northern Paiutes and Washos occasionally served as guides across Sierra passes and a group of the former joined Fremont in 1846 - 1847 in his campaigns against the Mexicans of coastal California.

It is to be suspected also that the great expansion of warfare and slave-raiding which occurred in the Oregon Country and northern Rockies during this period very much affected Nevada-Utah native groups. Columbia River-Oregon tribes capable of raiding northern California for slaves were also capable of raiding northern Nevada, while Plains Indian war parties could easily have attacked the Shoshones of northeastern Nevada and northern Utah. It is highly likely, therefore, that few groups in the Great Basin were immune from influences, including slave-raiding and disease, likely to lead to significant internal changes and boundary dislocations.*

   In summary, the Mexican-Indian Period, while not witnessing any great expansion in the extent of non-Indian territorial control, was an era of significant change for native peoples. Although many positive elements can be cited, such as greater unity, increased sophistication in dealing with aggressors, more adequate military ability, and the adoption of certain useful traits (such as agriculture in the Central Valley), the general trend of the period is negative. Aside from the fact that thousands of Indians were enslaved, forced to labor as neophytes or serfs, killed, flogged, separated from loved ones, and pushed into apathy and alcoholism, is the clear evidence that the still-free groups were greatly weakened by disease and warfare. Thus, although the area of free Indian territory remained much the same as in 1821, the numbers of Indians living there were greatly reduced, and those that remained were being more frequently abused by alien incursions.

   By 1848 the native population of California had been reduced to about 100,000, with perhaps as many as 100,000 Indians dying of sickness and warfare in one generation after 1820-1821. Thus the Mexican era was apparently more destructive to the native population than the Spanish period had been (although the loss of at least 50,000 persons between 1769 and 1820 may not be accurate since it does not reflect the possible effects of epidemics in the interior).

   Nonetheless, the Native American population might well have ultimately recovered (as immunity to disease developed) and remained dominant in the Far West were it not for the Anglo-American invasion. At the time the latter event commenced, in 1845 - 47, some 6,000 ex-mission Indians were still residing along the coast (along with 7,000 predominantly-Indian Mexicans and 700 Europeans) and more than 100,000 natives in the interior of California, Nevada, and Utah. The Far West was still overwhelmingly Native American, but a drastic change, for which neither Mexicans nor natives were ready, was in the offing.

---

* For example, James C. Adams in 1854 joined a group of Mewuk in their annual excursion from the Toulumne River over the Sierras to Walker Lake, where they were accustomed to spend the summer. Such movements could easily have spread the epidemics of the 1830's into Nevada.

The Anglo-American Invasion

    The United States-Mexican War had little immediate effect upon the
Native Americans of the Far West, since the United States' armed forces
concentrated upon subduing Mexican settlements and not upon controlling
the vast areas belonging to Indians. The U.S.-Mexican War did not, therefore, result in the conquest of the entire so-called "Mexican Cession"
area. On the contrary, this war merely marked the beginning of an era
of military conquest which did not finally cease until a small group of
Utes and Southern Paiutes in the area of southeastern Utah were subdued
in 1915 (although the bulk of the region was conquered by the 1870's).

    Nor did the United States acquire, as so many school maps assert
the "Mexican Cession" area as a result of the Treaty of Guadalupe
Hidalgo of 1848. The Mexican government could only cede to the United
States that which she possessed and quite clearly Mexico possessed no
sovereignty except in coastal California, southern Arizona, and central
New Mexico. Many decades of warfare, and the expenditure of many thousands of dollars and lives, were necessary before the United States could
assert meaningfully that its laws were operative throughout the Far West.
It is simply another example of anti-Indian prejudice, and of ignorance,
that school maps award the Far West to the United States in 1846 (Oregon)
and 1848, ignoring thereby the existence and continued independence of
numerous native groups.

    The conquest of the bulk of California and Nevada was not accom-
plished primarily by regular soldiers, although they played an important
role, especially in remote areas and in later phases of fighting. The conquest was rather the direct result of the westward movement of a vast horde
of armed civilians, single men and family units, very much resembling the
ancient "hordes" of Central Asia in their mobility, warlike nature, and
indifference to the boundary claims and property rights of already established but alien peoples. Unfortunately for Native Americans, these
invaders often possessed a hatred of Indians which went beyond the mere
desire for acquiring Indian property to the wish for the complete extermination of native peoples. Unfortunately also, these invaders possessed
a form of society which provided no real means for Indian absorption (as
had the Spanish and Mexican) and forms of government which tended to be
immediately responsive to the vilest wishes of the westward-moving masses.

    Thus it is not surprising that a historian such as H.H.Bancroft
could, in the 1880's, assert that
          the California valley cannot grace her annals with a
          single Indian war bordering on respectability. It
          can boast, however, a hundred or two of as brutal
          butchering, on the part of our honest miners and
          brave pioneers, as any area of equal extent in our re-
          public. The poor natives of California had neither
          the strength nor the intelligence to unite in any for-
          midable numbers; hence, when now and then one of them
          plucked up courage to defend his wife and little ones,
          or to retaliate on one of the many outrages that were
          constantly being perpetrated upon them by white per-
          sons, sufficient excuse was offered for the miners
          and settlers to band and shoot down any Indians they

met, old or young, innocent or guilty, friendly or hostile, until their appetite for blood was appeased.

The United States possesses many sordid chapters in its history, but perhaps none is more sordid than that relating to the conquest of California, typified as it is by great brutality and callousness and what closely approaches genocide. This process cannot be examined in detail, since the bulk of California Indians were conquered, and died, in innumerable little episodes rather than in large campaigns. This fact, of course, makes the sequence of events all the more distressing since it serves to indict not a group of cruel leaders, or a few squads of rough soldiers, but, in effect, an entire people; for the conquest of the Native Californian was above all else a popular, mass enterprise.

A few Indians seem to have naively expected that the United States' armed forces would sympathize with the native viewpoint in the Southwest, since both groups had been fighting against the Mexicans. But, of course, the Anglo-Americans, as soon as the U.S.-Mexican War was terminated, adopted the Mexican side of whatever controversies were in progress, since the Mexican leadership was "white" or "nearly-white", and since the property interests of the two ex-enemies coincided. (It should be noted that throughout the Americas the United States has almost always supported white or near-white elites against the brown or black masses, betraying thereby a deepseated racial and cultural bias).

Quite understandably then, United States forces became involved in warfare against Indians even before the war with Mexico was officially ended. Thus the long struggle of the Central Valley natives against the Mexican ranchers became, by 1846, a struggle also against Anglo-Americans, with U.S. troops campaigning to protect their new subjects in the San Jose area. Similar skirmishes occurred in the south.

The Anglo-American invasion of California and adjacent areas really commenced with the Gold Rush of 1848, although the initial phase (from May 1848 to the spring of 1849) did not involve extensive warfare. The incoming miners, many of whom were Mexicans from California and Sonora, South Americans, and Europeans, were intent upon finding gold rather than upon acquiring land. They likewise were greatly influenced by the Mexican attitude, which favored the 'hiring or commissioning of Indians to do as much of the prospecting and rough work as possible. Many ex-neophytes were brought from the coast and large numbers of interior natives, both ranch-hands and free Indians, were encouraged to prospect. Such settlers as John Sutter, P. B. Reading, and Charles Weber were especially prominent in using Indian miners, Weber making an advantageous agreement with José Jesus, a former neophyte alcalde of San Jose Mission who had returned to the Rio de Estanislao to fight against the Mexicans and who had succeeded Estanislao upon the latter's death. José Jesus supplied Weber with Indian miners who were so successful in locating coarse gold that they were responsible for a rush of other miners to the Stanislaus River watershed. Other old-settlers in California, such as Isaac Williams, used Indian miners in the Southern California mountains as early as 1849. Many other natives searched for gold on their own, using the metal as a means for obtaining food in an environment fast becoming difficult to survive in by means of their traditional economy.

Generally speaking, the 1848-early 1849 phase of the Gold Rush was localized in the central Sierra foothills, the numbers of miners were not as numerous as in later years, and inter-ethnic hostility was diminished by the relative ease with which gold was located. Nonetheless, hostilities did occur in the most crowded districts, the Colomas and Consumnes both suffering briefly from warfare. Elsewhere, Trinity River natives (probably Hupas) forcibly drove away miners and minor friction was common along the various emigrant routes from Oregon, across Nevada, and along the Colorado River.

During 1849 the Gold Rush changed in character as tens of thousands of Anglo-Americans with lesser thousands of Mexicans and others poured into California. During the next few years the miners expanded rapidly northwards to the tributaries of the Feather and Yuba rivers, southwards to the Kern, stormed by sea and land into the Trinity-Klamath region, and even prospected extensively in such areas as Sonoma-Mendocino and Southern California. The Anglo-Americans also became increasingly hostile towards any class of non-white miners and even against non-Anglo Europeans.

Everywhere the miners went hostilities soon developed and understandably so, since the invaders refused to respect any native rights. Villages were uprooted, women were raped or carried into concubinage, men were casually murdered, and, everywhere, the native food supply was ruthlessly destroyed. The Indians responded with retaliatory attacks which almost always led to the organization of campaigns by irregular militia or vigilante-type units. These campaigns often resulted in the near-extermination of whatever Indians might be in the vicinity, including women and children.

A few incidents can be cited here to illustrate the predominant character of warfare in California in 1849 and the 1850's. At Big Oak Flat in 1850, for example, one writer witnessed the following:

> We had been there only a few days when one night
> a band of Mt. Indians made a raid on some of the
> Miners on the Flat and robbed them of a Horse and
> other valuables, killing one Miner and wounding
> another with their arrows. The Miners followed
> the Indians for 25 miles up into the Mountains,
> then they found their settlement, and killed old
> Men, Squaws, and Children, the Bucks having fled.
> I am thankful that I did not join them as their
> acts were more foul than the Indians'. (Charles
> E. Pancoast, A Quaker 49'er, 1930, p.298).

A few years later a group of Wintu living in the McCloud River area were invited by the whites to come to a feast for the purpose of making peace.
> About three hundred Indians came....They had been
> there several days, feasting and dancing, when some
> Num-soos from Trinity Center came and warned them
> of danger, telling of a similar trick played on
> their people at a place called Kal-le-ke-le where

many were slaughtered.... Then Dol-le-ken-til-le-ma
[a leader] warned his people to be on their guard.
The Indians began to slip away quietly.... The chief
then noticed that whenever an Indian left the table,
a soldier followed. This alarmed him, so he watched
his chance and slipped down to the river. A soldier
followed. The chief dived and when he came up the
soldier fired at him, but he dived again and escaped.
The forty-five Wintoon warriors remaining at the
table were all massacred by the soldiers and volunteers. (C. Hart Merriam, Studies of California Indians,
1955, pp. 20-21).

The natives of the Clear Lake region during 1848-1850 experienced
a sequence of events not by any means untypical. Two white men, Stone
and Kelsey, had settled in the Clear Lake area where they established a
Mexican-style ranch operation using Indian labor (which, however, they
abused more than the average Mexican ranchero would have, with frequent
flogging, torture, seizing of women, and even murder). In 1849 Kelsey
led a futile expedition to the gold regions, taking a number of Clear
Lake Indians along as virtual slaves, few of whom survived. Finally
in the fall of 1849 the exasperated and starving Pomos, led by two
Indian cowboys, Shuk and Xasis, executed Stone and Kelsey.

The killing of two white men, even though guilty of great wrongs,
naturally led to a military campaign against the Clear Lake natives. The
first expedition, in 1849, failed to reach the Indians, who were hiding
on an island but in May 1850 Capt. Nathaniel Lyon led a large force,
equipped with boats, to the lake. According to army reports, 60 out of
400 Indians were killed on the island while at least another 75 were
eliminated near the Russian River in Mendocino County. That this was a
"massacre" is revealed, first, by the fact that the soldiers suffered only
two non-fatal casualties while more than 135 natives were being killed,
and, second, by the Indian version of the event:
The next morning the white warriors went across in their
long dugouts. The Indians said they would meet them in
peace so when the whites landed the indians went to
wellcom them but the white man was determined to kill
them. Ge-Wi-lih said he threw up his hands,.. but the
white man fired and shot him in the arm....many women
and children were killed on around this island. One
old lady...said she saw two white man coming with their
guns up in the air and on their guns being a little girl.
They brought it to the creek and threw it in the water.
And a little while later, two more men came....This
time they had a little boy on the end of their guns and
also threw it in the water. A little ways away...
layed a woman shoot through the shoulder. She held her
little baby in her arms. Two white men torge the woman
and baby, they stabed the woman and the baby.... She
said when they gathered the dead, they found all the
little ones were killed by being stabed, and many of the
women were also killed stabing.... This old lady also
told about the whites hang a man on Emerson island....

The Indian was hung and a large fire built under [him].
And another Indian was caught.... This one was tied to
a tree and burnt to death. (William Ralganal Benson,
"The Stone and Kelsey 'Massacre' on the Shores of
Clear Lake in 1849," Calif. Hist. Society Quarterly,
September 1932, pp. 266-273).

The Indians of California and the southeastern Great Basin were
continually subject to slave-raids in this period to supply servants
for the towns and ranchos of California and New Mexico. In 1853 E. F.
Beale visited San Pablo Rancho in Contra Costa County where he found
ninety sick and starving Indians who were "survivors of a band who were
worked all last summer and fall and as the winter set in, when broken
down by hunger and labor and without food or clothes they were turned
adrift to shift for themselves." These natives had been brought from
the same Clear Lake area mentioned above by Mexican-Californians who
made a business of capturing and selling Indians. (Stephen Bonsal,
Edward Fitzgerald Beale, 1912, p. 177).*

Extreme cruelty in warfare was not limited to the first few years
of fighting. As late as 1858-1863 horrible massacres were perpetuated
in northwestern California as when the citizens of Eureka slaughtered
some 60 unsuspecting natives of all ages and sexes at Humboldt Bay, or
when almost all of the males of the Wailaki and Lassik groups were killed
during a "round-up" of Indians along the Eel River. One should also not
forget the planned extermination of almost 2,000 Yanas (most of whom were
working on white ranches) by Indian-hating white vigilantes in the area
east of Redding and Red Bluff during the single year of 1864. (See
Theodora Kroeber, Ishi in Two Worlds, 1967, for further details).

It must not be thought that all Indians were more or less passive
victims of miners and slave-raiders. Many native groups, from Klamath
River to the Colorado, offered notable resistance during the early 1850's,
resistance which sometimes won the admiration of their violence-admiring
foes. In Southern California, for example, the Quechans and Hamakhavas,
although generally tolerant of inoffensive travelers, defended themselves
well when offended. In 1850 a group of outlaws led by John Glanton, who
had been scalping Apaches (and Mexicans) for money in Chihuahua, took
over a ferry being operated on the Colorado at Yuma. The Anglo gang not
only robbed travelers but destroyed a rival ferry operated by the Quechans.
Finally on April 21, 1850 the Quechans rose up and wiped out the outlaws,
only thereby to gain the animosity of Indian-haters who held that no
Indian should ever be allowed to kill any whiteman, no matter how bad. In
the fall of 1850 125 white militiamen attacked the Quechans but the Indians
were soon able to force the invaders to retreat back to the coast.

---

* Sad to state, northern Indians, such as the Klamath, were still
raiding southward to the Pit River country for slaves to sell in
Oregon as late as 1857.

United States troops established a post at the site of Fort Yuma in late 1850 and peace prevailed until 1851 when many Southern California natives, exasperated by white encroachment and by attempts to collect taxes on Indian property, planned a general revolt. Antonio Garrá, a Kupanga-kitom, was the chief architect of the revolution but he was soon joined by Quechans, some southern Cahuillas, Kamias, Luiseños, Chemehuevi Paiutes, and Hamakhavas, and messages were sent to the San Joaquin Valley tribes. During 1851 and 1852 warfare raged along the Colorado River and in San Diego County, with the river and desert areas being for a time completely under Indian control. Garra was eventually tricked into being captured by a group of pro-white Cahuillas and subsequently strong U.S. forces defeated the Quechans, but only after a bitter and protracted campaign featuring the destruction of the native food supply.

By the mid-1850's the greater part of central and southern California was conquered, although a little fighting occurred in the San Joaquin Valley in 1857-1858. Much of extreme northern California, all of eastern California, almost all of Nevada, and most of western Utah were still under Indian control, however, and a new phase in warfare tended to develop. The still-free Indian groups generally lived in isolated, rough or desert regions and many had profited from the experiences of their less-fortunate brothers in terms of being more knowledgable about fighting whitemen. Therefore, it was generally necessary for large bodies of regular troops or organized militia to proceed against them.

The most notable areas of resistance centered among the Hamakhava (1850's and early 1860's), Southern Paiutes (to at least 1869), Owens Valley Paiutes and Shoshones (1850's to 1865), Northern Paiutes (1860's and, for a few, into the 1870's), Western Shoshones (early 1860's), Modocs (to 1873), Pit River groups (to 1867), and Hupas, Whilkuts, and Karoks (to 1864). In all of these wars the Indian people exhibited great bravery in the defense of their homes or in their efforts to insure a food supply for survival, but they also tended to exhibit the disunity so destructive of native efforts at liberation generally. There was no simultaneous general uprising against the invaders occurring over a wide area. Instead each group tended to rebel or fight only when pressed to the wall itself and not in alliance with other people in anticipation of what might be their own fate at some future date.

The Native Americans of the Far West won a number of notable victories, as when the Northern Paiutes defeated a large militia force sent against them at Pyramid Lake in May 1860, when many Hupas, Karoks, and Whilkuts successfully fought a war of attrition for five long years between 1858 and 1864, when a small body of Modocs under Kentipoos (Captain Jack) courageously held off an overwhelming force of regular U.S. troops in the Modoc lava beds for over three months in 1872 - 1873, and when the ever-diminishing Yahi fought stubbornly for their freedom from 1850 until 1870 and then chose to live a life of complete concealment rather than surrender.

Unfortunately, the many heroic instances of resistance by Indian people ordinarily failed in the long run simply because of the overwhelming numer-ical superiority possessed by the invaders. It is worth noting, however, that the native groups which fought the hardest often received the best and largest reservations, while those who were defeated early or who were relatively passive usually received small or no reservations. Perhaps deservedly, those Indians who served as auxiliaries or scouts of the whites quite often received nothing at all for their efforts.*

By 1873 the California-Great Basin region was militarily under the control of the Anglo-American invaders, but at what human and moral cost! The California census of 1870 reveals only 31,000 Indians surviving, a decline of perhaps 70,000 in two decades. But the conquest itself did not end with the military phase - in fact it was only beginning.

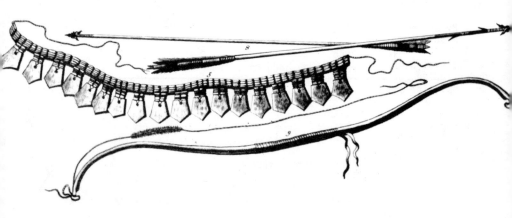

5. Ground shell necklace, probably also used as money. 8. Hunting arrows. 9. Reflexed bow. Old drawings of G. Langsdorf. Courtesy Bancroft Library, Berkeley, California.

---

* It should be noted that the United States during this period often followed a policy of not providing lands or services, except sporadically, for completely pacified or un-warlike groups.

III. THE CONQUEST: POWERLESSNESS AND POVERTY

The First Thirty Years: Stealing From the Dying

The first thirty years of the conquest were the hardest to bear, especially in California. That this is true is starkly evident in the fact that the native population fell to a mere 16,000 in 1880, indicating a loss of 15,000 in the decade of the 1870's (an almost 50% drop) and a loss of some 80,000 during the entire thirty year period (an 80% decline).

To be conquered at all is a very sad fate, but to be conquered by those who hate and despise you is the worst of all possible situations. The Native Californians were unfortunate in that they were overcome by a people whose view of them was so filled with hostility that it easily supported genocide:

> We will let those rascally redskins know that they have
> no longer to deal with the Spaniard or the Mexican, but
> with the invincible race of American backwoodsmen, which
> has driven the savage from Plymouth Rock to the Rocky
> Mountains, and has headed him off here on the western
> shore ...., and will drive him back to meet his kindred
> fleeing westward, all to be drowned in the Great Salt Lake.
> (Horace Bell, Reminiscenses of a Ranger, 1881, p. 116)

Along with hostility came contempt and prejudice, as exemplified by numerous viciously racist statements included in works about California written during the period after 1849. Even a more balanced writer such as H. H. Bancroft could write in the 1880's that "we do not know why the Digger Indians of California were so shabbily treated by nature; why with such fair surroundings they were made so much lower in the scale of intelligence than their neighbors...."

The Anglo-Americans as a whole felt little sympathy towards peoples considered to be both hostile foes and inferior creatures. Bancroft typified white-Indian relations in California during this era as "one of the last human hunts of civilization, and the basest and most brutal of them all." Quite naturally, this brutality extended far beyond the realm of actual warfare and affected every facet of the natives' life, especially wherever whites were numerous.

What were the conditions faced by Native Americans in the first decades of conquest? In practical terms, the Indian existed with neither legal rights nor protection since the constitution of the State of California, adapted in 1849, deprived him illegally of citizenship*, since the legislature soon prohibited Indian testimony in the courts, and since white attitudes made the killing, raping, or enslavement of an Indian no crime at all. A similar situation existed in Nevada (and to a lesser extent in Utah

---

* Under the Treaty of Guadalupe Hidalgo the United States was bound to recognize Indian citizenship in ex-Mexican areas, but the U. S. ignored this requirement.

where Mormon attitudes were more sympathetic to the Indian as a person).
This point must be strongly made: that the Indian, after conquest,
existed at the complete and absolute mercy of whatever sympathy or bar-
barity existed in the white population. And there was precious little
sympathy!

The white settlers and their governments adopted the unconstitu-
tional attitude that the Indians possessed no property rights whatsoever
and that they were "trespassers on the public domain."* Thus although
native villages might be allowed to exist for years in an out-of-the-way
or undesireable location, the villagers generally gained no "squatter's
rights" through longevity of residence and could be removed at will by
anyone. For many years, then, most Indians possessed no land or security
of residence since reservations served only a small proportion of the
population.

Conquered natives were constantly faced with the prospect, not
merely of being driven from their homes, but of being seized and forced
into servitude or concubinage. The Los Angeles Basin was a major center
of Indian labor exploitation, with natives either retained as peones
(unable to move because of debts or having nowhere else to go) or literally
worked to death as captive-labor, purchased at auction in Los Angeles
(as late as 1869) or simply seized in the countryside. Northwestern
California was also a center for Indian slavery. An 1861 report asserted
that

> In the frontier portions of Humboldt and Mendocino
> counties a band of desperate men have carried on a
> system of kidnapping for two years past; Indian
> children were seized and carried into the lower coun-
> ties and sold into virtual slavery.... The kidnappers
> follow at the heels of the soldiers to seize the
> children when their parents are murdered and sell them
> to best advantage. (37th Congress, 2nd Session,
> Senate Ex. Doc. No. 1, v.1, p. 759).

The California legislature adopted legislation in 1850 which made
it possible for any Indian to be declared a vagabond and sold to the
highest bidder for laboring purposes. Throughout the state Indian women
were commonly seized and forced to serve as servants or concubines, in
some cases being cast adrift after a time, in other cases becoming a
common-law wife (legal marriage between whites and Indians was long prohibited in both California and Nevada).

Another widespread form of servitude developed in both California and
Nevada due to the non-possession of land on the part of the Indians. As
whites seized all of the desireable fertile lands the natives who survived the military conquest found that they had to reside on either non-
productive ground or on a white farm or ranch. In either case, survival

---

* This doctrine, which is still held, in effect, by the U.S. government,
blatantly violates both the Fifth Amendment to the Constitution and
the Treaty of Guadalupe Hidalgo.

depended largely upon being able to acquire food in the white economy
since hunting and gathering had become exceedingly difficult. Thus most
natives were forced by economic circumstances to become agricultural
laborers or house servants for white people. Our histories of labor
ordinarily ignore this fact, but prior to the Chinese the Indians served
as the great exploited agricultural laborers of the Far West.

The vast majority of Indians, therefore, were dispersed as squatters
in the rough places or as tenants on white farms and ranches, in either
case largely dependent upon white employment and whatever|wages (if any)
were offered. In many areas, in fact, the natives labored only for room
and board and protection, since to be expelled from the farm might mean
death at the hands of white terrorists or by starvation.

Indian labor was especially important in northern California, in the
fertile valleys of Nevada, and in Southern California. In 1852 it was
said that
> they [the Luiseños and Kamias] are a large majority of the
> laborers, mechanics, and servants of San Diego and Los
> Angeles counties .... The Indian laborers... are almost
> the only house or farm servants we have. (John W. Caughey, ed.,
> The Indians of Southern California in 1852, 1952, pp. 16,21).

Unfortunately, the Indian laboring class was not well cared for and by
1880 there were not enough Indians left to comprise an important part of
the labor force, except in a few rural localities.

The fact that the whites of California and the Great Basin desired
cheap labor was certainly a major factor in preventing the establishment
of adequate reservations. Other factors were, of course, the usual
white greed for land and the failure of most Indians to pose a serious
enough military threat to justify a "generous" policy.

In 1848, when the United States asserted its claim to the Far West,
the coastal zone of California included numerous villages or settlements
of ex-mission Indians. These villages possessed property rights under
Mexican law, which rights the United States was required to respect by
the Treaty of Guadalupe Hidalgo. The United States, in spite of suggestions
to the contrary made by a few experts on Mexican law, chose not to recognize any such titles and, as a result, virtually every village was destroyed during the 1860's - 1880's by aggressive Anglo entrepreneurs and
ranchers. Theoretically, of course, the Indians might have appealed to
the courts but in practice they could not during these years because
their citizenship rights and their right to testify against whites were
both denied. The viciousness of the white population as regards the ex-
mission Indians is illustrated by the fact that when, in 1870, an effort
was made to set aside the valleys of Pala and San Pascual as reservations the surrounding whites rushed in to seize the land and the Indians
were effectively intimidated. The federal government opened the land to
whites again in 1871.

Elsewhere in California and the Great Basin were Indian groups who
had never been conquered by Spain or Mexico but whose property rights were
theoretically protected by the Treaty of Guadalupe Hidalgo (since the
United States chose to base its title upon this treaty), by the Fifth

Amendment to the Constitution (which prohibits the seizure of private property by the federal government without "due process" and "just" compensation), and by the customary practice of the United States (which recognized "Indian title" as valid until quieted by treaty). Unfortunately, however, the federal government was extremely negligent in the Far West, allowing local white desires to become fiat in defiance of constitutionality.

In 1851, after vast hordes of whites had already inundated California, the President chose to empower three commissioner-agents to regulate Indian affairs in California. These agents, in conformity with standard procedure elsewhere, toured the state, negotiating eighteen treaties with a large part of the native population. The agents found the natives generally anxious for peace and willing, apparently, to cede most of their lands to the United States in return for eighteen reservations totalling some 7,500,000 acres where they would be congregated, temporarily supplied with food, and aided in becoming agricultural. The text of a typical 1851-1852 treaty included the following:

> A treaty of peace and friendship made and concluded at
> Camp Barbour, on the San Joaquin River,... between...
> the United States, and the undersigned chiefs, captains,
> and headmen of the... How-ech-ees, Chook-cha-nees,
> Chow-chil-lies, Po-bo-nee-chees, and Nook-chees...
> [The Indians acknowledge the jurisdiction of the United
> States and relinquish all claims to ceded territory].
> To promote the settlement and improvement of said tribes
> or bands, it is hereby stipulated and agreed that the
> following district... shall be, and is hereby, set apart
> forever for the sole use and occupancy of the aforesaid
> tribes of Indians.... To have and to hold the said
> district of country for the sole use and occupancy of
> said Indian tribes forever. [Certain rights, such as for
> roads, are reserved to the U.S.]. And provided further,
> that said tribes of Indians... shall at all times have
> the privilege of the country east of the aforesaid
> district... to the foot of the Sierra Nevada mountains,
> to hunt and to gather fruit, acorns, etc.... (Quoted in
> William H. Ellison, "The Federal Indian Policy in Cali-
> fornia, 1846 - 1860," Ph.D. dissertation, University of
> California, Berkeley, 1919, pp. 206-8).

The treaties negotiated in California were implemented in three ways; first, many Indians were actually persuaded to leave their other lands and to congregate upon the reserves in 1851-52; second, the agents purchased large quantities of supplies for the Indians (although much was diverted for the profit of the agents and other whites); and, third, the Indians throughout the state were gradually required to give up their old lands as if they possessed no title. Thus one can argue that the treaties in question were transformed from mere tentative agreements into actual contracts binding upon the Executive Branch of the United States, since, in effect, the treaties were made binding upon the natives.

In any event, Congress, under pressure from California whites, rejected the treaties and caused them to be hidden in the archives. One might well agree that the reservations set aside in 1851-1852 were still bonafide Indian property, both because of the implementation of the treaties by the U.S., and because the "Indian title" had not yet been surrendered to the federal government; but such an argument matters little since the "White Power" of the day decreed otherwise.

The natives of eastern California, the Colorado River, and Nevada were not even visited by treaty-makers, except for the Western Shoshones, Goshute Shoshones, and Yahuskin (Northern Paiute). During 1863 - 1864 treaties were negotiated with the above groups, but no formal cessions of land took place nor were any lands guaranteed to the Indians (except in the case of the Yahuskin who agreed to give up all of their territory in order to settle at Klamath Lake Reservation).

It can be said, therefore, that the United States seized the Indian lands of California and the Great Basin and allowed these lands to pass into the hands of whites (or to become a part of the so-called "public domain") without benefit of even the remotest shred of legality. Can the federal government possess title to property forbidden to it by the Constitution? This interesting question has not yet been settled for Indians although, of course, the answer is "no" if the seized property belongs to whites. (See Jack D. Forbes, "The Public Domain and Indian Property Rights in Nevada,"Nevada State Bar Journal, July 1965).

Some efforts were made on the Indians' behalf by the federal government during these years but they were usually either confined to simple peace-keeping maneuvers or to small scale, insufficient programs which chiefly benefited white agents and speculators. In 1847 three persons were appointed as Indian agents for California. They had no money to spend, which may have been just as well since the commissioner-agents appointed in 1850 spent nearly $800,000 during 1851-52, very little of which benefited Indians. Cattle, blankets, and flour destined for the natives were either never delivered (with "kickbacks" for the agents) or were sold to Indians and whites. Blankets were cut in half when being distributed to Indians so as to supply a larger number with half-blankets and thereby create a surplus of whole blankets which were then sold to whites. In brief, these agents of 1851-52 set the pattern for later federal appointees who, almost without exception, used "the Indian business" as a lucrative step towards wealth.

In 1852 E. F. Beale was appointed as superintendent of Indian affairs for California, with an appropriation of $100,000 for "presents" to keep the natives quiet. Beale, influenced by the plans for the eighteen reservations rejected by Congress and by a proposal of Benjamin D. Wilson to establish eight reserves ("pueblos") for 9,000 Indians in the southern half of the state, advocated the establishment of mission-style reservations. Here the Indians would be gathered and instructed, under the watchful eye of an agent and nearby soldiers. (The only difference between this plan and what was being done farther east was the use of federal

employees as supervisor-instructors rather than federally-subsidized
missionaries).*

    Beale asked for $500,000, received $250,000, and immediately began to
lavish his entire effort on one site, the Tejon Reservation (at the extreme
southeast end of the San Joaquin Valley). The site was a poor choice
because it had white claimants (who were never bought out) and because it
probably never could have supported a large population. Beale acquired
supplies for 2,500 Indians (paying very high prices for beeves and other
items) but an employee later stated that there were never more than 800
there including 600 local Tejon-area natives who had already been growing
crops before Beale arrived. Beale himself reported in 1854 that he had
gathered 2,500 Indians at Tejon but a friendly visitor found only 1,200
three months later. In any event, Beale neglected tens of thousands of
Indians, including many who were in desperate condition, in order to
provide supplies for a few hundred, most of whom were not directly threatened
by white encroachment. Furthermore, the improvements made by Beale were
eventually lost because they were made on what became private property.**

    Beale was succeeded in 1854 by an agent who established Nome Lacke
Reservation in Colusa County, Mendocino Reservation at Fort Bragg, and
Klamath Reservation along the lower Klamath River. In 1856 Nome Cult or
Round Valley reserve was established along with "farms" at Fresno, Kings
River, and Tule River. Perhaps as many as 6,000 Indians were thus provided for, but at tremendous cost due to the fact that the whole operation
was really designed to enrich the superintendent and his accomplices.***
One aspect of these years was that the reservation Indians were often forced
to look for food on their own (in spite of rations - the latter were
re-sold by the agents to whites) and their labor was also sold to whites
by the government employees. The superintendent also allowed white squatters
to gain footholds on many of the reserves.

    Various investigations were made, including one by J. Ross Browne
who summarized the policy of the 1850's as follows:

            The results of the policy pursued were precisely
            such as might have been expected. A very large amount
            of money was annually expended in feeding white men

---
* Beale is often given credit for initiating a new approach to reservations,
  however, similar ideas were advocated by Utah agent John Wilson in 1849
  and by Oregon agent Joel Palmer in 1853. Farmer-instructors were actually
  working with Indians in Utah as early as 1851 and formal "farms" were laid
  out in 1855.

** In 1855 Tejon reserve was greatly reduced in size. Just what Beale did
   for the Tejon Indians is unclear. His successor found only 700 Indians
   at Tejon, living in native-style houses, and gathering wild foods for
   part of their subsistence. Beale later became the owner of Tejon and
   thereafter used the local Indians as laborers.

*** In 1856 it was claimed that 10,000 of 61,600 California Indians were
    residing on the reservations.

and starving Indians.... At all events, it
invariably happened, when a visitor appeared on the
reservations, that the Indians were "out in the
mountains gathering nuts and berries.... Very few
of them, indeed, have yet come back.... In the brief
period of six years they have been nearly destroyed
by the ... government. What neglect, starvation,
and disease have not done, has been achieved by the
co-•peration of the white settlers in the great work
of extermination. (J. Ross Browne, The California
Indians, pamphlet, no date).

In 1859 the federal government virtually abandoned the reservations,
leaving the Indians more or less on their own and allowing white squatters
to seize most of the improvements. Between 1860 and 1866 all of the
reserves and farms, with the exception of Round Valley and Tule River,
were extinguished or sold. Thus the Indians lost again, including the loss
of many miles of ocean-front property along the Mendocino coast. Was it
legal for the federal government to sell or abandon these "Indian"
reservations? Obviously, "Executive Order" reservations, established by
the President, were insecure places at best.

To take care of some of the northwest Indians expensive land was
rented from white owners on Smith River in Del Norte County (1861 - 66)
while in 1864 the Hoopa Valley Reservation was established to appease
natives who had been at war for five years and the Colorado River Reservation was set aside for the river tribes (1865). Meanwhile, in the
Great Basin, the Utah Superintendency established a number of "farms"
(small reserves) in Utah during 1855 and in 1859 briefly set aside two for
the Shoshones (one at Deep Creek and one at Ruby Valley, the latter being
six miles square in size). In 1859 also the Pyramid Lake and Walker
River reserves were set aside for the Northern Paiutes.* These latter
were the only reserves set aside in Nevada until 1873 (when the Southern
Paiutes received a tiny reserve at Moapa), and both were administered in
a typical inefficient and corrupt style. In 1877 the Duck Valley Reservation was established and at the same time some "farms" were rented from
whites for the Western Shoshones.

During the 1870's some effort was made to establish schools for California and Nevada Indians (most could not attend public schools) but
the early facilities provided were crude and frequently operated by the
local agent's wife whether she knew how to teach or not. In California
a new experiment was also attempted wherein the Quakers were to administer
the northern reservations and the army the rest, but it was the Methodists
who actually took over in 1870. The Baptists were assigned to work in
Nevada but did nothing and, all in all, very little happened in California
either. In many instances, the church appointees behaved no differently
from their predecessors, as for example, when in 1873 - 1876 Tule River

* In 1865 two Washo reserves of 360 acres each were authorized in
Washington but the local agent failed to take action because there
were "no suitable lands."

Farm was abandoned in favor of a mountainous tract which could support only one-quarter of the agency population. In 1874 a reservation was set aside for Chemehuevi Paiutes on the Colorado River and two years later eight small tracts were reserved for Southern California Indians. Almost all of the latter were surveyed in such a way that the native villages were left out and worthless lands included, or the areas set aside included lands already patented to whites.*

The first thirty years of the conquest presents, therefore, a rather sordid picture at best. Not only were Indians being killed in warfare and dying from sickness and starvation by the thousands but federal agents, in connivance with local whites, saw this tragedy as merely presenting them with an opportunity for making money. At the same time the white population generally exhibited a tendency to deprive Indians of their land and their labor with as little recompense as possible.

It should be noted that although philanthropical endeavors did occur in California in relation to "white causes" during this period (such as helping the Sanitary Commission during the Civil War), no movement developed whose purpose it was to come to the aid of the Indians even though the circumstances of slavery, starvation, et cetera, were well known. These thirty years, and what they reveal of Anglo-American character, cannot be forgotten. Nor can the fact be ignored that the modern Indian people of the Far West possess a burden of conquest from these and subsequent years, a burden which many still carry.

Native Survival

That American Indians survived at all during those thirty years is in itself rather remarkable and is testimony to the fortitude of the Indian people. Those Indians who resided in heavily white-controlled regions had to make revolutionary adjustments in order to survive, although for those in coastal Southern California the adjustments were similar to those of the late Mexican period. Everywhere in the heavily occupied regions the native people had to alter their economy, as has been pointed out, in the direction of becoming a rural proletariat or, to a lesser extent, an urban laboring class. Changes in styles of dress, housing patterns, and food habits followed rapidly as traditional items were hard to acquire. Many Indians became dependent for a time upon cast-off white material goods with which they clothed themselves, developed utensils, and built their houses. Gradually, many developed a positive desire to emulate white styles of dress and living because to do so was an indication of being a "civilized" person and was rewarded by white favor.

It should be pointed out, however, that during the transitional period in their changing material culture Indians were generally the butt of jokes because of the odd combinations of Indian and non-Indian practices which were often followed. White people generally had little understanding

_____

*In 1875 Malheur Reservation was established in eastern Oregon, serving Northern Paiutes of Nevada and Oregon, but it was mismanaged, coveted by whites, and soon abandoned.

of the difficult processes of acculturation taking place.

Many Indians resisted the Anglo-American conquest in passive ways, such as preserving native religions and ceremonial practices, maintaining such crafts as basketry, holding traditional dances, keeping their native language, and holding to their sense of identity as a people. Others, however, succombed to the alien pressures and became more and more non-Indian, especially in the coastal zones of central and southern California. In these areas many surviving Indians intermarried with Mexicans and by 1889 one observer could report that the Indians north of San Luis Obispo were becoming lost in the Mexican population. In the Los Angeles-San Diego region a similar process occurred, with the younger people often preferring the Spanish language and Mexican dances to their native traditions. In the rural areas many of these Mexicanized Indian groups survived as distinct communities but in the towns they became simply Mexican-Americans.

Along the Colorado River, in the desert areas, throughout great sections of Nevada, and in isolated pockets in northern California other Indian groups attempted to maintain their native cultures virtually intact for long periods of time. The Hamakhavas, Quechans, and Cocopas, for example, maintained traditional inter-tribal warfare until the 1860's, and in one case to 1880, along with their religions, ceremonies, and basic orientation towards life (in spite of a somewhat altered material base). In isolated regions a few small native groups simply stayed away from whites, while farther north Winnemucca (a Northern Paiute leader) and a large number of followers retreated into the rugged areas of northern Nevada and southeastern Oregon in order to live as in the pre-conquest period. In northern California, a small group of Yahi survivors chose to conceal themselves in their beloved Mill Creek canyon and to cut off all contacts with the outside world.

Still another form of resistance was in the development of religious movements based upon traditional dreaming and curing behavior but modified in the context of conquest. One of the better-known of these movements, the Adventist or so-called Ghost Dance religion, apparently developed in Nevada in ca. 1869 when a Northern Paiute religious leader, Wodziwob, dreamed of the return of the Indian dead and that dancing would aid in their reappearance. Other preachers, such as Numataivo (father of Wovoka), Winawitu, Weneyuga, and Winnemucca spread this doctrine in the 1871-72 period to Idaho, northeastern California, and elsewhere. In 1871 a Northern Paiute missionary visited Indians on the North Fork of the San Joaquin and converted Joijoi, a North Fork leader. The latter subsequently made several trips to Nevada, learning songs and dances from a Paiute known as Moman. Joijoi staged dances in the San Joaquin Valley and other converts soon spread the adventist movement southwards to Tejon and northwards among various Yokuts-speaking groups.

Other missionaries apparently carried the songs and dances to the Mewuk where, in 1871-72, "Old Sam" was reported to be a great orator and prophet who said that mourning at death was not necessary since the dead were to return. About 1872 also Indians at Pleasanton revived the central California Kuksu religion in connection with adventist doctrines. This revived Kuksu movement was then spread by native missionaries to the

Mewuk, Maidu, Pomo and Wintun peoples where it survived for some time
although the adventist songs and dances were abandoned farther south
and in Nevada after 1875.

The Indians of the Far West were unaware of the possibility of
engaging in political or quasi-political action during this period and,
with one exception, they confined their movements to "mystical resistance"
or to warfare. The one exception was Sarah Winnemucca, a brilliant
daughter of Winnemucca who had managed to acquire a little schooling.
During the 1870's Sarah wrote letters on behalf of her people and then in
the late 1870's commenced an active campaign on behalf of Indian rights
as a public lecturer and lobbyist, which activity culminated in two books,
Life Among The Piutes (1883) and Sarah Winnemucca's Solution To The
Indian Problem (ca. 1885).

The potential for Indian political-civic activity was vastly improved
when it became possible for natives to testify against white men in
California in 1873. It also seemed as if the Fourteenth Amendment (1869)
had given many or all Indians citizenship rights since the amendment
asserted that "all persons born or naturalized in the United States and
subject to the jurisdiction thereof" were citizens of both the United
States and of the state in which they lived. Many whites in California
and elsewhere believed that Indians were included but during the 1880's
the United States Supreme Court held otherwise in two blatantly uncon-
stitutional and racist court decisions. Legally, therefore, Indians were
held to be aliens but unlike other aliens they were also held to be
"non-persons"and beyond the protections of the Bill of Rights.

The Next Forty Years: 1880 - 1920's

After the period of open violence had ceased the Indian people
settled down to a still-traumatic life as conquered aliens ultimately
without legal privileges and subject to the ever-present threat of terror.
But as warfare became confined to Arizona, northern Mexico and the Four
Corners region, and as it ceased altogether in the United States after
1915, a changed attitude began to appear among many white individuals.
Gradually, that "moral conscience" in which Anglo-Americans have always
taken such an inordinate amount of pride began to assert itself, especially in those sections of the country where there were few Indians.
Of course it appeared after the majority of California Indians were dead
but at least it did finally appear.

In the late 1870's, as already mentioned, Sarah Winnemucca began
lecturing and writing on behalf of her Northern Paiute people. She was
soon joined by others such as Standing Bear of the Poncas who lectured in
Boston in 1879. Listening to Standing Bear was Helen Hunt Jackson, a
wealthy New England author who soon decided to devote the remaining years
of her life to the Indian cause. Jackson's A Century of Dishonor (1881)
and Ramona (1884) drew the literate white population's attention to the
plight of the Indian in general and of the ex-mission Indians of Southern
California in particular. Although vicious attacks upon the Indian
people were more typical of the writing of the 1880's (as for example
Theodore Roosevelt's Winning of the West, 1889), such works as Jackson's

and Sarah Winnemucca's served to awaken a strong tide of pro-Indian sentiment, especially in New England. In 1882 the powerful Indian Rights Association was organized. Religious denominations also became more concerned and a number of "Indian associations" appeared which were essentially devices for supporting various Christian missions. Unfortunately, as shall be pointed out, many of these "friends of the Indians" proved to be enemies in disguise, but others did bring about improvements in Indian affairs.

In spite of their greatly reduced numbers most far western Indians still possessed no land recognized as their own. During the 1880's and 1890's several new reserves were created, such as Fort Yuma (1883) Hoopa Extension (1891) and the Washo allotments (1895). Aided by the Indian Rights Association the Southern California Indians won a court fight to obtain title to the village of Soboba, while the Sequoya League (a "friends of the Indians" group active between 1901 and 1911) helped the Warner's Ranch natives obtain new lands when they were ousted from their ancient villages in 1900 - 1901. Thereafter, exceedingly small parcels were occasionally purchased or set aside for "homeless" Indians, especially between 1910 and 1929 (most of these "rancherias" in California or "colonies" in Nevada were designed to provide residential sites only). The Owens Valley Indians were to receive a large reservation (66,000 acres) suitable for grazing purposes in 1912 but for some reason the Indian Bureau never actually made it available to them.

The setting aside of these additional lands must be viewed in perspective. First, they provided homes for only about one-half of California-Nevada Indians; second, most provided no opportunity for future economic development; and, third, these "postage stamp" reserves, as they were called, were set aside during a period when much larger quantities of land were being transferred to white ownership or being set aside as national parks and national forests.*   Millions of acres of timberland, grazing land, and some agricultural regions were still available during this period and much of it could have been made useful for Indians but was not. The reader should realize that 87% of Nevada still remains today as so-called public domain, thus clearly indicating that the whites of the period in question were not over-generous in meeting native land needs. (Congress often attached riders to appropriation bills forbidding the acquisition, by Indian tribes, of additional lands even with their own funds). Millions of acres also remained under federal control in California during this era.

Although we should applaud the efforts of the "friends of the Indian" in spurring the government to acquire some additional land for natives it is quite obvious that setting aside land for parks and timber reserves was far more popular and successful in this period. Likewise, the Indian people actually lost a great deal more land than they obtained, as will be noted below.

---

* The new national forests often posed a threat, in fact, to
  Indian villages. Likewise, Indians continued to be ousted from
  their homes as late as 1910.

Raw corruption gradually declined in the Bureau of Indian Affairs
during the period in question but Indian people were still the victims
of great abuses. Perhaps the greatest of these was the Dawes Allotment
Act, pushed through Congress in 1887 by a strange combination of western
anti-Indian interests and New England reformers. Unfortunately, the
humanitarianism of the followers of Helen Hunt Jackson (who had died in
1885) was often warped by their white superiority complexes; that is, the
reformers felt that they knew what was good for Indians without asking
Indian people. And what was good for Indians was, of course, to force them
to become Anglo-Americans through a process of destroying tribal organizations and dividing up economic assets among individual families. It
should be pointed out that this process, of giving individual plots to
families, had been tried many, many times before and had almost always
failed (due primarily to white chicanery but also to native traditions of
collective ownership).

Additionally, the Dawes Act provided that after each family had
received its 40 to 160 acres the balance of the land was to be declared
"surplus" and opened to whites.*   This was a key part of the act from
the western view point.

It might be asked how it came about that Congress could by legislation both alter the form of corporate assets and also confiscate
a portion of them, but it must be remembered that Indians were not thought
of as possessing any constitutional protection. (It is especially ironic,
of course, that the allotment act was put into effect during a period when
whites were moving more and more in the direction of corporate, i.e.,
collective enterprise rather than individual enterprise. This was nowhere
more true than in California).

In any event, many Indians were pressured into accepting allotments,
in part as the only means for gaining security of title or citizenship
(the latter was made available to allottees). Such far western reserves
as Walker River, Klamath River, and Hoopa were allotted or partially
allotted, although most California-Nevada reserves were totally unsuited
for such a process, being too small, too rough, or too sterile. The result
was not surprising. Klamath River reserve was abolished entirely by 1892
while whites were able to gain control of key sections at Walker River
and Hoopa. Elsewhere the allotments did not work out well, even where
retained by Indians, because of federal red-tape, marginal quality, and
lack of capital for development. Federal regulations (and the assumption
that the Indian population would remain static) produced complicated heir-
ship problems which even today make many allotments virtually useless.

In brief, the Dawes allotment plan proved to be a disservice to
Indians and a net gain for white land-grabbers, not because Indian families
did not desire to have their own farms and ranches but because it was an

---

*The money obtained, held in trust for the Indians, was spent for
government operations.

inflexible bureaucratic plan conceived and executed by outsiders. Indian people were not given a chance to work out their own solutions to the land problem.

During this period Indians also continued to lose land in various other ways. For example, in Nevada the Pyramid Lake Paiutes lost a 20,500 acre timber reserve (set aside in 1864, then abandoned "informally" after having never been developed but still being shown on maps as late as 1910), and the entire southern part of the reservation around the town of Wadsworth. Both areas were lost due to the influence of the Central Pacific Railroad and in neither case were any legal formalities followed by the government. Additionally, during the 1890's Senator William Stewart of Nevada sought to abolish the Walker River Reservation entirely and diminish the Pyramid Lake reserve still further but fortunately his efforts were blocked by the Board of Indian Commissioners (a body which contributed to improvements in the Indian Bureau during this period).* In the early 1900's white squatters succeeded in occupying the southern portion of the Walker River Reservation and by 1906 the Indians were forced to give up that area and Walker Lake in exchange for arid desert lands.

Other examples of land lost to the Indians included the Klamath River Reservation of forty square miles of which, in 1893, the Indians received only 9,000 acres, and the Paiute Reservation of 66,000 acres located north of Bishop. The latter was finally lost to the natives in a rather mysterious way through the machinations of the City of Los Angeles (which during the 1920's was seeking to gain control of as much land as possible in the Owens Valley area). As late as 1954, when hearings were held in Bishop, the head of the Indian Bureau in California could not explain what had happened to the 66,000 acre reserve (but the latter's value was being subtracted from the award to be made to Indians for lands seized by the federal government on the grounds that the reserve still existed).

Another manner in which Indians effectively lost the use of their land was through leases (managed by the Indian Bureau) with white ranchers and farmers. In 1925 some 57,000 acres were leased in California, 19,000 were "farmed by Indians," and the balance, more than 400,000 acres, were not being utilized for any agricultural purpose apparently (most being useless).

In 1919 Malcolm McDowell conducted an investigation into California Indian affairs on behalf of the Board of Indian Commissioners. McDowell's excellent report is sprinkled with recommendations for reform including the following:

---

* Senator Stewart did not succeed in taking away much Indian land but, ironically, he did get an Indian school, Stewart Institute, named after him.

The adoption of a California Indian policy, with
appropriate legislation to make it effective,
predicated upon the acknowledgement of a legal
debt due the Indians because they were dispossessed
of their lands without due process of law and
without compensation, and based upon the principle
of exact justice and not upon sentiments of pity or
charity. (Fifty-first Annual Report of the Board
of Indian Commissioners, 1920, p. 40).

Mr. McDowell commented at length upon the "strange" fact that the
procedure followed in other parts of the United States, in quieting Indian
titles, had not been followed in California. Unfortunately, McDowell was
näive since "exact justice" as regards land rights has never been extended
to California or Nevada Indians in the fifty years since his report was
written.

The period from the 1880's through the 1920's was an era during which
the conquered native population was constantly brought under greater and
greater bureaucratic control. Although without constitutional basis, the
Indians were reduced legally to the status of "wards" and were regarded as
possessing virtually no rights over their "own" reservations (actually the
government made it very clear that the reservations belonged to the
government and not to the Indian people).

Indian agents in this period often possessed as much power as they
wished to award to themselves, including authority to suppress Indian
ceremonies, cut adults long hair off, expel "difficult" persons from the
reservation, imprison offenders, make assignments of land to "cooperative"
persons, offer agency employment, recommend certificates of competency,
and otherwise control and manipulate the native population. The degree
of totalitarian control actually exercised naturally varied from region
to region and was generally in direct relation to the proximity of a given
reservation to an agent's headquarters. Those Indians not residing on
reservations and those at a distance from the agency were comparatively
free from supervision.

Most Indian children were, in one way or another, affected by the
schools operated by the Indian Bureau. By 1910 51.3% of California
Indian youth, ages 5 to 20, were attending school (as compared with 61.6%
for all rural children) while by 1920 60.4% were in school (68.5% of all
rural children). The vast bulk of these pupils were enrolled in the
elementary grades.

The Indian schools (along with a few public schools) had succeeded
only very slowly in reducing English illiteracy so that in 1910 63.4% of
California Indians over 21 were still illiterate while 16.6% of those
between 10 and 20 were non-readers. By 1920 these figures had declined
to 46.2% and 9.1%, respectively, as compared with 6.4% and 1.9% for all
classes of the rural population. Nevada, unfortunately, was even farther
behind with 82.6% of the adult Indian population and 43% of those ages 10
to 20 still illiterate in 1910. By 1920 these figures had become
66.9% and 33% as compared with 7.9% and 3% for all classes of the rural

population of the state. Quite obviously something was lacking in a
program that after some forty years still saw one-third of older school-
age youth illiterate in Nevada and one-tenth illiterate in California,
not to mention rates of two-thirds (Nevada) and one-half (California)
of the adults still non-literate.

> In 1882 Helen Hunt Jackson found that the Southern California Indians
> are all keenly alive to the value of education. In every
> village that we visited we were urged to ask the
> government to give them a school, In one they
> insisted upon ranging the children all in rows, that
> we might see for ourselves that there were children
> enough to justify the establishing of a school.
> (Jackson and Kinney, "Report on the Condition of the
> Mission Indians...," 1883, p.12).

The slow progress actually made by Indian pupils was, apparently, in sharp
contrast to the initial enthusiasm of both parents and young people. In
part this situation can be blamed upon the poor quality of instruction
received in Indian schools (in spite of evidence that there were some
individual teachers with great skill and dedication), but in large measure
it must have been due to the over-all orientation of the schools. Education, during this era, was conceived of as a means for destroying the
native heritage and "liberating" the individual Indian so that he could
take his place in society as a "brown-white man." The Indian schools were
totally divorced from the culture of the native people and were essentially
anti-Indian in almost every respect. It would be quite understandable if
most Indian children left that kind of classroom as quickly as possible.
On the other hand, some pupils were able to attend vocational boarding
schools which sometimes gave them a "trade" even if it alienated them from
their Indian heritage.

In 1915 only 316 Indian pupils were attending public school in
California but by 1919 this number had increased to 2,199. In general,
this was the result of a campaign carried out by Indians and the Indian
Board of Cooperation and a new government policy of integrating Indians
in public schools in areas such as California and Nevada where the native
population was intermixed with white communities. Resistance to integration on the part of whites was widespread in California and Nevada at
first but gradually prejudice was overcome (in great part due to the fact
that the federal government paid the local school districts on a per-pupil
basis).

By 1919 eleven-thousand California Indians were residing on federal
"trust" land (reservations or rancherias) with another 5,200 to 14,000
scattered elsewhere. Of the 12,725 Indians served by the Indian Bureau
in 1920-1921, some 5,029 were of mixed racial ancestry with 2,308 of
these of one-half or less Indian descent. Since it is highly likely that
a greater proportion of non-reservation Indians were of mixed ancestry,
it would seem likely that approximately one-half of the California native
population was of mixed background by 1920.

In 1882 - 83 probably less than 1,000 Nevada Indians (out of 5,000) were
residing on "trust" land but by 1927 about 2,500 were on the larger

reservations with 2,000 at the various colonies and about 500 on their own.

General conditions in the Far West were far from good in 1919-1920, after more than a half-century of conquest. McDowell wrote in 1919 of the majority of California Indians that

> more than all else, they have for generations been treated by their white neighbors as an inferior people and have been accepting that appraisement quite as a matter of course.... They get their own living with the work of their own hands.... With apparently few exceptions the California Indians are seasonal, or casual, work people. The earning time for the great majority is the growing seasons.... [Others] of them find employment in sawmills, on the surface of mines, in logging camps, and on railroads and public roads. During sheep shearing these Indians are in demand.... They herd cattle, milk cows, and do general farm labor. The women who live near cities and towns go out by day as domestics and laundresses.

This description was also applicable to most Indians in Nevada, including perhaps a majority of reservation natives, since the latter very often had to become seasonal workers in order to earn a living.

During this era the ways of living of the Indian people were further transformed and, on the whole, their material existence came to approximate that of poor whites except in so far as a few native arts and crafts survived. In clothing styles, house construction, methods of transportation, and personal ornamentation "white ways" became the rule, with native clothing disappearing except for ceremonial occasions and with most Indian-type structures (such as community "round houses" and men's sweat houses) being allowed to deteriorate and disappear. Generally, Indian people were under great and continued pressure to imitate white behavior and with the exception of a few arts and crafts, such as basketry, there was no significant tendency in the non-Indian community to encourage any retention of the ancient heritage. Most younger Indians were, of course, deeply influenced by the anti-Indian heritage bias of their educational experiences and, even when "turned off" by the schools, were under great psychological pressure to conform to the dominant society.

Indian people were often rather passive during these forty years. This is, of course, not at all surprising in view of the enormity of the shock of the preceding period of warfare and disorganization and of the immense power and prestige available to those whites who intervened in Indian affairs. Indian people operated at a great disadvantage and to resist at all required great tenacity of spirit or brilliance of perception. The easy course was to bend with the hurricane, accepting white views on all matters from dress to religion.

Spiritual resistance was most in evidence during the early years of this period, what with the revival of the adventist (so-called

PLATE 1. Essie Parrish actively preserves the basket-making heritage of the Kashia Pomo people at Tsununu-Shinal in Sonoma County. Photo courtesy Mrs. Essie Parrish.

PLATE 2a. Sarah Winnemucca, out-standing Nevada Indian writer and lec-turer, and daughter of Neh-meh leader Winnemucca (about 1880). Courtesy of S. W. Museum, Los Angeles.

PLATE 2b. A Western Shoshone young warrior, known to the whites as "Char-lie" (about 1880). Courtesy of S. W. Museum, Los Angeles.

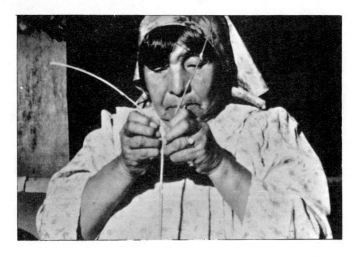

PLATE 2c. Wessie (or Wazzie) George, a Neh-meh (Northern Paiute) living at Stillwater, Nevada, splitting willow stems for basket. S. W. Museum photo.

PLATE 3. A young Pomo man navigating in Clear Lake in a tule boat (about 1880). Photo courtesy of S. W. Museum, Los Angeles.

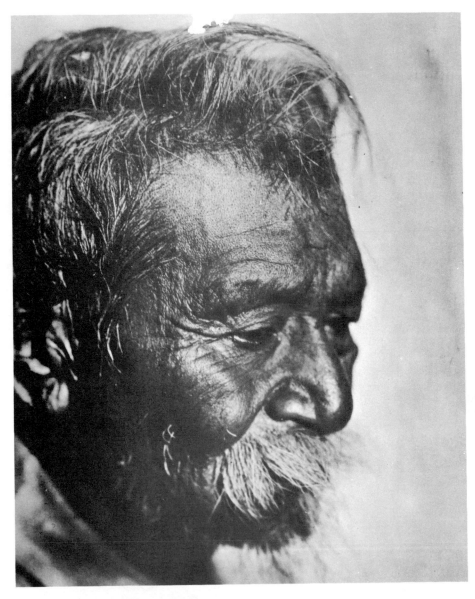

PLATE 4.   A Koshónomo Pomo man (about 1880–1900).   Photo courtesy of
S. W. Museum, Los Angeles.

PLATE 5. A California Indian basketmaker in Yosemite Valley (before 1900).
Photo courtesy of S. W. Museum, Los Angeles.

PLATE 6.   A Mewuk settlement in the Sierra foothills during the period when Indians were driven off all the best sites (about 1880).   Courtesy of the Bancroft Library, Univ. of California, Berkeley, California.

PLATE 7. San Francisco Bay Area – Central California Indians with dance headdresses (early 1800's). Reproduced through the courtesy of the Bancroft Library, Univ. of California, Berkeley, California.

PLATE 8. Tachahagáchile, A Kato (Nungahl) man (pre-1900). Photo courtesy of S. W. Museum, Los Angeles.

PLATE 9.   A Hamakhava girl.   (Colorado River).   Courtesy S. W. Museum, L. A.

PLATE 10. A Nim (Mono) or Neuma (Owens Valley Paiute) girl with winnowing basket (about 1880). Photo courtesy S. W. Museum, Los Angeles.

PLATE 11. A Maidu woman (probably before 1910). Photo by E. S. Curtis, courtesy S. W. Museum, Los Angeles.

PLATE 12.   Noverto León, a 105 year old Soboba (Atahum) man (about 1900-
1910). Reproduced through courtesy of Bancroft Library, Berkeley, California.

PLATE 13. A Pomo village near Clear Lake (about 1890). Reproduced through the courtesy of the Bancroft Library, University of California, Berkeley, Calif.

PLATE 14. William Robert Cooke, Yurok Indian and a prominent member of the California Indian Education Association from Susanville.   Photograph by Dennis Galloway.

PLATE 15. Frank Canizales (center), an active young Mewuk leader (1969). Photograph by Dennis Galloway.

PLATE 16. Jack Forbes and David Risling talking with Long Beach State College Indian students at a California Indian Education Association meeting (1969). Photograph by Dennis Galloway.

"Ghost Dance") movement by Wovoka, the continued functioning of the
revived Kuksu religion of central California, and the survival of various
curing procedures among a number of groups. Wovoka, a Northern Paiute,
became nationally famous when, in 1887-1890, his songs and dances spread
rapidly from the Walker River of Nevada to the Plains Indians. Wovoka's
teachings, emphasizing rededication to a life of virtue and the consequent
return of the Indian dead, were opposed vigorously by Indian Bureau officials and the movement rapidly collapsed in Nevada (and never appreciably
spread into California). Nonetheless Wovoka was greatly respected by
many Indians, and along with numerous other Indian doctors, maintained a
tradition of ancient native practices which has endured, to a certain
extent, to the present day.

In the Pomo region the Maru religion, an outgrowth of the adventist -
Kuksu revival of the 1870's, continued to function. In that area and
elsewhere in California individual native doctors periodically experienced
revelations (usually in dreams) which caused them to develop variations in
either the Maru religion or the practice of spiritual doctoring. Bureau
officials attempted to discourage the native religious movements but often
with only very gradual success. In 1919 it was reported, for example,
that at Hoopa "some of the old tribal customs and superstitions remain;
the medicine man is still somewhat in evidence; some of the old-time dances
bring the Indians together once in a while...."

On the Walker River Reservation the agent attempted to interfere
with native dances and doctoring but met with resistance. In 1912 the
Indians, with the help of a sympathetic white attorney,drew up a petition
asking for the removal of the agent but the effort was largely a failure
since the Indian Bureau approved of the suppression of native religion,
dancing, and other "excesses." (See Jack D. Forbes, ed., Nevada Indians
Speak, 1967, pp. 168-176).

Many other kinds of resistance were offered by individual Indians,
as with pupils frequently running off from boarding school, or with
occasional violence, as when in 1910 - 1911 a group of Indians under
"Shoshone Mike" briefly raided in northern Nevada. Quite different was the
response in 1904 of the Yokayo Pomo people to the efforts of a white man
to acquire part of the property which they had purchased for their Indian
community some twenty years before. The Yokayo took their case to court
and won, thereby protecting their unique Indian-controlled community.

As early as 1882 the people of the Round Valley Reservation began
struggling against federal bureaucrats, utilizing varied forms of resistance. In that year the agent wrote that

> from the time I struck the first blow to prepare
> the buildings at Camp Wright for a boarding
> school, I have met with opposition from nearly
> all parties.... and even the Missionary, who was
> here at the time said, "The Indians will not let
> their children come, and they will burn the
> buildings before they will let you take their
> children into them."

As predicted, the boarding school buildings were burned on the nights
of July 20 and July 23, 1883. The agent wrote that

> this is but the out crop of the spirit of hostility
> to the school that has been more or less expressed
> since I began to prepare the buildings for that
> purpose. Added to this the spirit of insubordination
> ... has shown itself lately....

Five of the "largest boys" of the school later confessed to the burnings.

During 1911 - 1914 a new wave of opposition to policies being followed at Round Valley Reservation and boarding school developed. In
1911 the girls burned their dormitory down, in 1912 the girls set fire
to their temporary dormitory on two occasions, and in 1914 the boys twice
attempted to burn their dormitory and actually succeeded in burning down
the main school building. The then-superintendent wrote that

> I have every reason to believe that the action of
> the pupils... is the result of the feeling manifested
> by the parents of the children and discussed in
> their presence while at home.... There has always
> been among these Indians a very strong feeling
> against the government school.

The Round Valley Indians were aided by the Rev. F. G. Collett, a Methodist
preacher who had organized the Indian Board of Cooperation in 1913.
Collett helped the reservation residents circulate a petition seeking the
removal of their Indian Bureau supervisors and an investigation followed.

> The Indians were not allowed to tell their stories
> [except] in the presence of Superintendent Wilson....
> We cannot fully appreciate how hard this made it
> for the Indians to relate their grievances, only as
> we take into consideration that the Indians are
> desperately shy and incomprehensively afraid of
> ridicule and are cowed under a system that makes
> them dependent creatures and that the children
> had been most cruelly flogged on their bare backs
> until they had suffered for weeks from the outrages
> perpetrated by these government officials. (Records
> of Col. Lafayette Dorrington, 1915-1923, Item 102,
> various boxes, Federal Records Center, San Francisco).

Indians also expressed their resentment of federal policies by seeking
to obtain public schools. A Captain Odock of an Indian group near Colusa
appealed for a school in 1910, with the result that ultimately an all-
Indian public school district was established. Rev. Collett's Indian Board
devoted much of its energy between 1913 and 1915 to helping Indians in the
Lake-Mendocino area establish new public school districts or gain admittance to already existing non-federal schools.

The Indians of Lake County, also with the aid of Rev. Collett, discovered another means of advancing their position by means of a court case. Ethan Anderson attempted to register to vote with the Lake County Clerk but was refused and a test case was set up which eventually reached the State Supreme Court. Ethan Anderson won his right to vote in 1917 and thereby won citizenship rights for all California Indians who did not reside on the larger reservations (Anderson v. Mathews, 174 Cal. 537, 163 Pac.902). During 1915 and 1916 Lake County area Indians held many meetings to raise money for the case and also to plan challenges to county welfare practices.

Quite obviously the Native Americans of California were beginning to learn how to engage in political-legal resistance. By 1919 it was reported that

> the rancheria Indians...living in Mendocino, Lake, and Sonoma Counties... have organized themselves into an association under the name of the Society of Northern California Indians. This organization was effected under the guidance of Rev. Father Raymond, O.M. Cap. of St. Marys Church, Ukiah... the coming together of these rancheria Indians, with the set purpose of forming an organization of any kind, is significant and interesting. A few years ago it would have been impossible to unite these rancherias into an organization....

McDowell sat in on a conference of the SNCI at Ukiah where fourteen rancherias were represented.

> The purpose of the society is to promote the advancement of and to secure a peaceful and prosperous existence for the Indians; to obtain and publish a history of their people; to establish a legal department to advise the Indians, and to suggest and obtain remedies for unsatisfactory conditions; to work together for more and better schools for their children and to arrange for lectures on agriculture, stock raising, domestic science, etc. .... These are non reservation Indians - Pomos, Concows, Noyos, Sansels, Ukies, Wylackies, and Nomelackies - who, with some exceptions, live on tracts of land owned by the Government.... They want to be more like white men: they want water piped to their little cabins... they want better living conditions; they want their children to have more and better school facilities.... (Fifty-first Annual Report of the Board of Indian Commissioners, 1920, p.69).

Somewhat comparable developments took place in Southern California where the natives organized the Federation of Mission Indians to improve conditions and promote concerted action. But

at the federation meetings expressions of ill
will or hostility to the Government were occasionally heard. Grievances were aired and
complaints, both legitimate and trivial, were
uttered. As a result, and under orders of the
Department of Justice, some 57 Indians were
placed under arrest on the charge of conspiracy
against the Government.

The Indian Bureau was able to attempt to deny free speech and assembly
rights to Indians because of its doctrine that Native Americans were
not protected by the Constitution. Fortunately, friendly whites organized the Indian Welfare League to help the Indians and in March 1922
the Board of Indian Commissioners intervened, finding that the bureau's
policy was both "ill advised and utterly futile." Conditions among the
ex-mission Indians were in a bad state - they were "suspicious and their
resentment seemed to be justifiable." (Report of the Board of Indian
Commissioners, 1923, p. 22).

        Thus by 1920 the Indians of the Far West were beginning to experi-
ment with new forms of concerted action ranging from petitions, to law
suits, to organizing in order to make their desires known. A new era
had not yet dawned, but its birth could be anticipated.

IV. THE NATIVE AWAKENING

The Struggle for Equality of Citizenship

In 1924 the United States Congress, fifty-five years after the passage of the Fourteenth Amendment, finally extended citizenship to all Indians. But Indian people did not thereby acquire citizenship rights equivalent to those of whites. A long period of struggle against the Bureau of Indian Affairs, the various state governments, and local white prejudice was still to be necessary.

For complex reasons, all of which were extra-constitutional, the U.S. Supreme Court had come to hold that Indians were "wards" of the federal government. Still later the court came to assert that "wardship" did not end when citizenship was granted. In 1923 the court held, for example, that

> This duty of protection and power [of the federal
> government] extend to individual Indians, even though
> they may have become citizens...."The civil and
> political status of the Indians does not condition
> the power of the government to protect their property
> or to instruct them. Their admission to citizenship
> does not deprive the United States of its power or
> relieve it of its duty." (Cramer v. United States
> with quote from U.S. v Kagama [1886], in C.S. Goodrich,
> "The Legal Status of the California Indian,"
> California Law Review, March 1926, pp. 161 - 162).

The Bureau of Indian Affairs interpreted the granting of citizenship in 1924 as not affecting its authority.

> The act of June 2, 1924... did not in any way alter the
> control of the Office of Indian Affairs over the tribal
> or individual property of Indians. Nor did it change
> the laws that apply to the person of the Indian. The
> unallotted Indian living on a reservation is still not
> subject to state laws, and he is subject to United States
> law for only certain specified offenses (L. F. Schmeckebier,
> The Office of Indian Affairs, 1927, p.90).

It should be borne in mind that the only special constitutional power over Indian Affairs possessed by the federal government relates to the regulation of "commerce" with the "Indian tribes," the same power which the federal government possessed in relation to interstate commerce. The Constitution does not provide the federal government with any special authority over individual Indians, whether aliens or citizens, nor does it provide that government with any explicit powers over Indian property or territory.

During the 1920's, and ever since, American Indian people have existed in a legal "no man's land" as a result of conflicting congressional statutes, state laws, bureaucratic rulings, and non-constitutional court decisions. First, Indian property or territory had gradually changed from being regions ("domestic dependent nations") not a part of any state and simply under federal "protection" to areas held "in trust" by the federal government for Indians (a vast and significant change). Further, Indian areas in California and Nevada were held, again by extra-constitutional processes, to be actually owned by the government and simply made available for Indian occupancy as a kind of "gratuity." All of this is quite significant because it relates closely to the question of "termination," a concept developed quite early but not widely implemented until the 1950's. If Indian lands were beyond state jurisdiction because of their former sovereign political character and "protectorate" status, then the withdrawal (or "termination") of federal supervision did not per se alter the local tax-free status of those lands; but if Indian lands were the trust property of the United States then the lands were threatened with state jurisdiction and local taxation at any time when the federal government chose unilaterally to alter that trust status. The whole question of the legal status of Indian reservations has also been greatly affected by a hodge-podge of conflicting federal statutes adopted without any prior resolution of the question outlined above.

Second, individual Indians were often unable to be either citizens or "wards" because the two concepts, in spite of the Supreme Court, are quite obviously in conflict. Many states, regarding Indians as federal "wards", refused to make state and local services and voting rights available to individual natives, while the federal government, regarding them for certain purposes as citizens, sometimes discontinued its welfare programs. This was especially a problem for non-reservation Indians in the Far West but it was also a problem for groups residing on rancherias and colonies, since these small tracts were often not regarded as being true reservations. The full range of federal services tended to be available only for persons residing on large reservations.

As citizens one might suppose that at long last Indians acquired the protection of the Bill of Rights, but such was not usually the case. As has been seen, as late as 1922 the Indian Bureau sought to arrest Southern California Indians (some or all of whom were citizens) for merely criticizing the bureau. In a similar manner, the Indian Bureau sought forcibly during the 1920's to suppress the native religion at Taos Pueblo in New Mexico, in clear violation of the First Amendment, while everywhere the bureau cooperated closely with Christian missionaries.

The federal government was actively engaged in efforts to forcibly change native cultures, as in seeking state laws to suppress the peyote-using Native American Church (in addition to the police-state tactics utilized on reservations). The bureau also sought to interfere with traditional marriage practices on reservations and advocated repressive state laws:

> I think it not untimely to suggest the need for legislation subjecting all Indians to the laws of citilization respecting their marital relations... there is still too much disregard of the sacred principle upon which conjugal happiness... depend.... The vicious practice of Indian custom marriage and separation is deplorable.... The tribal courts [run by the bureau] ... are not sufficient

to deal successfully with the loose marital relations
of barbaric origin and there should be some means
provided for involving State law more effectively...
before we can have the right beginning of progress
toward civilization. (Report of the Commissioner of
Indian Affairs, 1922, p. 20).

During this period a renewed effort was made to suppress native dances of
religious significance. The Commissioner wrote in 1923 that

A long-time tendency of the Indians has been to give
too much time to dances, powwows, celebrations, and
general festive occasions.... To correct this
practice a letter was widely circulated among the
Indians last year ... [with] an earnest appeal...
that they shorten somewhat the length of these
gatherings and omit from them use of harmful drugs
[peyote], intoxicants, gambling, and degrading
ceremonials. (Report of the Commissioner of Indian
Affairs, 1923, pp. 20 - 21).

This paragraph does not fully convey an idea of the actions that were
actually taken to suppress "degrading ceremonials," such as the arrest of
many leading men at Taos referred to above.

The awarding of citizenship did not at first diminish the great power
exercised by bureau officials, including especially local superintendents
of "agencies." To understand this situation, one must picture each
reservation as a colony administered by civil servants who, formally at
least, answered only to their bureaucratic superiors in Washington rather
than to the people being "served." Indian reservations were communities
where the ruling bureaucrats possessed the power to disburse appropriations from Washington, the power to award jobs and land-use privileges,
the power to control the local police and courts (in which the Constitution
did not operate as a limitation upon procedure), the power to control
who received piped water, who obtained a road nearby, who obtained sewage
services (when available), the power to influence the securing of jobs
from white employers, the power to control movement to and from the reservation, the power to award rights to attend bureau vocational institutes,
and, later, the power to award scholarships to colleges and universities,
among other powers. Struggling with these all-powerful, non-elected
officers of the federal government were largely unorganized people who
were also exceedingly poor, under-educated, and without powerful allies
(since very often the local bureau officials had tie-ins with local busi-
nessmen, farmers, and ranchers due to the awarding of contracts and lease-
rights). Very often also the Indian people were very much afraid to
challenge the local bureau officers, not merely because any such action
would endanger them in very concrete ways, but also because of a deep
general fear of "white power" imposed by the experience of being conquered.

The terrible power of the Indian Bureau over the lives of individual
Indians (and still greater power over the lives of communities) meant that
many Native Americans could always be found who would serve as "front-men"

and "tools" of bureau officials. Acting out of fear or self-interest
many Indians made themselves accomplices of the colonial system and
served to make it virtually impossible for Indian people to speak with
a firm, united voice.

Unfortunately, the power of the Bureau of Indian Affairs still
remains almost as great today as it was in the 1920's, especially in
relation to smaller and less well-organized Indian communities. The
reforms of the 1930's, the Indian awakening, the rise of competing state
and federal agencies (such as the Office of Economic Opportunity), and
the decline in bureau services in areas such as California have all
conspired to reduce somewhat the more blatant and obvious violations of
Indian peoples' rights to local self-determination, but bureau officials
still possess powerful tools for controlling individual Indians
(principally in the awarding or withholding of such items as jobs,
scholarships, road projects, public works, and economic development programs, but also in terms of influencing who gets what lands and under
what conditions, et cetera).

Courageous individuals and small groups resisted the bureau's total-
itarianism during the 1920's and 1930's, but with varying success at the
local level. In part this was because the Indian Bureau has always displayed a remarkable ability to project an appearance of making changes
while actually resisting change. For example, in 1932 the superintendent
of the Sacramento Agency, Oscar H. Lipps, wrote a pamphlet which ostensibly placed the bureau on the side of reform in California Indian
affairs. But Mr. Lipps' program included such items as 1) recommending
a California Advisory Committee on Indian Affairs to be composed entirely
of non-Indians, and 2) the expenditure of $12,000,000 of the Indians'
own money (an expected award from a land claims case) in "a carefully
prepared program... worked out in advance by the State and Federal
agencies cooperating... to rehabilitate the needy and neglected
Indians of the state...."

Mr. Lipps, the man "speaking on behalf" of California Indians and
exercising great power over the lives of, in his words, "these primitive
people," stated:

> The California Indians are not by nature the low,
> degraded, intellectually inferior people they are
> generally believed to be. They are a retarded race
> and their seeming intellectual inferiority is due
> more to their treatment, poverty and lack of oppor-
> tunity than to any inherent incapacity. While not
> the upstanding, proud and noble bearing type of the
> quaintly picturesque and brilliantly arrayed Plains
> Indians, still they possess average native intelligence,
> and, given a chance, the majority of them can be
> developed into useful citizens and as such contribute
> something of value.... (Oscar H. Lipps, The Case of the
> California Indians, U.S. Indian School Print Shop,
> Chemawa, Oregon, 1932).

During the 1930's reforms were made in federal policy towards Indians, the principal one being that local native groups were to be allowed to incorporate, possess constitutions, and elect a "tribal" or business council. This small measure of local self-government was rapidly taken advantage of by many far western groups, including in the first year (1935) the Pyramid Lake Paiute Tribe, the Reno-Sparks Indian Colony, and the Washoe Tribe of Nevada and California. National reforms in bureau policy were also attempted but, unfortunately, these reforms were entirely dependent upon the continued good-will of Congress and the appointment of pro-Indian officials. No power at the national or regional levels was actually transferred to democratically-chosen Indian boards and therefore it was possible for many of the reforms to be reversed or sabotaged during the late 1940's and early 1950's, whenever a new president chose an unsympathetic Commissioner of Indian Affairs or Secretary of the Interior.

The reforms were often also meaningless at the local level since the same bureau officials as before possessed the same power either to control tribal council elections or to manipulate the council members. Gradually many Indian groups were indeed able to acquire some independence and authority but others remain, to this day, under practical bureau domination (or else the council members and local bureau officials comprise a "partnership" oligarchy which controls local affairs).

Nonetheless, a new spirit came to pervade the bureau during the 1930's which could not entirely be reversed even during the reactionary years of the 1950's. For example, the outright opposition to Indian traditions largely disappeared except in the schools (and it was diminished even in the latter), the "image" of respecting Indian opinions came to be valued, the loss of Indian land was largely halted, and many persons of Indian and part-Indian descent were allowed to rise in the bureau hierarchy. (The latter, of course, has a negative aspect since it serves as one of the means for preventing many educated Indians from criticizing the government).

As the relative power of the Bureau of Indian Affairs declined only a portion of the authority lost was acquired by Indian communities. A significant part of the bureau's power passed instead into the hands of white-controlled state and local agencies and this process has tended to accelerate in recent years. For example, during the period after 1912 and through the 1930's numerous small public school districts were established in both California and Nevada to serve Indian populations. The bulk of these districts were potentially controlled by Indians (although many were, in fact, controlled behind the scenes by the bureau, by white missionaries, or by white superintendents). During recent decades, however, virtually all of these districts have been abolished and consolidated with larger districts, thus ensuring white control.

Increasingly, therefore, and without solving the problems created by continuing Indian bureau power, Indian people have been forced to turn their attention to state-level politics. At the state-level Indians faced the hard fact that, due to small numbers, they could generally possess no direct representation in the legislature and were dependent upon difficult-to-tap "good-will" rather than possessing any reliable source of influence. Unfortunately also, both the governments of California and Nevada have

tended to adopt a paternalistic approach to Indian affairs, typified by
the establishment in California of a State Advisory Commission on Indian
Affairs, composed entirely of non-Indians, in 1961.

In the 1950's, as will be discussed below, the Bureau of Indian
Affairs commenced the termination of its services to California Indians.
Indian people were concerned and so were state officials who were not
anxious to accept responsibility for communities which normally were
still lacking in such fundamentals as paved roads, clean water, sewage
facilities, and defined property lines. The legislature therefore established a Senate Interim Committee on Indian Affairs which held hearings
beginning in 1954. The committee did signal service in calling attention
to the gross insufficiency of the bureau (conditions were not too dis-
similar from those described in the special investigations of 1882 and
1919) and an opportunity was provided for the, by then numerous, Indian
organizations to testify. Unfortunately, the legislators chose to rely
entirely upon white federal and state officials to "do something" and
the result was virtually nil.

Since 1961 a California state advisory commission, composed of
whites and almost always employing white staff, has been in existence but
it has not served to provide Indians with a voice in California Indian
affairs (a few appointed Indians have merely served on an advisory committee to the advisory commission). More significantly, the one concrete
accomplishment of the commission, the Progress Report to the Governor
and the Legislature was researched, prepared, and edited by non-Indians.
Their recommendations, while often praiseworthy for their concern for
material progress on reservations, are much weakened by being written by
non-Indians unable to comprehend the fundamental problems of Indian people.
Not surprisingly these non-Indians could not, without repudiating their
own commission and staff, come to grips with the issue of powerlessness,
nor could they face up to land problems whose discussion might irritate
powerful white interests.

In 1968 an effort was made by the existing California advisory commission to transform itself into a more powerful agency but with an all-
white membership. Indian people, through intensive lobbying, succeeded in
amending the bill so as to establish an all-Indian commission. This
latter amended bill then passed the Senate but was ultimately killed by
the chairman of the existing all-white advisory commission, Senator
William Coombs (who, as author of the original bill, possessed the traditional legislator's right to withdraw a piece of legislation bearing his
name).

In Nevada one Northern Paiute, Mr. Dewey Sampson, briefly served in
the legislature, but otherwise the Indian people were unrepresented at
the state level until 1965. In that year the newly-formed Inter-Tribal
Council of Nevada and allied tribal councils succeeded in persuading the
legislature to establish a State Commission on Indian Affairs to be
composed of at least three Indians (out of seven members). John Dressler,
the Washo chairman of the Inter-Tribal Council became commission chairman
and Alvin James, a Northern Paiute, became the first executive secretary.

An important step forward has been the continuing development of Indian-controlled organizations, such as the National Congress of American Indians (1944) and numerous local groups in California and Nevada. Unfortunately, the N.C.A.I. has never been strong in the Far West and most California-Nevada groups became embroiled in the land claims cases to such an extent that their effectiveness on other fronts was seriously handicapped.

Of recent significance has been the development of state-wide inter-tribal councils, particularly in connection with the handling of grants from the Office of Economic Opportunity and other federal agencies. In the early 1960's efforts were made to organize such a council in Nevada but bureau opposition led to failure. During 1963, however, the BIA changed its position and a number of Indian leaders were ready to move in any case. The result was the establishment of the Inter-Tribal Council of Nevada Inc., which initially represented only a few reservations and colonies but has since come to include virtually all such communities, and has successfully encouraged the funding of numerous development-action projects in Nevada. The Native Nevadan, published by the council, has become an excellent means of communication for most Nevada Indians.

Unfortunately, the fact that the initial meetings of the Inter-Tribal Council of Nevada took place at the BIA office and that a U.S. Public Health Service officer played a major advisory role led many Indians to adopt a hostile position. Furthermore, factionalism already existed among Nevada Indians and, in general, those who were militantly opposed to the government position in the claims cases tended to stay away from the Inter-Tribal Council. Those who supported the council tended, generally, to be persons who were more willing to cooperate with white officialdom while those in opposition tended to be extremely suspicious of all white-controlled agencies.

The Inter-Tribal of Nevada might well have failed except for the fact that it has become virtually the sole vehicle for the disbursal of federal grant money to Indians in Nevada. Again we see the power of the federal government, in that its selection of particular Indian agencies for the receipt of funds powerfully affects native internal politics.

In California a movement to establish an inter-tribal council also developed but under slightly different circumstances. The Office of Economic Opportunity made the decision during 1964-1965 not to fund local tribal groups directly, but rather to use coordinating groups such as inter-tribal councils. During 1966 O.E.O. stimulated, more or less artificially, an effort to create an Inter-Tribal Council of California. Unfortunately, the federal representatives became involved with only one of the many factions in the state with the result that the persons controlling the Inter-Tribal Council have not been nearly as representative as in Nevada. Repeated efforts to secure funding and to achieve a broader base were unsuccessful but finally in 1968 the O.E.O. "Indian Desk" decided to make a grant to the council. Still, the future of the Inter-Tribal Council of California is uncertain at this writing and it is especially unclear as to whether the council can avoid becoming enmeshed still further in personalistic factional politics.

In general, those Indians supporting the Inter-Tribal Council of California are individuals who, in the past, have been "cooperative" with the Indian Bureau and who are willing, for one reason or another, to work with white officialdom. The opposition, as in Nevada, includes many natives who have become completely disillusioned with the federal government and who generally oppose the California claims case. These Indians in California and Nevada, whom this writer denominates as "militant traditionalists," are informally allied with such groups as the Survival of the American Indians, Inc. of the Pacific Northwest (who staged the "fish-ins"), the traditionalist Hopis, and Mad Bear's Iroquois (who fought against Kinzua Dam). In 1968 traditional Indians radically opposed to federal policies organized the American Aboriginal Traditional Conference in an Oklahoma meeting but whether this grouping will have any important effect in the Far West remains to be seen.

A few California and Nevada Indians have also been active in the National Indian Youth Council and its off-shoot for the 1968 Poor People's Campaign, the American Indian Citizen's Coalition. A small number of individuals, mostly young, participated in the summer demonstrations in Washington D.C. By and large, though, this development has had little impact upon the large majority of Indian people in California and Nevada, many of whom, although critical of the government, are not inclined to stage demonstrations or to develop alliances with other minorities. During 1968 also a new pan-Indian organization was developed in the San Francisco bay area, called United Native Americans. The UNA, under the leadership of Lehman Brightman, a Sioux, has been quite active but its future impact is uncertain at this date.

The future of the struggle for Indian equality largely depends upon Indian people overcoming factionalism and achieving a greater degree of unity. Whether this can be accomplished in a society where powerful and well-funded white agencies constantly intervene in Indian affairs is conjectural at best.

The Struggle for Land and Compensation

Since 1920 Native Americans have had to continue their efforts to achieve a better economic position in the face of continued white attacks upon the Indian land base, continued existence of a large number of landless Indians, and the opposition of the federal government to a willing recognition of its debt for land illegally seized in earlier years.

Many Indians still did not possess adequate reservations during the 1920's, as in Inyo County where 759 of 1,418 natives were reportedly still "homeless" in 1925. Small plots were being acquired by the Indian Bureau, but on a very protracted and unsatisfactory basis. The setting aside of so-called public lands for national forests, national parks, et cetera, continued to take precedence over the meeting of the Indians' land needs, both during the openly anti-Indian (and corrupt) adminis- tration of Warren G. Harding, and under the later, somewhat improved, administrations which followed. Similarly, the leasing of "public" lands to white ranchers, miners, and farmers possessed a higher priority with the Interior Department.

By 1920 many Indian people in California had become somewhat familiar with the idea of using the courts as a means for achieving justice. The Indians of northern California, aided by Rev. F.G. Collett decided at that time to seek compensation for the lands seized illegally during the 1850's. In 1920 Congressman John E. Raker introduced a bill which proposed that any California tribe or band could sue the United States for lands taken away, utilizing private attorneys of their own choosing. Raker's bill and similar ones which were introduced each year through 1927 were all defeated, in great measure because of the opposi- tion of the Indian Bureau. The BIA, the supposed "guardian" of the Indians, was actually disposing of Indian lands during this period (Secretary of the Interior Albert B. Fall was himself seeking lands belonging to the Mescalero Apaches) and, not surprisingly, was hostile to such court cases.

In April 1922 a number of delegates representing California Indians journeyed to Washington D.C. to attend an Interior Department hearing where they hoped to get a reversal of the department's stand in opposition. The Commissioner of Indian Affairs reported that:

> At this hearing it was made clear that the previous adverse report would not be modified, as the depart- ment was unwilling to approve any bill that had for its purpose compensating Indians for the value of lands ($10,000,000) involved in the eighteen treaties which were rejected by the Senate in 1852.... (Report of the Commissioner of Indian Affairs, 1922, p.18)

The department did agree that landless Indians should be provided with homes and that the poor should get further aid, all administered by the bureau. (It is rather ironic that the Executive Branch during the 1920's, ostensibly dedicated as it was to "rugged individualism" and economic conservatism should favor the "dole" for Indians and oppose what was essentially a self-help measure. The basis for this opposition would seem to have stemmed from a fear of allowing Indians access to the courts, and a basic hostility towards Native Americans achieving any measure of independence from the federal bureaucracy.) During the late 1920's various white organizations began to respond to Indian interest in the matter of land claims. In 1926, for example, the influential Commonwealth Club of San Francisco issued a report on native affairs including a recommendation for federal legislation allowing for a fair determination of California Indian claims. In 1927 the State legislature authorized the state attorney general to bring suit against the United States on behalf of the Indians, provided that Congress approved authorizing legislation; and in the following year Congress did approve such a measure.

The bill finally approved, originally introduced by Rep. Clarence Lea of Lake County, empowered the California attorney general to submit the claims of California Indians to the U.S. Court of Claims "for determination of the equitable amount due said Indians" and recognized the failure to secure the lands and goods guaranteed in the eighteen treaties as "sufficient ground" for the suit. California Indians were defined as those resident in the state on June 1, 1852 and their descendents.

Unfortunately the bill was weak in several respects. First, the Indians were unable to retain their own counsel and while the use of the California attorney generals saved money, they also were elected partisan office-holders subject to replacement each four years (actually three different men, U. S. Webb, Earl Warren, and Robert Kenney, served while the suit was in court). Second, the bill was amended so as to preclude any award exceeding $1.25 per acre, awards were to be limited to the value of what was promised in the 1851-52 treaties, all federal expenses for California Indians over the years were to be deducted from the award as "off-sets," and the award (if any) was to go to the U.S. Treasury "to the credit of the Indians of California," earning therein 4% annual interest. The award was to be "subject to appropriation by Congress for educational, health, industrial, and other purposes for the benefit of said Indians...and no part...shall be paid out in per capita payments...." (Kenneth M. Johnson, K-344 or the California Indians vs. the United States, 1966, pp. 64-5).

Thus Congress in effect recognized the validity of the cessions of lands made by the California Indians in 1851-52 (about 75 million acres) but did not recognize the validity of the United States' treaty obligations to the natives (about 8 million acres) except in terms of possibly awarding a belated $1.25 per acre with no interest (as it turned out). Quite obviously, if the Indians' cession was valid the United States' establishment of eighteen reservations was equally valid and the Indians were entitled to recovery of the land, or if not that, at least to its actual value plus damages. Many other inconsistencies were also involved, as in deducting federal expenses which often never benefited Indians or which were used for coercive purposes; including in the suit many California Indian groups not a party to the treaties; and proposing to use the award monies for future federal expenses. Clearly, the Congress of 1928 was not in either a generous or a fair mood, but at least some kind of action could commence.

The case was initiated in 1929 but disappointment soon set in as the California attorney general (U. S. Webb) awakened to the realization that the Hoover Administration was going to bitterly fight the suit. "To the Department of the Interior [the case] was an uninvited intruder in their domain, inspired by ignorant do-gooders." To the Department of Justice it was "a raid on the treasury." (Johnson, K-344, p.67). As a result Webb, in 1932, filed an amended petition which made a stronger case for Indian title, asserting that in 1851-52 the Indians "were the owners and entitled to the use, occupancy, and possession of certain lands ... amounting in all to more than seventy-five million acres...." Repeated efforts were also made between 1930 and 1943 to obtain amendments to the 1928 authorization act so as to make it possible for the Indians to obtain a more generous settlement but Congress was hostile on each occasion except in 1935 and in that year President Franklin D. Roosevelt vetoed the legislation.

The Interior Department and Executive Branch continued their efforts to see to it that the Indians received next to nothing by procrasti- nating on the matter of computing the "off-sets" and then, finally, in 1934 coming up with a total of $12,500,000 allegedly spent on California Indians in almost one hundred years. This total wiped out more than two- thirds of the value of the properties promised in 1851-52 (figuring the land at $1.25 per acre) and exceeded congressional appropriations for the period (it was finally reduced to $12,029,099, the figure for appropriations, after the Court of Claims refused to allow deductions for corruption, diversion of funds, et cetera).

Webb then adopted delaying tactics in the hope of getting federal legislation allowing the Indians to receive interest but this effort was a failure. In 1939 Earl Warren became attorney general and the case was reactivated; and finally in 1942 the question of liability was settled.

> The plaintiffs [California Indians] are entitled to
> recover the value of the land set out and described
> in the ...treaties... [and goods promised]. As this
> claim does not involve a taking of land by the Govern-
> ment for which just compensation shall be made, but
> only compensation for an equitable claim, no allowance
> of interest is permitted or allowable.(Johnson, K-344, p.73)

This was a strange decision indeed, denying "just compensation" and holding that "equitable" did not include interest, but the result should not be too surprising as Indians have not done well in the federal courts as a general rule. Warren tried to obtain a new trial but was turned down and in 1943 his successor, Robert Kenney, appealed to the Supreme Court without success.

During 1943 and 1944 Kenney attempted to reach a settlement on the basis of the unsatisfactory rulings of the Court of Claims. In essence, an agreement with the government attorneys secured a settlement of $5,024,842 for the Indians after the "off-sets" of $12,029,099 were

subtracted from the value of the treaty promises (land, goods, and
services) set at $17,053,941. Many Indians were extremely unhappy but
Kenney went ahead and made the settlement in December 1944, almost
two decades after the case had begun. In 1950 Congress finally adopted
legislation providing $150 for each California Indian (leaving a
portion of the award still in the U.S. Treasury).

The settlement of the 1928 case was, in effect, a shrewd bargain
for the federal government and another fleecing for Indians. The
Indian people had been made to pay for almost a century of Indian Bureau
expenses relating to California, including funds spent on forcibly
removing natives from their homes and on lining the pockets of crooked
officials. Or, from another perspective, the government had obtained
about 8 million acres of prime land for a 1950 cash expenditure of about
60¢ per acre coupled with $12 million in previously already paid for
"services." But this is not the whole story, because the government had
already realized more than enough income from the lands in question to
pay for the full settlement given the Indians. Therefore, it can be said
that the government quieted the Indian's claim at no expense to itself
whatsoever and it may well be that the government actually made a
profit (if the 8 million acres were sold to whites for more than $2 per
acre or if proceeds from timber sales, leases, et cetera, are considered).

The settlement of the 1928 - 1944 case was certainly not "equitable,"
nor was it legally sound. As to the latter, it should be pointed out
that all California Indians had subtracted from their award money the
value (at $1.25 per acre) of reservations (600,000 acres) set aside for
only a part of the California Indian population; that all California
Indians were to participate in the award money regardless of whether
or not they had any real legal interest in the eighteen treaties of
1851 - 52; and that each person of California Indian descent was treated
as having an equal interest in the award regardless of whether he
possessed sixteen Indian ancestors living in 1851-52 or only one.

One interesting effect of the procedure followed in the case was the
apparent transfer of title to some 600,000 acres of established "Executive Order" reservations from the federal government to the California
Indians collectively, or at least to individual reservation groups. No
deeds have been issued to Indian people as a result of this case but it
would seem clear that in making the Indians pay $1.25 for each acre of
existing reservation land the federal government made Indian ownership
effective. But which Indians?   Since the California Indians collectively paid for each and every reservation acre it could be argued that
each Indian possesses an interest in each reservation. But the legal
confusion created thereby is great indeed, especially since the
600,000 acres paid for included lands already patented to individuals
and, often, resold to whites. One could go on, but it should be clear
that the procedure followed in the 1928 - 1944 case can be criticized
from many viewpoints and it may well be that future law suits will be
required to settle the confusion.

The total land claims of California Indians were not settled by the
1928-1944 case since part of the state was not covered by the eighteen
treaties and since the payments made under the latter did not really
constitute "just compensation" (the total gross award being $17,000,000
in exchange for the cession of some 67,000,000 acres of land).

In 1946 Congress authorized the creation of an Indian Claims Commission with broad powers to deal with any and all of the remaining
claims of Indian groups. The commission procedure was such as to facilitate claims cases which might never have received separate congressional
approval, but cases taken to the commission could not be appealed and
normal constitutional provisions relating to just compensation were
bypassed. In any event, many California Indians pressed for a new case
which would settle all of the remaining claims and such a case was initiated in 1947 with private attorneys.

The details of this case are in many respects similar to that of
1928-1944 except that about 60 million acres were involved. After sixteen years of litigation the various attorneys agreed to a value of
47¢ per acre ($29,100,000) and in a series of meetings held in 1963-64
people of California Indian descent voted, 11,427 to 3,310, to accept
the settlement. In May 1965 the commission made the settlement final,
although the per capita distribution of the award must still await
congressional legislation and a new census to determine all who are
eligible.

The Indian Claims Commission case suffers from many of the same
legal and procedural liabilities as did the 1928-1944 case and, in
addition, raises questions about the constitutionality of this entire
approach to the settlement of native land claims. Suffice to state
that the Indians were never afforded Fifth Amendment protections nor,
specifically did they possess the option of securing title to any of
the claimed land. The federal government, in effect, acquired a clear
title to millions of acres of so-called public land for 47¢ per acre
in what amounted to a "forced sale." As to the "generosity" of the
government, one should note that California's national forests grossed
$36,336,621 in timber sales for the federal government during fiscal
1968 alone.

The procedure followed in the California claims case has also
served to deepen factions among Indians in that state, since many natives
have been very unhappy with either the amount of compensation or the
failure to allow them to have the option of obtaining land instead of
dollars. Those Indians desiring to retain a portion of their ancient
territory will receive about $800 as payment for about 1600 acres but
with that $800 can not purchase even one acre of good land. In
addition, many Indians believe that they were not dealt with fairly by
their attorneys, that the voting at meetings was irregular, and that
persons with small amounts of Indian ancestry and of non-Indian self-
identity should not have been allowed to influence the outcome of the
case. It should also be noted that individual groups which might have
voted against the settlement had no separate voice but were simply part
of a collective "California Indian" vote.

On the other hand, many Indians are pleased that at least some additional compensation will be available and look forward to future litigation to settle for the value of losses in mineral rights, timber, and other kinds of property.

Other native groups in the Far West have become involved in their own cases before the Indian Claims Commission, including groups which extend partially into California. The Washo, Northern Paiute, Western Shoshone, Southern Paiute, and Colorado River cases are all in various stages of development and all closely resemble the unified California case in general character. Resistance to the entire concept of seeking compensation for land before the commission is greater than in California, however, especially among the Western Shoshone people. Many, perhaps a majority, of the Shoshone are opposed to the "sale" of land which they regard as being rightfully theirs or as belonging to the Creator. But "their case" still grinds on towards a cash settlement because the government needs only to obtain authorization from one reservation council to engage attorneys for the entire "people" (however defined), and because no other option is available in practical terms (primarily due to the extra-constitutional position of Indians).

Very little compensation has been thus far received by western Indians and when it does come it will often come in a manner unacceptable to many Indians, the authorizing legislation being ordinarily drawn up by non-Indian federal officials, attorneys, and congressmen.* On the other hand, many Indians will feel proud that at least some token payment has been forced from a reluctant government and that the cases, although imperfect, can represent something of a moral victory for the natives.

Interestingly, the years of litigation and expected awards have led to many changes in native life including attendance at numerous meetings, the development of many new organizations, the acquisition of some degree of knowledge about legal procedures, the appearance of "Claims Case Indians" (people who never had identified themselves as being of Indian descent until the prospect of money arose), and the reinforcement of extreme suspicion of the government on the part of those opposed to the cases. Finally, many Indians have been forced by the cumbersome nature of the litigation to devote time to the claims controversies which might better have been spent on other matters.

Indian people have also continued to be involved in defensive struggles to protect their land and wealth throughout the last forty years. For instance, the Owens Valley [Indian] Board of Trustees in 1958 adopted the following resolution:

_____

* Incredibly, the BIA drew up a proposed bill in the Northern Paiute case and had it submitted in Congress prior to any discussion with Indians. A comparable development occurred in 1967-68 in relation to the California case.

We should also like to have the 66,620 acres of land
known as the Paiute Indian Reservation... be opened
to use by the Paiute Indians as grazing land and that
they be reimbursed for all grazing fees, mining royal-
ties and the like received by the federal government
since 1910 plus interest on this property. This land
was paid for at $1.25 per acre out of the money
received by the Indians of California [in the 1928-
1944 claims case]. The land obviously is the property
of the Mono and Inyo County Paiute Indians...although
they have been denied the right to use it.

An incredible series of correspondence followed, between Leonard Hill,
BIA director for California, and State Senator Charles Brown, in which
Hill made it very clear that his office intended to make no effort to
restore the 66,000 acres to the Paiutes and that he was inclined to be
opposed to seeking more land for Indians. In a letter of November 24,
1958 Hill stated that

It is the policy of the bureau in California to conform
to the mandate of Congress as expressed in House
Concurrent Resolution No. 108 passed July 27, 1953.
This resolution states: "That it is declared to be the
sense of Congress that at the earliest possible time,
all of the Indian tribes and individual members thereof
located within the States of... California... should
be freed from federal supervision and control from all
disabilities and limitations especially applicable to
Indians...." Aside from keeping the Indians informed
of the availability of public domain land which may be
allotted under existing authority [none was available],
we see no particular remedy for the plight of the Mono
Basin Indians. (Progress Report.. by the Senate
Interim Committee on California Indian Affairs, 1959,
pp. 68, 73 ff).

Clearly then, the California BIA intended to use the 1953 "termination"
resolution (to be discussed below) as an excuse for continuing what had
long been bureau practice, that is, to refuse to protect, or to work
for, the interests of California Indians when those interests clashed
with white interests (as in this case, with the City of Los Angeles).
It should be noted that the 1953 joint congressional resolution was
without the force of law, being merely the expression of the desires
of a particular Congress and not being binding upon any subsequent
Congress. As shall be noted below, however, such resolutions have
been transformed into "administrative law" by the California BIA.

    Another example of the continuing struggle for land relates to the
repeated efforts of the Pyramind Lake Paiute Tribe to obtain the
removal of illegal white squatters from their reservation, to obtain
their share of Truckee River water, and to preserve the existence of

Pyramid Lake itself. In 1938 the Indians commenced legal proceedings
to recover their lands from the squatters in the face of repeated efforts
by anti-Indian U.S. Senator Pat McCarran of Nevada to persuade Congress
to give the whites title to the disputed land. In 1944 the Supreme Court
finally ruled in favor of the Northern Paiutes but it was still necessary
to evict the squatters and that required another seven years. The whites,
with the aid of Senator McCarran, resisted every step of the way, finally
blocking the use of irrigation ditches needed to make the recovered lands
usable. The bureau had aided the Indians through 1949 but by 1951 the
reactionary policies of Commissioner Dillon Myer and Interior Secretary
Oscar Chapman put them on Senator McCarran's side. The government attempted
to prevent the tribe from retaining its private attorneys while McCarran
did everything possible to prevent the Indians from developing their
lands.

Many Indian organizations came to the aid of the Pyramid Lake Paiute
Tribe and the battle over their right to hire their own attorneys was
largely won. The water problem has not, however, been resolved to this
day since white farmers continue to drain water away from the Truckee
River which should be going into the reservation. A new water scheme,
the Washoe Project, currently threatens the very existence of Pyramid Lake,
the major future economic resource of the tribe.

Indians have also had to struggle to protect their lands from termination and from such federal and state projects as flood-control dams.
Current plans of the Army Corps of Engineers envision the flooding of the
Round Valley Reservation in California, while numerous reserves have been
flooded in other parts of the country. Unfortunately, the Indian people
have not been in a position to resist the power of federal agencies in
most such instances. The allotment system, although in moth-balls from
the early 1930's to 1950, has also continued to erode the native land
base since lands patented to individual Indians have usually passed to
white ownership. Thus today the best areas of many reservations are in
the hands of non-Indians.

The Struggle Against Discrimination and Poverty

In 1920 the census counted 17,360 Indians in California and 4,907 in Nevada, while the Bureau of Indian Affairs reported 16,241 in California and 5,900 in Nevada. A special 1928 count of California Indians eligible for possible claims awards enumerated 23,542 persons of full or partial California native descent although the 1930 census identified only 19,212. It would appear, therefore, that at least 4,000 persons of California Indian descent were "passing" as Caucasians or as Mexican-Americans by the latter year. By 1950 at least 17,000 persons of California Indian ancestry were not counted by the census as Indians.*

A 1926 bureau report identified 18,913 California Indians of whom only 8,197 were "full-bloods" while 4,149 were one half or more of native descent, 3,844 were of less than half native descent, and 2,723 were unclassified "Mission Indians." Nevada possessed 5,692 Indians including 3,434 "full-bloods," 702 one-half or more Indian, and 286 less than half Indian. By 1931 less than one-half of California Indians were enrolled with the bureau (10,490 of some 24,000) and 1,841 of these were not residing on trust land. During the 1950's and 1960's estimates indicate that only 8 to 9,000 persons, or less, have resided on trust land, with perhaps 32,000 other California Indian individuals living elsewhere. Thus it is clear that in California Native Americans receiving federal assistance have declined in number while the over-all population has increased; and that intermixture with non-Indians has proceeded fairly rapidly. In Nevada, on the other hand, intermixture has proceeded more slowly and a larger proportion have remained on trust land (4,362 of 5,700 in 1927 and 4,200 of 6,700 in 1960, although the latter relationship may be invalid since 1964 - 1965 estimates placed the actual Nevada Indian population at 8,525 to 9,385). By 1960 only about 2,500 Nevada Indians (out of more than 7,000 individuals) were residing on those reservations with meaning-ful agricultural potential.

California and Nevada Indians have ordinarily been the victims of poverty and discrimination, both induced, tragically, largely through the actions of the federal government and other white agencies. The period since the 1920's has unfortunately witnessed only a very gradual and, in some cases, negligible change in Indian material conditions of life. In great measure, California and Nevada Indians have been victimized by a federal policy which has not only been hostile in the sense of seeking to acquire native land, suppress native culture, and rigidly control native affairs but also in the sense of positively discriminating against California-Nevada groups within the context of federal Indian programs. That is, the federal government has tended to "short-change" the small tribes and groups of the Far West in relation to the range of services made available to the larger tribes found elsewhere. In great measure this continuing pattern of discrimination stems from the earlier failure to establish large, viable reserves for most far western Indians.

During the 1950's and 1960's discrimination against California Indians in particular was greatly accelerated by the so-called termination policy referred to earlier. For many years a group of basically

---

*By 1950 36,094 persons were enrolled as being of California Indian descent.

anti-Indian congressmen had sought to abolish the reforms of the 1930's
and to carry the Dawes Allotment concept to its logical conclusion.
They sought, in other words, to abolish tribes as corporate entities,
to divide up all tribal assets among individuals, to sell those
assets not so divisable, and to expose the land transferred to individuals to local taxation. The results of such a program had long been
made crystal clear by the operation of the Dawes system. Indian property
would rapidly be dissipated by sale to whites and no tribal organizations would exist to either protect native interests or to engage in
corporate-level economic development projects. Without a doubt many
of the groups pushing for a renewal of the Dawes program desired the
above results, since congressmen from states with powerful white timber,
mining, and stock-raising interests have been rather prominent in the
movement.

During the 1950's a reactionary trend both within the bureau and
in Congress made it possible for the Dawes program, now called simply
termination, to be successfully pushed. In 1953 P.L. 280 and House
Concurrent Resolution 108 initiated the process. P. L. 280 transferred
many powers (over law and order, for example) to state jurisdiction
without, however, sufficient clarity of language to ensure a smooth
transition. H.C.R. 108, already quoted above, called for the termination
of California Indians and required the Secretary of the Interior to
produce a bill by January 1, 1954 designed to accomplish that purpose.

The BIA produced a series of bills which were totally unsatisfactory,
not merely from the native viewpoint but from the perspective of the
State of California. Basically, California Indian communities were to
be cut off abruptly from federal services with their state of poverty
and under-development left "as is." The California Legislature had
endorsed the idea of termination in 1953 but during 1954 made an abrupt
change, largely as a result of the hearings conducted by the State
Senate Interim Committee on Indian Affairs. The committee found that
most reservations were simply unprepared for termination, with a multitude of problems often including undefined boundaries, no roads, no
water, no sanitation, substandard housing, and 2,600 complicated heir-
ship cases. The state was unwilling to accept the financial responsibility for correcting the failures of bureau management and opposed
the BIA termination legislation.

Many California Indians fought against termination also, including
groups such as the Council of California Indians, the California
Indians' Congress, and the Federated Indians of California Inc. Only
one group, James Martinez' Mission Indian Federation of California,
completely favored the 1954 termination bills. The combined opposition
of Indians, of such groups as the American Friends Service Committee,
and the State of California led to the defeat of the 1954 legislation.

In 1957-1958 the State Senate Interim Committee conducted another
investigation and found that "with minor exceptions... very little has
been done to carry out the recommendations set forth in the [1954-55]
report" to prepare Indian reserves for termination. In spite of that fact,

the committee in 1957 recommended termination legislation which, by its nature, reveals that their opposition to the 1954 bills was not based upon any pro-Indian bias.

Briefly, the committee's proposed bill would: 1) close tribal membership rolls so as to even exclude future-born children,; 2) allow an Indian individual to initiate court proceedings to divide up tribal property; 3) require each tribe or the Secretary of the Interior to draw up a plan for the "distribution and disposal" of much reservation property; 4) require the Secretary of the Interior to draw up a plan for the "distribution and disposal" of the balance of reservation property, with the lands being divided or sold; 5) allow for a referendum on the plans but give the Secretary of the Interior authority to override any adverse vote unless Congress takes specific action to halt him; 6) authorizes the Secretary (at his discretion presumably) to help provide training for Indians; and 7) revokes all tribal constitutions and corporate charters after the above process has occurred.

This plan was incorporated in several bills, one of which, H.R.2824, was passed into law as P.L. 85-671 on August 18, 1958 and was made applicable to 44 rancherias in California, exempting (temporarily, at least) the larger reservations.

The California termination plan was neither necessary, just, nor wise. If the legislators were sincerely concerned about freeing Indians from the control of the Indian Bureau that could have easily been accomplished by sponsoring an Indian-controlled non-profit corporation, or corporations, which could have contracted with the federal government for the carrying out of the service functions of the bureau. Numerous examples of federal contracting with white non-profit (and profit-seeking) corporations existed as readily applicable precedents.

The termination legislation as proposed and adopted was quite obviously designed to destroy Indian communities, render economic development impossible, and place Indian individuals at a competitive disadvantage with whites. Let us examine this thesis further.

First, the only feasible units available for Indian economic development, the tribal corporations, were to be abolished by fiat, without a vote of the members. This would be comparable to the forced dissolution of a white corporation or, more accurately, of a white non-profit municipal corporation. Second, the internal affairs of tribal corporations were to be transferred, in fact, to the Secretary of the Interior and Congress for the transitional period and those organizations were to be prevented from controlling their own membership rolls. Third, Indians were to be completely individualized. All reservation property was to be either sold or divided into individual parcels, with none being held in corporate ownership. This is especially ironic in a state such as California where agriculture and the timber industry are overwhelmingly corporate in character. How were Indian individual owners of a few acres of timber, farmland or grazing land to compete with white corporations? Fourth, Indians with virtually no cash income (many were unemployed and on local welfare) could not be expected to do anything but sell or lease their individual parcels.

It should also be pointed out that the California termination plan
was developed in a completely elitist manner by whites who did not
involve Indians in any of the major decision-making steps, whether at the
bureau, congressional, or state level. In this respect, as in others,
the enactment of the 1958 legislation revealed the same tendency towards
a decidedly anti-democratic procedure in so far as Indians are concerned
as had the Dawes Act of 1887, the Cherokee Removal of 1838, and many
other nineteenth-century actions.

The termination philosophy of the 1950's embodied the incredible
stance of putting people "on their own" who had been robbed of their wealth,
denigrated for years, neglected in terms of essential economic and educational development, and subjected to stultifying experience of decades
of bureaucratic manipulation without returning any appreciable quantity
of their former wealth and without taking a single meaningful step to
insure their ability to compete in a complex society dominated by their
former oppressors. Finally, the termination philosophy, in its high-
handed and presumptuous assumption of the right to destroy Indian tribal
organizations and native community life, could be said to have posed a
potential threat to all forms of local group self-direction in the United
States. Perhaps it is indeed far-fetched, but it is nonetheless con-
ceivable that one day coercive programs directed against whites might be
justified by the precedent established by the treatment of Indians.

In any event, the Bureau of Indian Affairs' Sacramento office moved
forward vigorously to high-pressure as many rancherias as possible into
being terminated, without, however, fully informing the natives of other
alternatives and without providing essential services needed for an
orderly transition. More significantly still, on the basis of a mere
concurrent resolution of a single Congress, the BIA commenced the termination of services to virtually all California Indians, whether included in
the 1958 legislation or not. By administrative fiat only, the bureau
withdrew college scholarships, vocational education, economic development programs, water and sanitation development projects, et cetera,
from California Indians while still offering these services to Indians
elsewhere. The Public Health Service likewise eliminated medical
services for most Indians in California, while the BIA persuaded the
State of California into acquiescing in the cutting off of Johnson-
O'Malley funds (designated to subsidize public schools serving Indian
pupils living on tax-exempt land).

This extremely discriminatory and short-sighted policy was resisted
by a few Indians but they lacked any influential allies until the Indian
Services Division of California Rural Legal Assistance Inc. (an OEO-funded
agency) began to call attention to what was taking place. In August 1967
the CRLA pointed out that

> the government seems to have pursued this policy
> [of termination] almost fanatically, in a blind
> rush to cut the Indians loose from its protection
> and benefits, no matter how harsh the effects on
> them.... Still the federal government continues

to pursue the termination policy indiscriminately
and relentlessly, inducing the Indians to terminate
by unfulfilled promises and in proceedings shot
through with legal irregularity. ("California Rural
Legal Caseload," August 1967, p.21).

CRLA staff repeatedly badgered the Sacramento BIA office with evidence
of irregularities and made it clear that HCR 108 lacked any validity.
The Ad Hoc Committee on California Indian Education, a new all-Indian
group, also called for the restoration of Johnson-O'Malley funds and,
together, CRLA and the Ad Hoc Committee succeeded in getting congressional pressure placed upon the bureau.

Finally in June 1968 Commissioner Robert L. Bennett announced that
he had ordered the restoration of certain services to California Indians,
including the right to attend BIA vocational-special schools and to
receive college scholarships. A few months earlier Leonard Hill was replaced as director of the Sacramento BIA office, thus presumably preparing the way for a policy reversal. The "latest word" is that
termination is "dead" as a policy (not merely because of what happened
in California but due to the sad experiences of the Menominee, Klamath,
and other terminated groups), but it is highly unlikely that such a
continually popular approach to liquidating Indians can be buried as
long as whites control Indian affairs.

Nevada Indians were also specifically threatened with termination
when a bill was introduced in Congress in 1954 which would have cut-off
services from eight groups in the state. On April 16, 1954 hearings were
held in Reno, Nevada where most Indian representatives testified that they
were not ready for termination without the solution of many specific
problems. The Nevada bill was not as bad as those of California
since it at least provided for the option of corporate ownership of
property, but it otherwise was similar to the previously discussed legislation. The bill was defeated.

It should be clear from the foregoing that little in the way of
economic development occurred in these years on California or Nevada
reservations, although in the latter case OEO money has recently facilitated some advancement. It is most depressing indeed to read the 1966
report of the California Advisory Commission on Indian Affairs or the
various reports of the California Rural Legal Assistance and to realize
that very little has been done to improve conditions on most California
reservations since the 1958-59, 1954-55, and 1919 reports referred to
earlier. The quality of life of Indian people has improved in many cases,
but such change has come about largely because of individual, off-
reservation employment and not because of on-reservation development.

California and Nevada Indians have also continued to suffer from many
of the same kinds of discrimination experienced by other poor, non-white
groups. The most blatant forms of racism would appear to have largely
disappeared but many Indians have experienced police brutality, hostile
justice courts, discriminatory landlords, and prejudiced employers.
Additionally, of course, Indian people suffer daily from the anti-Indian

or stereotypical nature of television" westerns," and from the general
pro-white bias of the communication media and advertising.

California Indians in 1960 constituted that portion of the California
population with the lowest income and highest unemployment rates.
Indian males, on a statewide basis, possessed a median income of $2,694
(as compared with $3,553 for blacks and over $5,000 for whites), while
13.4% of males over 25 earned less than $1,000, 31.6% earned less than
$2,000, 45.2% earned less than $3,000, and 74.8% earned less than $5,000.
Thus at least one-half of California Indians were below the "poverty-
level" statistically, although this is an under-estimate because Indian
families were much larger than the average (25.4% were composed of seven
or more persons as compared with 12.9% for all non-whites and 4.9% for
whites). "Rural Farm" (i.e., reservation) Indian males had a median
income of $1,769 (as compared with $3,298 for whites).

Statewide Indian unemployment in 1960 was 15.1% for males (as compared with 12.7% for blacks and less than 5% for whites), while unemployment was even higher in rural areas as in the Trinity-Klamath region
(21.7% for males). (American Indians in California, State Department of
Industrial Relations, 1965).

Nevada Indians also suffered from high unemployment and low-income
rates in 1960. Unemployment for non-white males in Nevada was reported
at 10.1% (as compared with 5.9% for whites), while Indian rates stood at
8.2% in Elko County, 12.1% in Ormsby County, and (with blacks) at 13.2%
in Washoe County. The median income for non-white males was $3,184
($4,903 for all males), while 19% of non-white families or single indivi-
duals received less than $1,000, 32% received less than $2,000, and 45%
received less than $3,000 (as opposed to 24.5% for whites). (Elmer
Rusco, Minority Groups in Nevada, 1966, pp. 34-37).

In recent years new problems have arisen due to the fact that sizeable
numbers of California and Nevada Indians have migrated to urban areas.
More significant still has been the almost-forced migration of tens of
thousands of out-of-state Indians into the San Francisco-San Jose and Los
Angeles areas thanks to a modern "trail of tears" known as the Relocation
Program. Relocation was commenced during the reactionary period of the
1950's as a device for reducing population on overcrowded reservations,
as a partial substitute for an unwillingness to spend money for on-reservation development, as a means to encourage "assimilation," and as a means
for improving the income of individual Indians. The program has been
highly praised and severely criticized but, in any event, it has had the
effect of contributing heavily to the growth of urban Indian populations
and has made many natives into virtual commuters between reservation and
city. Perhaps as many as one-third of the relocatees give up and return
home while still others move back and forth, being relocated several times
in some cases.

There is no question but what it is a traumatic experience for rural,
tribally-oriented people to be moved, not to the nearest small city, but
to the very heart of a modern metropolis, especially when the counseling

afforded the relocatees is marginal at best. Then the relocatee is
placed in a job (any job, literally) after, perhaps, some brief training
(which may or may not be related to his first job) and for a few weeks
he receives minimal financiallassistance. Thereafter, he is on his own
in a strange city and, not surprisingly, a high proportion end up on "skid
row" or as local welfare recipients (in many respects it can be said that
the BIA is contributing directly to the increased welfare expenses of
our urban complexes). Innumerable personal tragedies occur, hidden beneath
a mountain of statistics relating the number of initial jobs which have been
secured, et cetera.

On the other hand, many relocatees are able to gradually adjust to
the city, thanks in great measure to|another new phenomena, the appearance
of urban "Indian centers" and "friendship houses." Whatever fellowship
is to be found (aside from the many bars catering principally to Indians),
whatever counseling is to be secured, whatever social life is available,
is usually in association with one of these Indian centers or with the
clubs which have grown out of them. These valuable organizations, so
essential to whatever success the relocation program has had, receive no
support from the BIA and little from any federal agencies. This has been,
in part, a beneficial circumstance because it has allowed most such
centers to come under Indian control.

Joining the relocatees have been thousands of self-relocated Indians,
individuals whose personal experiences have led them to seek greater
opportunity in the city. It would appear that the self-relocated individuals adjust better to urban life in spite of having to obtain their
own first jobs, pay their own bus fare and obtain their own housing.

Together these various groups are creating a new kind of Indian life,
not completely pan-Indian (because tribal clubs and frequent trips "home"
maintain a certain degree of tribal exclusiveness) but nonetheless something of an amalgamation. More significantly, the BIA may well have mis-
calculated if"assimilation" and "getting rid of the Indian problem" was
one of its goals in fostering urbanization. Not only do the various clubs
and centers preserve and even expand upon the Indian heritage but the
urban Indian is fast becoming politically militant and sophisticated. It
may well be that urban-trained Indians will help to awaken their rural
brothers and succeed in transforming Indian affairs in this republic.
Certainly it is clear that urbanized Native Americans are far more willing
to engage in demonstrations than are their rural relations.

Significantly, as of the 1960's, only (at most) 9,000 Indians reside
on reservations in California, less than 40,000 reside in smaller cities
and rural areas, while at least 50,000 are living in metropolitan zones.
A sizeable proportion of Nevada Indians now reside in the Reno-Sparks
and Carson City areas but those cities cannot be regarded as affording
a truly urban environment.

The Struggle for a Better Education

Between the 1920's and early 1940's the Bureau of Indian Affairs ceased to have any appreciable role in California-Nevada Indian education, thanks in great measure to Indian efforts to establish local public schools or to gain admittance to existing schools. This latter was facilitated by the case of Piper v. Big Pine School District (1924) in which Indians won the right to attend public schools.

Unfortunately, the public school movement failed to yield the results anticipated by the more optimistic, especially where the schools were controlled by white individuals basically hostile towards the Indian heritage and prejudiced against native pupils. Prior to World War II it was rare indeed for an Indian to graduate from high school in California and a high school education was simply not available to many Nevada Indians living in highly anti-Indian areas such as Douglas County. (It was not until the 1920's that Nevada Indians were able to receive a high school education and then, in a real sense, only at Carson City High School. In 1926 there were no Nevada Indians enrolled in grade ten or above at any federal school).

A college education was simply beyond the realm of possibility for California and Nevada Indians before World War II and the number of college graduates from that period can be literally counted on one hand.

The post-war period witnessed some improvement but not primarily due to any change in the schools as such. Anti-Indian personal prejudice did decline but basically the public schools, now increasingly under white control, retained the same mono-cultural Anglo-American curriculum as in earlier years. History was white history, literature was Anglo or European literature, music was in the European tradition, art was Anglo-European, cooking was white cooking, sewing was white sewing, crafts were white crafts, and so on. Needless to state, no effort was made (and none has ever been made) to teach any California or Nevada Indian language in any school below the college level (although the Indian-controlled Kashia Reservation Elementary School is currently teaching a few words of the Kashia language). English language instruction was almost always designed for the pupil from a middle-class English-speaking home.

In spite of these handicaps native far western Indian pupils, stimulated by the pressure of exceptional parents or teachers, began to graduate from high school in larger numbers after World War II and this, in turn, has made it possible today for college graduates to number about two score and college students to number in the dozens.

The majority of Indians have not, however, been able to advance beyond the upper years of high school on the average, and in some areas few still advance beyond the junior high school level. In 1957 a field worker for the American Friends Service Committee in northern California reported:

> The drop-outs of Indian students appear to be generally high in those counties in which Indians form a sizeable

proportion of the county population.... Drop-outs
do not seem to occur on an unusual level in the
elementary schools but begin to develop as students
go on up through the high school. Very few Indian
students go on to commercial, vocational, or college
training.... As examples, of approximately 100
Indian students who entered Ukiah Union High School
in the five years ending in 1952 only two were
graduated.... In Round Valley one elementary school
is entirely Indian, the white parents of that district
do not allow their children to attend this school and
recent attempts to unify with the adjacent white
school have met with defeat on the basis of the racial
issue. (Letters of Frank A. Quinn in Progress Report...
by the Senate Interior Committee on California Indian
Affairs, 1955, pp. 56, 58).

The 1960 census revealed that 43.3% of the Indians in California
14 years and older had not gone beyond the eighth grade (as compared
with 25% for whites and 36% for blacks), that only 56.7% had completed
one or more years of high school, that only 7.6% of males had completed
one or more years of college (as compared with 12.7% for blacks, and
over 25% for whites), and that only 1.8% of males had completed four
or more years of college (as compared with 5.5% for all non-whites and
10.7% for whites). The median school years completed for all Indian
males in California was 9.7 (as compared with 10.6 for non-whites and
11.7 for the total population). The rural median was, however, much
lower (probably 8.9 or less) while the urban median was about 10.6 (as
compared with 10.7 for non-whites and 12.0 for the total population).
(American Indians in California, 1965).

Indians would appear to have been receiving two years less schooling
than the California population as a whole in 1960, and probably two and
one-half years less than the white population. Still further, Indians and
Mexican-Americans were at the bottom of the educational ladder among
minorities, with the Mexican-Americans pulling ahead of Indians at the
college level. The 1966 report of the State Advisory Commission on
Indian Affairs summarized conditions by stating that

> few Indian students finish high school, few attend
> college, and many who have graduated from high
> school receive an inferior education because of a
> lack of teacher concern or the failure of the school
> system to devise compensatory teaching techniques to
> cope with students of differing cultural backgrounds.

Educational conditions in Nevada are, if anything, more severe than
those of California. The median school years completed for Indians twenty-
five and older in Elko County stands at 7.9 years and for all non-whites
in Nevada at 8.8 years (as compared with 12.2 for whites). Almost 17%
of the adult Indians have never been to school (compared with 0.7% of
whites). Approximately 1.7% of Indian adults possess four years of
post-high school educational experience (as compared with 8.7% of Nevada
whites). (Elmer Rusco, Minority Groups in Nevada, 1966).

This disappointing state of affairs convinced many Indians and
non-Indians that the educational programs of the school serving Indian
pupils had to be radically altered and that Indian people themselves had
to become meaningfully involved in educational issues. Both white-
controlled segregated schools (the BIA schools) and white-controlled
integrated schools (the public schools) had apparently failed and many
Indians began to look back towards the successful Indian-controlled
schools of the past, especially those operated by the Cherokees and
Choctaws.

In 1964 the American Indian Historical Society, founded in San Francisco by Mr. and Mrs. Rupert Costo, began publishing The Indian Historian
along with special research reports. The AIHS was especially concerned
with bringing an Indian viewpoint to bear upon historical writing but
it also became concerned with many related issues including the white
biases of school textbooks and the non-Indian orientation of school curricula. During the fall of 1966 the historical society, with a grant from
the Rosenberg Foundation, conducted workshops for teachers at Beaumont,
Hoopa, Fresno, Berkeley, and San Francisco. The society also launched
an Indian historical, artistic, and cultural center in San Francisco,
called Chautauqua House, and successfully fought for the removal of an
anti-Indian text used in the Oakland schools. More recently, The Indian
Historian has been transformed into a valuable professional-quality
journal contributing to the enrichment of contemporary knowledge about
Indian history and culture, while society members have continued to
work for the improvement of school programs.

Another development contributing directly to increased Indian involvement in education grew out of a Conference for Teachers of California
Indian Pupils held at Stanislaus State College in March 1967. The conference, funded by a grant from the legislature, brought together several
dozen teachers, administrators and Indian adults. The latter, not being
willing to see the conference become merely another discussion session,
organized themselves into the Ad Hoc Committee on California Indian
Education with the purposes of seeing that the recommendations of the conference conformed to Indian viewpoints and that a major state-wide all-
Indian meeting on education would be held.

The report issued as a result of the Stanislaus Conference contained
many useful recommendations, including ones favoring increased Indian
involvement in education, the convening of an Indian education conference,
and calling for the development of California Indian-oriented courses for
teachers and Indians in the universities and colleges of the state. But
the Stanislaus report was not comprehensive, nor did it have the backing
of a large enough group of Indians to make it a truly powerful tool for
bringing about change.

During 1967 the Ad Hoc Committee, under the chairmanship of David
Risling Jr. (Hoopa), proceeded to hold numerous regional meetings designed
to involve large numbers of Indians in an educational movement and to
prepare for a state-wide conference. The latter, with the help of the
Rosenberg Foundation, was held in October 1967 at North Fork, California.

The North Fork Conference brought together about 200 Indians who thoroughly analyzed the problems involved in Indian education. The conference proceedings, including numerous specific recommendations, were then edited and published as California Indian Education: the Report of the All-Indian Statewide Conference. This represented an extremely significant step forward since the North Fork Conference was the first all-Indian, Indian-controlled conference on education ever held anywhere in the United States and California Indian Education is the first comprehensive statement dealing with education ever prepared by a large and representative group of Indian people.

Basically, the North Fork Conference called for increased Indian involvement at all levels of the educational process. It especially emphasized the role of the Indian family and community in the education of children and advocated the development of Indian-directed out-of-school educational projects. Stress was placed upon the value of the native heritage and the schools were called upon to transform their curriculum so as to insure that an Indian element existed in all aspects of the school's program.

The North Fork Conference also called for the restoration of Johnson-O'Malley funds (with the proviso that they be used to advance the quality of Indian education under the direction of a panel of Indians), for Indian participation in the control of BIA schools, for the development of Indian-oriented higher education programs, and for Indian membership on the State Advisory Commission on Indian Affairs. During 1968 the Ad Hoc Committee continued its activities, sponsoring successful conferences in Hoopa, Oakland and elsewhere and making strong efforts to implement the recommendations of the North Fork Conference.

California Indians can be justly proud of the fact that in the activities of the Ad Hoc Committee and the American Indian Historical Society they have set a national precedent and have launched programs which are truly of national and even international significance. Unfortunately, however, the struggle for a better education for Indians is just beginning. Johnson-O'Malley funds have not been restored to California, no significant changes have occurred in colleges and universities, and only a few school districts have as yet modified their programs.

But the Indian people of California have awakened and are demanding that changes take place. It is certain that this awakening will soon have a direct impact upon Indian education both in California and elsewhere.

V. BASIC CONCEPTS FOR UNDERSTANDING NATIVE HISTORY

AND CULTURE

Who Is An Indian?

The term "Indian" or "Indio" is, of course, an unfortunate result of the early Spaniards confusing the Americas with India. The Native American people, the persons residing in the Americas when Columbus arrived, possessed no universal or even widespread name for themselves as a group since they knew of no other kind of people to contrast themselves with. The name "Indian" has come to be used by natives themselves although quite often Native Americans have been also called simply Americans (during the co-lonial era), indígenas (indigenes or aboriginies), naturales (natives), et cetera.

But regardless of the name, who is an Indian or Native American today? There is no clear answer to this question, since different people apply different definitions. Generally, how-ever, most definitions rest either upon a "cultural" or a "racial" basis, with the former being used most widely in Latin America and the latter in Anglo-America. For example, in Mexico most people are very proud of being of indigenous (Indian) ancestry but do not consider themselves to be Indians unless they speak an Indian language and live in an Indian community. A Mexican of pure Indian descent participating fully in the Mexican national culture does not ordinarily think of himself as an Indian (al-though he may be aware of his Indian background and even oc-casionally refer to himself as "indio" in certain contexts). Likewise, the person of mixed racial descent is never considered to be an Indian in Latin America unless he resides in an Indian community and speaks an Indian language.

In brief, from the Latin American perspective, to be Indian is to live an Indian way of life. This means that Indianized Europeans and mixed bloods have on occasion been thought of as Indians.

In the United States independent Indian communities were often able to absorb Europeans and mixed-bloods into their ranks and to define such persons as being Indian, that is, as Delaware, Comanche, et cetera. The Anglo-American population tended, how-ever, to define such persons in a racial sense, as white men who had "gone Indian" rather than as Indians. Similarly, Anglo-American government officials have tended to keep rather close record of whether a person in an Indian community is "full-blood," "half-blood," "quarter-blood," et cetera, not being willing to fully accept a cultural definition of Indianness.

The tendency to define a person by his racial background rather than by his way of life (as is also very true in the case of United States citizens of African descent) is one facet of Anglo-American racism. (It is significant that Latin Americans, with less of a tendency towards racism, have tended to utilize cultural definitions rather than racial ones).

The conquest of American Indian tribes by the United States tended to deprive these tribes of the ability to absorb aliens, as they had done when they were still free. Because the re- sources left to the tribes have not been enough to support their own people, tribal groups have generally attempted to restrict "membership" rather than to welcome those outsiders who might wish to assimilate in an Indian direction. But perhaps more significantly, the federal government and certain state govern- ments have assumed the authority of defining what an Indian is. In Virginia and adjoining states many Indian tribes which had assimilated persons of African descent during the colonial pe- riod found themselves being defined by racist white govern- ments as mulattos or Negroes or of having some arbitrary defi- nition of Indianness forced upon them.

In Virginia an Indian was legally defined in 1924 as a person of one-eighth or more native descent who possessed no trace of African ancestry.* Generally speaking, the federal government defines an Indian as a person of one-quarter or more United States Indian descent who resides upon federal "trust land" (reservations, colonies, or rancherias) or who has preserved membership in a tribe occupying "trust land." A person of European descent or even of Mexican Indian des- cent who was allowed by a tribe to reside on tribal land, who married a person of one-quarter native descent, and who became assimilated into the local Indian culture would not be ac- cepted as an Indian by the federal government nor would his children be so accepted, although (as in the case of the Mexican Indian-United States Indian marriage) they might well be of five- eighths biological native descent. Generally speaking the fed- eral government takes the position that one-eighth "bloods" are non-Indian while one-quarter "bloods" are Indian, when both reside on "trust land."

To fully understand the peculiarity of this modified racial definition, one must be aware of certain facts. First, it is well to keep in mind that ordinarily assimilation and place of birth are the basic elements in defining identity. One does not, for example, ask a Scotsman how much Gaelic (Scottish) biological ancestry he possesses, nor does one refer to Scotsmen as being one-quarter Scots, one-sixteenth Scots, et cetera, on

---

*In 1930 persons with less than one-quarter "Indian blood" were allowed to become whites provided they had no other non-white ancestry. Indians as such still could not possess any African descent, except that those "domiciled" on a state reservation could possess up to one-thirty second part Negro background.

the basis of how much "original" Scottish ancestry they may
possess. The same thing is true for most populations around
the world, even including those, such as the English, Irish,
French, Greek, Chinese, et cetera, who have absorbed large
numbers of aliens. Generally speaking, each nationality defines its own membership and this is ordinarily on the basis
of how the individual involved defines himself. It is true
that extreme racial (or religious) differences may occasionally
slow this process down, but in this connection it is well to
keep in mind examples such as that of the Magyars and Turks
who have probably changed their predominant physical character (from "Mongoloid" to "Caucasoid") through absorbing European aliens and that of southern Arabs who have become largely
"Negroid" through a similar process, in all three cases preserving their sense of Magyar, Turkish or Arab peoplehood
while changing, in considerable measure, their biological
character.

It is probably impossible to clearly assert who is an
Indian in the United States today, although certain statements can be made. First, it is clear that the federal government's definition of Indianness is not a true definition of the
latter but is instead merely a description of the people
"served" by the Bureau of Indian Affairs and the "Indian Desk"
of the Office of Economic Opportunity. That is, a "quarter-
blood" residing on "trust land" and receiving BIA services
may, in fact, be less of an Indian, racially and/or culturally,
than a person residing off of "trust land."

Second, a purely "racial" definition of Indianhood cannot be applied, operationally, in the United States so long
as the Mexican-American population is regarded as being legally
"White with Spanish Surname," since this population is at least
as biologically Indian as that population being served by the
BIA.

Third, a "cultural" definition of Indianhood is rather
difficult to apply so long as persons of full-blood United
States tribal descent, living an Anglo-American style of life
in a non-Indian urban setting, are regarded in practice as
still being "Indian" (because of their physical characteristics, former tribal affiliation, and/or, perhaps, self-definition as an "Indian").

What one must do, perhaps, is to simply describe the different "kinds" of "Indians" who reside in the United States
without attempting to resolve the contradictions apparent
between the various groups. Let us consider, for example, the

following types of people:

1. Several million Americans are of "pure" biological
Native American descent and can be categorized as "racial
Indians." Within this group, however, only about 200,000-
300,000 are members of United States tribal organizations or
communities while an undetermined number of others have some
knowledge of being related to a specific Mexican or other
non-United States indigenous population.

2. Several million Americans possess a significant degree of Indian descent, but less than "full-blood." Only
about 200,000-300,000 of these persons are members of United
States tribal organizations or communities while an undetermined number of others have some knowledge of being related
to a specific Mexican or other non-United States indigenous
population. Quite obviously, these hybrids are not "racial
Indians" but constitute, in reality, a new mixed "race" of
their own. They have been called métis (in Canada), mestizos,
ladinos and cholos (in Latin America), half-breeds, half-
bloods, and Eurindians. Unfortunately, many of these terms
have also been used to refer to other kinds of hybrids or to
persons of mixed cultural, as opposed to mixed biological,
characteristics.

3. Approximately one-half million Americans belong to
tribal organizations or reside in Indian communities within
the United States. These persons are commonly thought of
as "Indians" in their local area or think of themselves as
"Indians," but in other respects they are an extremely varied
group. The various tribal groups vary, for example, from
ones whose members are exclusively of part-Indian ancestry
with little or no pre-European cultural heritage to ones whose
members are virtually all "full-blood" and whose culture is
significantly non-European. Additionally, many such "Indians"
do not, in fact, belong to a specific tribe or Indian community, but belong only to urban inter-tribal groups, Indian-
interest clubs, or to general categories of de-tribalized
hybrid populations such as "Mission Indians" in California
or "Lumbees" in North Carolina.

A very critical problem relating to defining a person as
an "Indian" simply because he belongs to a tribal or inter-
tribal organization arises from the fact that although a part-
Indian may be accepted as "Indian" in his own local community
or in a certain region, he may very often be regarded as a
"mixed-blood" or even as a non-Indian by people in other communities or regions. Still further, a "mixed-blood Sioux" may

be regarded as an "Indian" by whites or by non-Sioux, while
at home he may be regarded very rigidly as a "mixed-blood,"
that is, as a kind of person who is neither "Indian" nor non-
Indian (although he may be a member of the tribe and receive
BIA services).

Finally, reference should be made to the fact that many
persons who regard themselves as being of "pure" United States
Indian descent are, in fact, partially descended from the numerous Europeans, Africans, and Mexicans commonly captured
and/or adopted by tribes at an early date. This is especially
true for tribes formerly residing in the eastern half of the
United States or in areas adjacent to Mexican territory. In
the Far West Chinese and Hawaiian mixture was not uncommon among
certain Indian groups and in Alaska Russian, native Siberian,
and Chinese ancestry is present. The memory of being descended
from such early intermarriages has frequently been forgotten
or is known to only a few older persons and thus has no practical impact (except where a factional feud may lead to gossip
about such ancestry). Nonetheless, it is of some significance
in relation to any effort to equate "racial purity" with "Indianness."

In summary, the only type of person in the United States
who can be safely categorized as an "American Indian" under
any and all circumstances is an individual who is of unmixed
or virtually unmixed United States native ancestry and who
1) resides in an Indian community, 2) is a member of a tribal
organization, and 3) participates in the way of life of the
group to which he belongs; or, 1) resides in an urban setting
(usually temporarily), 2) maintains contacts with "home," and
3) participates in the activities of inter-tribal organizations
or tribal clubs.

All other classes of individuals may be categorized as
"Indians," "mixed-bloods," or even non-Indians, depending
upon what definition is being applied, by whom, and where.
Perhaps the most important criteria are self-definition and
how the individual is categorized in the community where he
resides, but neither of these yield a classification which
will be accepted by all Indian communities.

The problem of stating who an "Indian" is would, of
course, be in great measure resolved if we ceased to refer
to the peoples of the Americas as Cherokee Indians, Chickahominy
Indians, Hupa Indians, et cetera, and instead spoke of them as
Cherokee People, Chickahominy People, and Hupa People. This
style would conform to usage in all other parts of the world,
where, for example, we do not speak of Meo Asians, Shan Asians,

Dayak Indonesians, Basque Europeans, or Swazi Africans, but rather of Meo People, Shan tribesmen, Basques, and Swazis.

The use of the term Indian in the way in which it is commonly used (as will be discussed subsequently) implies that the natives of the Americas were one people, which is not true, linguistically or politically. It might be useful to speak of individual tribes as being part of a larger unit, as when we refer to "Buriat Mongols" because the Buriats speak a Mongol language, but this practice has tended to be followed only in certain regions of the United States (as in the Southwest with Mescalero Apaches, Jicarilla Apaches, et cetera).

In any event, there is no reason why we must add the word "Indian" to each group's name. Thus, we can speak of Pamunkies as easily as Pamunky Indians (and if we wish to make it clear that the Pamunkies reside in America we can refer to them as Pamunky-Americans, although the need for this is rather slight since we never find it necessary to speak of Hausa-Africans-- the context usually supplying information on geographic location).

Once we think in terms of specific peoples rather than of a vague group such as "Indians," then it becomes much easier to identify individuals ethnically. If a person belongs to the Shawnee Tribe he is, in fact, a Shawnee (provided, of course, that he is accepted by other Shawnees as a Shawnee) regardless of his ancestry. He may not be a Shawnee "Indian" but he is a Shawnee person.

This approach to ethnic definition has the virtue of taking away from whites the power to determine the identity of a person of native descent or affiliation and giving that power to the local tribal community, where it in fact belongs.

This approach poses some problems for persons who are descended from more than one native group and who have never chosen (or perhaps been able to choose) to affiliate primarily with one tribe or community. This is especially a problem for natives who reside in areas, such as California, where many of the pre-European community-republics were destroyed by white conquest and where few viable tribal organizations have subsequently developed. Since only about 9,000 California natives reside on "trust land" (out of a total of 30 to 50 thousand persons of Native Californian descent), it follows that large numbers possess no tribal organization to which they can belong since so-called "tribes," in California, are almost universally confined solely to organizations for persons who reside upon a specific piece of "trust land." Thus, for example, a person of Nisenan descent possesses no Nisenan tribe to which he can belong. He can only affiliate with some type of inter-tribal club or association or (if he resides on one of the very small reservations) with a local reservation organization. In point of fact, however, the Nisenan people (simply a language group before the conquest) possess little more than kinship relationships with each other and consciousness of being "Indians." They possess no means whereby persons who are partially descended from another native group or from a non-Indian can be "inducted" into membership in any Nisenan organization.

In California, therefore, (as along the Atlantic Seaboard) a caste of brown-skinned people is developing which cannot effectively identify itself with any specific tribe but which must be either "Indians" (without any other clarification) or simply "brown people." In some regions such people come to be known as "Marlboro County Indians" or "Auburn Indians," that is, they acquire rather meaningless geographical names. In still other areas, such people acquire vague nicknames as with "Mission Indians," "Moors," "Issues," and "Brass Ankles."

All of these latter developments, which collectively make it difficult for persons of native descent to maintain a meaningful and specific ethnic identity, are to be regarded as disadvantageous. To become simply a "brown person" with no specific history, no heritage, and no tribal identity around which pride can be developed, is to expose oneself to the worst possible kind of existence in a society which still, for all of its ideals, ranks people on a color basis and places great emphasis upon ancestry. The actual experience of detribalized people along the Atlantic Seaboard would certainly suggest that it is advantageous to retain as much specific heritage and tribal identity as possible.

This whole question is further complicated by the fact that existing tribal organizations, as specific incorporated bodies, are almost universally the creation of the federal government and stem from the manner in which Indians were "rounded up" or split up and forced onto particular reservations; while existing trans-reservation identifications (such as the concepts of "Apaches," "Yokuts," or "Southern Paiutes") are the creation of white anthropologists, historians or laymen and, in many cases, possess very little operational meaning for native people.

Of course, all of these problems relating to the loss of a specific tribal or ethnic affiliation are results of conquest and white dominance and can only be resolved when Native Americans assert themselves and grasp a greater degree of mastery over their own collective fate. In so far as identity is concerned, such a development would, in some cases, result in Indian people casting off white-imposed designations in order to create or recreate groupings which are truly meaningful and practical for their own lives.

What Are "Indian Cultures"?

All too frequently teachers who wish to discuss "Indian culture" in the classroom adopt the viewpoint that to do so they must deal with the "old" native way of life as it existed prior to European contact or at least prior to European conquest. "Indian culture," in brief, is perceived of as being a static thing which no longer exists (except perhaps in Arizona or New Mexico). It is generally described by laymen as an unchanging set of behavioral patterns and material objects uniformly used in the same way by all of the people in the "tribe" or group under discussion.

This viewpoint conveys a false impression of what "culture" is and also may serve to confuse pupils of both non-Indian and Indian background. The latter come to believe that to be a "real" Indian they must weave baskets, wear feathers, and dance to the beat of the tom-tom. This erroneous belief serves to deprive Indians of today of a sense of identity as Indians since most of them obviously can not live as native people did a century ago.

Unfortunately, many Native Americans also share the viewpoint of the teacher, as when they assert, nostalgically perhaps, that "Indian culture" is disappearing, that the young people are not learning "the old Indian ways."

Before discussing the above points further it is first necessary to say a few words about the concept of culture itself. This term, in its modern sense, is commonly understood as referring to the total way of life of a given people (as in the concept of "Comanche culture"), or to the somewhat related styles of behavior in a region (as with "Southwestern Culture"), or to the collective, although distinctive, ways of life followed by all human beings (as in "human culture"). Culture has also been defined by some anthropologists as referring only to those aspects of human behavior which are learned (that is, non-biological and non-environmental) and to the products of such learned behavior. This writer is disposed, however, to use the term to refer to the total patterns of behavior associated with a particular people, not attempting to separate out those aspects of behavior which are environmentally or biologically determined from those which are "learned." (Principally because it is, in many instances, impossible or at least very difficult to discuss many learned patterns when they are abstracted from their biological or environmental relationships. Thus, for example, it is meaningless to discuss color prejudice as a part of Anglo-American culture if the existence of biologically-determined skin-color differences are ignored).

In what does a culture (in the singular) consist? When does one pass from one culture to another? These are questions which confuse many persons who come into contact with socio-anthropological literature, and justifiably so, since few scholars are able to clearly define "a culture" or "a cultural tradition." Unfortunately for simplicity, human groups have commonly mixed together, separated, borrowed from each other, migrated, et cetera, to such an extent that few, if any, "boundaries" actually exist between behavioral traditions. Additionally, those "boundaries" between "cultures" which might be discerned by the scholar were, and are, largely imposed by himself upon the data and would not necessarily be meaningful to the peoples actually living in the particular area under study.

To illustrate the complexities involved, one might cite the situation in the early 1700's from Taos Pueblo (New Mexico) northeasterly into the plains. The Taos People possessed a settled horticultural tradition featuring large multi-story "apartment house" structures, an eleborate ceremonial life, et cetera, supplemented by some buffalo hunting and a few other traits (such as male hair style) more typical of Plains Indians. Ten leagues to the northeast lived the Apaches de la Xicarilla, a people with horticulture, irrigation ditches, pueblo-style single-story dwellings, and some emphasis upon buffalo hunting. Still further to the northeast were closely related Apache groups who practiced little or no horticulture, lived in tipis or brush huts, and pursued the buffalo and other game for the greater part of the year.

Quite obviously, these three peoples possessed three different "systems" or "configurations" of behavior and yet all shared traits with each other and, in fact, were in frequent, friendly contact with one another. One could probably assert that the three systems were three separate cultures, and yet, operationally, they seem to have "blended" together in such a way as to preclude any clear-cut boundary. However, this problem only arises when we think primarily in terms of material traits abstracted from socio-political and linguistic characteristics.

The Taos People, a Tiwa-speaking population, clearly possessed a distinctive sense of "peoplehood" confined to themselves. Although close linguistic and cultural relatives of the Tiwa-speaking Picuries and close friends of the Tinneh-speaking Xicarilla and Plains Apaches, the Taos clearly composed a separate, independent community-republic. This self-conscious concept of political separation must be thought of as a key element in their cultural system, having undoubtedly a great impact upon other facets of behavior.

The Plains Apache situation is less clear, for there is some evidence which would suggest that the Apaches de la Xicarilla were not a separate people from their semi-nomadic relatives to the northeast, since their dialects appear to have been very close and since the various local political organizations ("bands" or groups of related families) would appear to have acted in concert in a kind of a loose confederation during the late seventeenth and early eighteenth centuries. In this instance, it would seem that the socio-political ("peoplehood") unit (the informal confederacy) possessed several variations in material behavior, ranging from a quasi-Pueblo style of life to a Plains style of life. Can we then speak of a "Xicarilla-Plains Apache Culture?" Probably we can, since the extremely significant linguistic and "peoplehood" elements were uniform and since, after the 1730's-1750's, the remnants of these Apache groups largely came together as the Jicarilla Apaches of modern times (sharing a more uniform cultural tradition which leaned towards the Plains style of life).

It must be borne in mind that the dispersal patterns for various specific behavioral traits will not ordinarily conform one with another, nor will they conform with ethnic (linguistic and socio-political) boundaries. For certain scientific purposes it may, at times, be necessary to study various behavioral characteristics abstracted from linguistic and socio-political data (as when a scholar discusses the "Southwestern Cultural Tradition" and thereby ignores significant language and socio-political divisions). On the other hand, Native American peoples always operated within a conscious framework of social and political relations and one who wishes to understand native life as it was, and is, functioning must look at culture as an attribute of particular associations of people.

Thus, while it might be meaningful for the student of cultural evolution to create the concept of "Colorado River Culture," the several peoples along that stream would have certainly placed more emphasis upon belonging to the Quechan, Halchidhoma, Hamakhava, or Halyikwamai republics. This emphasis upon peoplehood rather than upon overall cultural similarity made it possible for the rather closely related Hamakhava and Halchidhoma to be almost continuously at war, while the Hamakhava were close friends and rather frequent associates of the quite culturally distinct Chemehuevi Nihwi ("Southern Paiute") people.

To summarize this discussion of culture one might make the following points:

1. The behavioral pattern systems of human groups are like currents in the ocean. It is possible to point out generally where a particular current exists, especially at its center or strongest point, but it is not ordinarily possible to neatly separate that current from the surrounding sea. Human cultural traditions flow together in much the same manner as currents and any attempt at charting boundaries must be regarded as only leading to rough approximations.

2. A culture, in the singular, is always possessed by a particular societal unit or "people," if the term "culture" is to refer to a living, functioning, integrated whole. If we accept the above, a culture can be said to consist in the system or configuration of behavior patterns exhibited by a particular people.

3. A culture according to this approach, may contain a number of behavioral options but must at least include some sense of "peoplehood" (shared by all individuals) and a common means of oral communication (a single language or, at least, one language available equally to all).

4. In speaking of closely-related systems of behavior we should perhaps speak of "cultures" (plural), as in "Colorado River Cultures," although it would probably be pedantic to make too much of this point.

5. The attempt to distinguish specific cultures one from another must always be fraught with difficulties even if socio-political units are regarded as the "container" of the culture. This is true because it is not always possible to clearly separate one "people" from another, especially in areas such as California and Nevada.

When we look at culture in connection with the life a particular people we find that their way of life almost always includes options or variations and, therefore, is never completely homogeneous. These options may be contradictory, they may endure for long periods of time, and they may be symptoms of the gradual shifting of a people's way of life from one pattern to another. For example, in the 1600's there was apparently no single, homogeneous Navaho way of life. Many Navahos were adopting Pueblo Indian traits at an increased rate, as well as Spanish-introduced items, while other, more isolated, Navahos were still oriented towards an earlier "Apache-like" way of life. But all were equally Navaho and all of the cultural traits being integrated into the lives of Navaho people were units within any generalized "Navaho culture."

We must also note that it is technically incorrect to speak of "Navaho culture," "Quechan culture," or "Sioux culture" without reference to a particular time period, unless it is fully understood that one is speaking about a fluid, changing "tradition" which has only one basic, unifying, element, that is, that it is associated with a particualar people. "Navaho culture" before 1000 was very different from "Navaho culture" of 1500 which in turn was different from that of 1700, which in turn was different from 1890, which in turn was different from 1960. Although there are some traits, such as language, which probably survive with relatively little change during this one thousand year period, the basic unifying strand is the fact that the modern Navaho is descended socio-politically from the Navaho of 1000 (although he is also biologically related to Apaches, Pueblo Indians, Paiutes, Utes, Spaniards, Mexicans, and other peoples).

If we take away such Pueblo Indian and Hispano-Mexican traits as blanket-weaving, cloth garments, the clan system, sand-paintings, much of the religion, silver-smithing, turquoise-working, sheep-raising, horseback-riding, agriculture, et cetera, we might be able to gain a better idea of how Navahos lived before 1000 A.D. But even the hunting and gathering Navahos of that early period did not possess an "original Navaho culture." Without a doubt, the Navaho way of life of 1000 was markedly different from that of their ancestors before they migrated to the Southwest. And, needless to state, one can continue this kind of analysis back to the very origins of all human behavior. In short, there is no point in time where a particular way of life can be said to be "original" or "pure" or "static." Cultural evolution constantly is in process and groups are continually borrowing from their neighbors as well as developing more or less original traits.

In short, so long as a people possess a sense of identity, of "peoplehood" (by means primarily of kinship ties and a self-consciousness of their own distinctiveness from "aliens") they can be said to possess a culture or way of life. It follows then, that the origin of the various specific traits is irrelevant as regards the question of whether or not a people possess a culture of their own.

Thus we can correctly speak of "Powhatan Culture" as existing today even though a large number of the current behavioral characteristics of the Powhatan people of Virginia are of European or alien Indian origin. In fact, it would not make any difference if virtually all of the traits of the Powhatan were of non-Powhatan origin, so long as the Powhatan people maintained themselves as a viable, distinct socio-political group with a "history" (largely internalized) of their own.

The Bulgarian people can be cited as a further illustration of this principle. The Bulgarians of today certainly possess a "Bulgarian Culture" but their modern language is of non-Bulgarian origin, they have migrated from their ancient homeland (the Volga-Don area of Russia), their religion is non-Bulgar (Greek Christianity and Islam), and so on. But the Bulgarian people have retained their identity and history as a distinct people descended from the ancient Bulgars of the steppes. They have not lost the possession of a culture by virtue of losing (and replacing) virtually all of their ancient behavioral patterns.

Indian cultures, then, continue to exist no matter what the origin of the particular traits found therein. (Pickup trucks are as Navaho as Navaho blankets). But there are two qualifying statements which must be made: first, as a people's social organization disintegrates, so too will the culture disintegrate; and, second, conquered peoples who do not control their own destiny may not possess a way of life which they feel to be an integrated way of life.

Regarding this latter point, we must understand that an independent or at least quasi-antonomous people ordinarily is free to accept or reject alien behavior patterns or products. They can, therefore, maintain a culture which is integrated and which is felt to be "their own." They are in control of the traits in question, and they are free to determine the manner in which the new trait relates to older elements of the culture. Conquered peoples, especially if experiencing a process of social disorganization, cannot ordinarily accept or reject alien behavior patterns. Thus when their culture changes it changes in a kind of hap-

hazard, un-systematic and socially disturbing manner (as
when, for example, Anglo-Americans appropriate native economic resources, reduce the natives to a state of poverty,
and force the latter to adjust as best they can).

Because of the fact of conquest, many modern Indian
groups, although possessing a modern culture, do not feel
that it is an integrated and harmonious whole. In point
of fact, such post-conquest cultures are often collections
of contradictory or irreconciled traits and it can be said
that the group possessing such a "culture of conquest" is
the victim of its culture rather than the master of its
culture. The resolution of this situation can only come
about when native groups possess enough self-confidence and
"power" to control the selection of their own patterns of
behavior. (Such a process does not depend upon the rejec-
tion of alien traits but rather upon their "rationalization"
within a harmonious system).

The possession of an integrated culture is perhaps
crucial for the psychological well-being of any class of
people. Only when a way of life is harmonious, integrated,
and rationalized can the individual understand his relationship to other individuals; and only then can he know what
kinds of behavior are acceptable or desirable under what
circumstances. It may well be that much of the alienation
and anti-social behavior found in modern mass cultures
stem from their being relatively non-integrated (non-under-
standable). Certainly, many of the tensions of Black Americans
derive from their not being able to deal successfully with
the contradictory traits within Anglo-American culture relative to race relations. One facet of the appeal of black
cultural separatism may well lie in the fact that it serves
to offer an understandable, non-contradictory, set of behavioral patterns and attitudes.

The educator or community aide must be continually
aware of the processes of cultural evolution and conquest.
He should encourage native peoples to become explicitly
conscious of the dynamics of culture change and of the
problems involved in possessing a non-integrated culture.
He should do what he can to facilitate the process whereby
Indian communities become masters of their own behavior.
Above all, the teacher must avoid the use of stereotypical
materials which, in effect, allow the white man to define
Indianness and Indian culture as something not possessed,
and not possessable by modern Indian people.

Systems of Classifying Native Groups

Teachers, Indian laymen, and others concerned with under-standing the history of Native Americans are unfortunately confronted with textbooks, maps, and guides which either clas-sify native groups in an erroneous manner or which use some system of categorization whose underlying assumptions are not fully explained.

One often, for example, sees maps of the "Indian Tribes of North America" 1) which give the impression of simultaneity for the various locations assigned to "tribes" when in fact the latter may be as much as two centuries apart [e.g., the location of the Leni-Lenápe (Delaware) may be as of the early seventeenth-century while the location of the Lakota (Sioux) is as of the mid-nineteenth century); 2) which give the im-pression of dealing with equivalent social units when in fact the groups shown on the map may vary from language families to loose confederacies to idiomalities* to actual political units; and 3) which assign all of the groups to a language family when, in fact, we possess only the weakest kind of evidence relating to the languages formerly spoken by many groups in northern Mexico, Texas, and the South.

Much of the published material available to teachers and laymen relating to Indians is misleading, especially when it stems from popular or general textbook sources. But scholarly sources can also be misleading in cases where the reader is not able to clearly perceive the assumptions of the author or does not understand the type of analysis being pursued.

A beginning point for misunderstanding consists in the fact that few sources are readily available which attempt to portray, via text or maps, an accurate idea of the native's own view of his socio-political life. The majority of the "tribes" or groups ordinarily mentioned in white sources are essentially the creation of non-Indians. In part this is due to the activity of white governments or missionaries, but in great measure it stems from the writings of scholars, principally anthropologists.

The names applied to native groups are very seldom the people's own names, in part because many groups depicted on maps were not self-conscious, named entities. But even when a native name has always existed, white writers have often persisted in using an alien term, as with Delaware (from

*An idiomality is a group of people who speak the same language and whose dialects are all mutually intelligible.

Lord De la ware) instead of Leni-Lenápe, and Navaho (or
Navajo) in place of Diné (Dineh). Indians themselves have
gradually been forced to "live with" or even to accept alien
names because of the pressure stemming from white "custom"
(and, occasionally, because of editors' demands for uniform-
ity).

The problem of named groups becomes more serious when
one finds that the units commonly dealt with in popular
sources actually had no socio-political reality in pre-
European times. For example, certain of the groups portrayed
on the usual map of Indian California are idiomalities--
groups of completely independent and perhaps even hostile
people who merely spoke the same language (e.g., Wintun,
Yurok, Shasta). Other groups commonly portrayed on such
maps are not even idiomalities but are in fact composed of
closely related, but different languages (e.g., Chumash,
Pomo, Mewuk, Maidu, Costanoan, Salinan, Coast Mewuk). Still
other groups are essentially fictitious creations of Spanish
contact and missionization (e.g., Diegueño, Juaneño, Luiseño,
Gabrieliño, Fernandeño, Serrano).

For the layman to be able to unravel the many layers of
invented groups in order to understand the functional reality
of native California life is a difficult task indeed. And
yet it is essential because a large percentage of Indians in
areas such as California are still living in a stage of socio-
political self-consciousness rather close to that of former
years and quite different from that implied by maps and textbooks.

The problem can best be understood by examining several
groups, such as the Maidu, Mewuk (Miwok), and Kamia-Diegueño.
Many maps simply assign the entire area of the Sierra Nevada
mountains and foothills from roughly Placerville to Lake
Almanor, California, to the Maidu. Other, more detailed maps
divide the Maidu region into three areas, occupied by "Southern
Maidu," "Northeastern Maidu," and "Northwestern Maidu." In
point of fact, however, the Nisenan, Maidu, and Konkow, respectively, all spoke separate languages and comprise, therefore, three separate idiomalities. To call all of them "Maidu"
is very misleading, when what is really meant is "the Nisenan-
Konkow-Maidu group of closely related languages," or, in brief,
a language family. But the process of classifying people according to a system of related languages is rather complex because, as in this example, the Nisenan-Konkow-Maidu group is
but a division of the California Penutian group of languages,
which in turn is now thought to be part of a still larger
assemblage of distantly related tongues.

The whole problem becomes still more complicated when we realize that the Maidu, Konkow, and Nisenan were probably not socio-political units but simply idiomalities. The real socio-political units were local community-republics (independent communities composed of at least one village), informal confederations of communities, and ceremonial exchange-kinship territories (which will be discussed below). Ideally our maps should illustrate these latter units. When space is lacking, however, we should speak of "Nisenan-speaking communities," "Konkow-speaking communities," and "Maidu-speaking communities," thus clearly specifying the kind of units being delineated.*

The groups commonly designated as Mewuk (or Miwok)-- Sierra Mewuk, Plains Mewuk, Bay Mewuk (Saklan), Coast Mewuk, and Lake Mewuk--pose problems very comparable to that of the so-called Maidu. Each of these groups possessed a language of its own, with the exception of the Coast Mewuk who possessed two languages. What we are dealing with is essentially a group of closely related languages (another branch of the California Penutian family) which, in turn, divides into two further subdivisions, that of the Mewko (Plains Mewuk) and the Mewuk (Sierra Mewuk), and that of the Tuleyome (Lake Mewuk), Hukueko (Marin County), and Olamentko (Bodega Bay), with the Saklan standing alone because of an insufficiency of evidence. Each of these six language groups (idiomalities) was ordinarily composed of a number of villages or local communities and in no instances, except perhaps in the case of the Olamentko and Saklan, did the socio-political unit conform to the idiomality. The Mewuk, Mewko, and Hukueko speaking groups appear to have been further divided by regional dialects.

The Kamia-Diegueño peoples of southern California present a little different problem from that of the above groups. The distinction between "Diegueño" and "Kamia" is purely artificial, being based upon the fact that certain Kamia-speaking people were missionized at San Diego Mission (while others were missionized in several Baja California missions and could be called Migueleños, Tomaseños, et cetera). The Kamia-speaking people compose a branch of the Kamia-Cocopa-Halyikwamai-Kohuana group within the Yuman division of the Hokan language family. The Kamia are, then, an idiomality (although it may be that the Cocopa, Halyikwamai, and Kohuana people should also be included in this idiomality, depending upon whether their various tongues were in fact mutually intelligible with Kamia). The Kamia were, however, on the margins of being a nationality, since there is considerable evidence that most, if not all, Kamia-speaking groups shared

*The term "tribe" should be avoided where possible because of its ambiguity.

a common historical tradition of being descended from the same
ancestral "first Kamia," that they shared a common sense of
"being Kamia," and finally, that they possessed intra-village
kinship ties by means of patrilineal lineages which were becoming non-localized.* (See Jack D. Forbes, Warriors of the
Colorado, 1965, for a more detailed discussion of the Kamia).
On the other hand, the Kamia nationality or proto-nationality
had not achieved political status since the various Kamia-
speaking villages, lineages and/or confederations were independent and occasionally mutually hostile. Thus we must still
refer to "Kamia-speaking communities" rather than to a unified
Kamia people.

The above analysis should serve to illustrate some of the
complexity involved in dealing with Native American linguistic,
social, and political units. The layman must understand that
there are many ways of classifying native peoples and, further,
that the various systems of classification may not correspond
one to another. Thus, for example, one can classify people on
the basis of language, beginning with extremely minor local
dialèctical variations and proceeding on to families of related
languages and super-families composed of extremely different
but probably related language families. This type of classification does not, however, always agree with a system based
upon political organization, since it is quite common for the
latter to embrace people speaking different languages (as, for
example, with the Comanche-Kiowa-"Kiowa Apache" confederation,
the Cheyenne-Sutaio confederation, the Minsi-Unami-Unalachtigo
confederation, the Iroquois confederation after the admittance
of the Tuscarora, Nanticoke, Tutelo, et cetera, and the Western
Apache-Yavapai mixed bands),

Long enduring alliance systems, although perhaps less
formalized than a confederation, operated as a part of the
political life of native groups and these systems often cut
across language boundaries, as with the Quechan-Kamia alliances
against the Cocopa, the Quechan-Hamakhava alliance against the
Maricopa, the Assiniboin Lakota-Cree alliance against the other
Lakota (Sioux) groups, and so on.

Very closely related to the political life of native peoples,
and integrally a part of their social-religious life, were the

---

* In this writer's usage, a nationality comes into existence when
  the people comprising an idiomality (a language group) become
  conscious of sharing an ethnic identity with the other speakers
  of their language. E.g., the German nationality came into being
  when the various German-speaking tribes and local groups developed
  a "pan-German" consciousness.

various ceremonial exchange systems. In the California area, for example, one finds that the people of various community-republics and villages had what appears to be a regular pattern of inviting the people of other specific localities to their ceremonies, and being invited to the other's celebrations in return. Such ceremonial exchange systems are particularly significant in California regions where distinguishable political units above the level of the village are absent, because the people who shared a common ceremonial life doubtless also shared kinship (it would be logical for mates to be acquired in conjunction with such a system) and, more significantly, probably operated as an informal political group (exchanging information, settling disputes, planning mutual activities, et cetera).

It seems clear that in many areas these ceremonial exchange systems, and likewise kinship ties, cut across language boundaries. This writer's study of the Tongva of Tujunga village in Southern California indicates, for example, that the Tujunga villagers and the not-too-distant Chumash-speaking villagers were intermarrying (See Jack D. Forbes, "The Tongva of Tujunga to 1801"). The Stonyford Pomo (Shoteah) and Wintun-speaking peoples were ceremony-sharers while these Pomo were somewhat hostile towards other Pomo-speaking people.

It must also be pointed out that many Indian peoples were bi-lingual or even multi-lingual. It is to be suspected that villagers in sedentary border areas, especially where intermarriage and ceremonial-sharing was frequent, were commonly bi-lingual from childhood (from infancy perhaps) and that the placing of such people in one or another language family is somewhat arbitrary. For example, it seems highly likely that the natives of the Chumash-Tongva border area (roughly the Los Angeles-Ventura county boundary zone) must be regarded as belonging to villages sharing something of a bi-linguistic and cultural unity. This seems likely to have been the case in the Chumash-Yokuts border area, the Hupa-Yurok-Karok area, and so on. (In general, it seems likely that wherever independent or autonomous sedentary community-republics bordered upon each other, where inter-village marriage was common, and where the people were friendly, any effort to utilize language groups as a basis for identifying social-political relationships is rather risky).

Another danger involved in a purely linguistic approach

to the classification of native groups consists in the fact that
a given people may physically resemble people of an alien tongue
more than they resemble people speaking a related language. Thus,
for example, the Hupa of northwestern California, although speaking a Tinneh (Athapaskan) language, share the same physical characteristics as the surrounding Yurok and Wiyot (Ritwan languages)
and Karok (a Hokan language). Quite clearly, the Hupa are "one
people" in terms of actual biological ancestry with their near
neighbors and their only apparent connection with distant Tinneh-
speaking peoples (such as the Navaho), is that somehow they possess a related language. In brief, if one were to be able to
construct a geneological chart for the Hupa it would be most
probable that their ancestry shared with the Yurok, Wiyot, and
Karok would be very much greater than that shared with Navahos,
Apaches, Sarsis, and other Tinneh language groups. Which relationship is functionally more meaningful, that of actual kinship
("blood") ties or that of a remote linguistic relationship?

In a very comparable manner, the Hupa shared quite similar behavioral patterns with their near neighbors, patterns very
different from that of distant Tinneh-speaking peoples. Still
further, the culture of the Hupa (and certain other nearby Tinneh
groups such as the Tolowa) was different from that of other Tinneh
peoples located in northwestern California (such as the Kato).
Areas of similar cultural configurations tend, therefore, not to
be the same as areas marked out by purely linguistic criteria.

Quite obviously, then, there are many ways for classifying
native groups, each with a different purpose or rationale. One
can utilize language, total culture, physical characteristics,
kinship, political organization, or socio-religious exchange areas,
among other characteristics, as bases for significant classification.
No one system can provide a complete picture of the interrelation-
ships existing between native groups, although certain characteristics are more likely to have been meaningful to the people themselves including especially socio-political relationships.

It is quite clear also that analyses of Native American
groups must consider the element of time, since much change has
taken place both before and after intensive European contact.
In the pre-European period, for example, one can note such phenomena as the gradual appearance of multi-village republics
along the Colorado River (composed, as it would appear, of
numerous small communities or bands gradually coming together
and developing a common sense of identity), the establishment by

Deganawidah of the Iroquois Confederacy ("The Great Peace") in New York, and the creation by Wahunsonacock and his kinsmen of the Powhatan Confederation in Virginia. In the post-European period one can note numerous changes, usually taking the form of the amalgamation of various previously independent republics into new unions as a response to foreign pressure (as in the Cheyenne-Sutaio merger and the unification of the Leni-Lenápe).

The evolution of Native American socio-political organizations did not, of course, cease with the European conquest. Some of the greatest changes have occurred under the pressure of action by non-Indian governmental agencies and through the influence of white systems of denominating Indian groups. Thus, for example, while we would be wrong to speak of "a Pomo people" before 1800 (instead we would have to refer to "Pomo-speaking peoples"), we would not be too greatly in error if we were to do so today. The various Pomo-speaking community-republics have been deprived, through the process of conquest, of their own political independence and, in many cases, of their territorial character (by relocation). In addition, the several Pomo languages are rapidly disappearing and, therefore, the surviving people possess very little reason for maintaining identity as, for example, members of the Yokayo, Kashia, or Hamfo communities. White writers constantly refer to them as "Pomo" and, in the absence of strong organizations, many Indian people have gradually come to accept the white designation. (This may not necessarily be an undesireable development since a unified Pomo people, several thousand strong, possesses more political power than a number of small groups of a few hundred individuals each). It would also appear that a number of Miyakama* (Yukian-speaking) individuals are being absorbed into the emerging Pomo ethnic group.

In summary, the individual who desires accurate information relative to the socio-political organization of native America must continually be alert to the complexities involved in cataloging human groups and to the appropriate time-period. He must also be alert to the fact that many errors exist in popular writings because the authors were not familiar with the basic first-hand accounts of native culture and history, but rather depended upon secondary sources whose systems of analysis were not fully understood.

The teacher or other individual who wishes to relate some aspect of his work to a particular native people must, in most

---

*The Miyakama are also known as Wappo, a corruption of the word "Guapo."

cases, check with the native people themselves in order to ascertain what they wish to be called and how they define their
present stage of social organization.*

Modern California Indians developing old basketry skills. Left to right:
Carol Vedola, Christine Campbell, Molly Jackson, Elsie Allen, Pomos.
Photograph courtesy of Mrs. Elsie Allen.

---

*Particularly useful in understanding some aspects of native socio-
political organization in the Far West are A. L. Kroeber, "The Nature
of Land-Holding Groups in Aboriginal California" in Aboriginal California, ed. by R. F. Heizer; and R. F. Heizer, Languages, Territories
and Names of California Indian Tribes.

VI. A COMMUNITY RESPONSIVE, MULTI-CULTURAL

APPROACH TO INDIAN EDUCATION

General Theoretical Principles

Jack D. Forbes in The Education of the Culturally Different (1968) as well as in several other monographs and articles, Mexican-Americans (1967), Afro-Americans in the Far West (1967), and "Our Plural Heritage," Frontier, (July 1964), has set forth much of the background for advocating community-relevant and community-responsive schools, and where culturally different communities are involved, multi-cultural and bi-lingual schools. The advocacy of this approach to education has now been taken up at the highest levels, as in the following statement made by U. S. Commissioner of Education Harold Howe II in May 1968 before an audience concerned with Mexican-American education:

> You are more familiar than I with the Mexican-American cultural factors that impede a youngster's transition from home to school. But I would say that the notion of Anglo-cultural superiority--over which youngsters and their parents have no control--is a much larger factor. Until the schools realize how our society projects this conviction of superiority, this cowboy-and-Indians mentality, and takes positive steps to correct it, they will not truly succeed with Mexican-American children. Some schools are taking positive steps that have shown promise of redeeming Mexican-American children from the near-certainty of educational failure. They emphasize a bi-cultural, bilingual approach which says, in essence, that Mexican-American children must learn the English language and Anglo ways--but that they can do so without having to reject their knowledge of the Spanish language and of Mexican-American ways.
>
> Some of these projects go farther. They suggest that maybe it is not a bad idea for Anglo children to learn Spanish, and to gain a familiarity with another culture. This idea has all sorts of good sense to recommend it. First of all, the evidence is clear that people learn languages best if they learn them young. It is rather paradoxical that in the southwest, some elementary schools have forbidden children to speak Spanish, while at the same time many of our secondary schools require students to learn another language-- and Spanish is one of the most popular electives. Mexican-American children offer their Anglo classmates a great natural teaching resource. It is time we stopped wasting that resource and instead enable youngsters to move back and forth from one language to another without any sense of difficulty or strangeness. (Report on Education of the Disadvantaged, v.I, no.4, May 15, 1968, p.12.)

Numerous efforts have in the past been made to improve the quality
of formal education available to minority pupils. Innovative efforts
range from the "Indian industrial boarding school" and "intensive
acculturation" approach of Colonel Richard Pratt after the Civil War
to contemporary "saturated service" compensatory efforts such as More
Effective Schools. None of these compensatory efforts, when instituted
by outsiders (i.e., by non-minority persons), have been unequivocably
successful (for a discussion of MES see The Center Forum, November 4,
1967, pp. 3-4 and The New Republic, September 23, 1967, p.18.)

There are undoubtedly many reasons for the failure of intensive
compensatory education efforts but doubtless the most fundamental is
that they are confined to the school as an institutional setting when
there is good evidence that the school is perhaps less significant as
an instrument for enculturation or acculturation than is the home and
community. Paul F. Brandwein has asserted that

> "for the first five (5) years of life... parents must be
> considered, in the most precise use of the term, as
> teachers of children....evidence points to these five (5)
> years at home as most significant, if not the most
> significant years, in the child's life ("Memorandum:
> Concerning a 'New' School System," ms., 1967)."

The Coleman Report (Equality of Educational Opportunity) would seem to
clearly indicate that the background and non-school environment of the
child is a powerful element in determining educational success or failure, while other research serves to show that some pupils possess
"disadvantages" upon entering school which the school is never able to
overcome (e.g. see Y. T. Witherspoon, "The Measurement of Indian
Children's Achievement in the Academic Tool Subjects," University of
Utah Bureau of Indian Services).

Educational researchers have long been aware that in most cases there
is a positive correlation between socioeconomic status (SES) and
measured intellectual ability (See, for example, Havighurst and Breese,
Journal of Educational Psychology, v.38, 1947, pp. 241-247).

Cushna points out that

> the educational process itself as well as the entire socio-
> economic spectrum depends upon the effectiveness of social
> interaction. The higher a family is upon the SES scale,
> the more child rearing efforts are invested in teaching the
> child the social graces, the ability to know how to meet
> the right people, and to say the right thing at the right
> time ("Some affiliative correlates of social class," 1966 ms.).

Another study indicates that:

Age does not appear to be a significant factor in
the Stanford-Binet performance of Negro American children
from ages 7 through 10; however, marital status of the
mother and her educational level exhibit important relationship to the children's performance.

These environmental factors appear to be more crucial
at ages nine and ten than at the younger age levels of
seven and eight.

Finally, the above conclusions suggest that the
intellectual development of minority and disadvantaged
children would benefit from action directed toward stabil-
izing their total family situation at an early age.
(Roberts, Dickerson, and Horton, "Performance of Negro
American Children Ages 7-10 on the Stanford-Binet by
Selected Background Factors," American Psychological
Association, Sept. 2, 1966, ms.).

The significance of family and community background can be vividly
observed in the academic success of Chinese-American pupils attending
the same or similar schools attended by unsuccessful Indian, Mexican-
American, or black pupils. The difference in achievement can not be
explained by the school but must rest in the strength and orientation
of the Chinese-American family and in the Chinese language and cultural
schooling received by the young people at home or in Chinese-operated
private schools attended after public school hours. The same phenomena
is observed with middle-class Negro children as contrasted with poor
Negro children, wealthy Latin American children as contrasted with the
children of migrant farm laborers, et cetera.

It is clear that compensatory programs will fail when they are
confined to the school since the school, as now organized, can have
little impact upon the home and minority community. On the other hand,
the Chinese-American experience would seem to indicate that a proud,
viable ethnic minority community, with its own supplementary educational organs, can protect its youth from the negative influence of medi-
ocre or poor schools.

James Coleman, in his Equality of Educational Opportunity,
Reconsidered, states that

it seems clear that the appropriate measure for studying
equality of educational opportunity lies in both dimensions: in the distribution of school resources, and the
intensity of their effect. Only if their distribution
was fully equal, and the intensity of their effect was
infinitely great relative to the divergent out-of-school
factors, would there be complete equality of opportunity.
Since the latter cannot be the case, then it can hardly
be even appropriate to speak of "equality of educational
opportunity," but rather to speak instead of the amount

of inequality. In a system with equal resource
distribution, but with less than infinite intensity
of effects, there remains a degree of inequality--
an inequality of opportunity not arising from the
school system, but arising outside and not overcome
by the school system.

The above, of course, overlooks the problem that "equal resource distribution" within the schools may exist quantitatively and yet quali-
tatively the school's programs may in fact be highly biased in favor
of one segment of the population. Nonetheless, it does point out the
fact that factors beyond the control of the formal educational system
are operative and must be dealt with.

It should be stressed, however, that an attempt to change the Indian
home and community by paternalistic-elitist reformers (whether Indian or
non-Indian) is not to be advocated. The Bureau of Indian Affairs has
often attempted to change Indian people during the past century, with
largely disastrous results. On the other hand, a "community development" approach which emphasizes Indian participation in educational and
non-educational programs will, it is believed, contribute gradually to
the diminishing of negative non-school factors.

It should be borne in mind that the negative aspects of Indian
community life, as regards education, stem largely from being a conquered, powerless people long denied the right to influence school
policy. This problem cannot be resolved by procedures which would
further strengthen feelings of powerlessness. Community-involvement
in decision-making and implementation is to be suggested as the key
resource available to school personnel.

The many arguments of James B. Conant, Frank E. Karlsen, McGeorge
Bundy, Murray Wax, Robert Roessel and others for a close interaction
of school and community-parents will not be reviewed in detail here
(see Jack D. Forbes, The Education of the Culturally Different: A Multi-
Cultural Approach, especially pp. 15 ff.). Nonetheless, some of the
evidence supporting emphasis upon community-involvement in education
will be cited.

As regards Indian education specifically it is necessary to stress
that only two formal educational systems have ever been clearly successful, and both of these were operated by Indians and arose out of Indian
needs. Until the late 1890's the Choctaw Republic operated its own
school systems in Mississippi and Oklahoma, developing about 200 schools
and academies and sending numerous graduates to eastern colleges.

As a result of its excellent public-school system the
Choctaw Nation had a much higher proportion of educated
people than any of the neighboring states; the number of
college graduates one encounters in any contemporary
record is surprising, and the quality of written English
used by the Choctaw both in their official and private

> correspondence is distinctly superior to that of the
> white people surrounding them (Angie Debo, The Rise
> and Fall of the Choctaw Republic, p. 242).

The Cherokee Republic developed a similar school system which was also
quite successful.

> It has been estimated that Cherokees were 90% literate in
> their native language in the 1830's. By the 1880's the
> Western Cherokee (Oklahoma) had a higher English literacy
> level than the white population of either Texas or Arkansas
> .... Since the federal government took over the Cherokee
> school system (with coercion) in 1898, Cherokees have viewed
> the school as a white man's institution....over which....
> parents have no control....it seems clear that the start-
> ling decline during the past sixty years of both English
> and Cherokee literacy in the Cherokee tribe is chiefly
> the result of recent scarcity of reading materials in
> Cherokee and of the fact that learning to read has become
> associated with coercive instruction, particularly in the
> context of an alien and threatening school presided over
> by (non-Cherokees).... As far as Cherokee society is
> concerned, we have historical evidence that Cherokees can
> learn to read both English and Cherokee and that most of
> them have ceased to do so (Willard Walker, "An Experi-
> ment in Programmed Cross-Cultural Education," 1965).

These programs were both brought to an end by the United States
government. The schools subsequently operated for Cherokees and
Choctaws by federal and Oklahoma state agencies have been typical "Indian
schools," with little or no parent-community involvement. They have
had, as Walker attests for the Cherokees, a negative impact.

Contemporary research findings relative to Indian education point
up the necessity for a close relationship between school and home, in
view especially of the psychological problems which accompany culture
change. As John F. Bryde has pointed out: "It seems unanimous in the
literature of the social scientists that mental health problems usually
accompany most culture changes." Bryde's studies of white and Indian
pupils in the same school showed that the

> Indian group revealed greater personality disruption and
> poorer adjustment. Notable among the more meaningful
> variables were: feeling of rejection, depression, anxiety,
> and tendencies to withdraw plus social, self, and emo-
> tional alienation.

Eighth grade Indians

> revealed themselves as feeling caught and carried along
> by circumstances beyond their control, hence they were

> more rejected, depressed, paranoid, withdrawn, and
> alienated from themselves and the others.... The
> centrality of the concept of alienation is suggested
> as the integrating pattern explaining the behavior
> of the Indian students studied (John F. Bryde, "Indian
> Education and Mental Health," 1967 ms.).

Recent unpublished findings of Bernard Spilka have confirmed Bryde's
analysis and have shown a close correlation between degree of "alienation"and lack of achievement. Similarly, the Coleman Report identifies
the feeling of "powerlessness" as being closely correlated with negative
achievement among Negro pupils.

William H. Kelly, a very experienced researcher in Indian education,
recently stated:

> The recognition of the place of the parent and of the
> community in the total process of socializing and educa-
> ting Indian children is implicit in almost all (current)
> research (in Indian education) and is explicit (in some).

> In every descriptive statement of the behavior of Indian
> children, attention is drawn to the psychological conse-
> quences inherent in the discontinuities that exist between
> the home environment and the school environment. The
> situation can be corrected to some extent through
> teacher training, changes in the attitudes of educators,
> and curriculum changes....

> The solution of fundamental problems of value orientations
> and biculturalism, however, will require more than research.
> It will require the kind of participation in, and under-
> standing of, the educational process on the part of Indian
> parents and leaders that will permit intelligent control
> of the destiny of their children after they enter school
> (William H. Kelly, "Current Research on American Indian
> Education: A Critical Review of Ongoing Studies," 1967).

The recommendations contained in the "Bundy Report" to the New York
City Schools reflect the same philosophy, in that

> the central purpose of [its recommendations] is to re-
> connect all the parties with an interest in the public
> schools of New York so that each will have more construc-
> tive power.... parents and neighbors shape the child's
> attitude. If peers and family regard the school as an
> alien,unresponsive, or ineffective institution in their
> midst, the child will enter school in a mood of distrust,
> apprehension, or hostility.... If, on the other hand,
> the community regards the school as an agency in which
> they can identify, which acknowledges a responsibility
> for pupils achievement-- in short as their own-- children
> will enter the school with positive expectations.

The ultimate test of a successful school system or educational institution is perhaps not so much the measurement of the progress of individual students along some arbitrarily-conceived curricular path, but rather how the communities served by that system or institution have enhanced their own lives, individually and collectively, because of the presence of that educational system. The Cherokee and Choctaw schools before 1890 were successful in that they arose from the felt needs of the Indian people themselves, attempted to meet those needs, and served as integral parts of the Indian society and culture. Most schools serving minorities today are in fact alien extra-cultural institutions controlled by powerful outsiders. These schools cannot meet the needs of on-going community self-development because they exist outside of the community, in a socio-cultural sense, and cannot effectively communicate with the people being served.

Finally, it is interesting that the National Advisory Commission on Civil Disorders has recommended that an important objective of programs affecting urban ghettoes should be

> removing the frustration of powerlessness among the disadvantaged by providing the means for them to deal with the problems that affect their own lives, and by increasing the capacity of our public and private institutions to respond to these problems.

These words sum up, in one important sense, the objectives of a community-responsive approach to education.

Suggestions for Personnel Training Programs

Much of the above discussion serves to illustrate the importance of having school personnel in minority schools who are trained especially for interacting with culturally different adults and pupils. It is now widely recognized that teachers need special training for working with minority pupils. One research study revealed that

> middle-class youngsters who have apathetic teachers are less affected than are poor children of lower-class neighborhoods who have such teachers.... Revolutionary revisions in techniques of instruction and teacher recruitment, selection, and preparatory programs appear to be necessary.... (study of 212 teachers and their pupils in 52 schools carried out by Albert H. Yee under a USOE grant. Education U.S.A., November 17, 1966, p.72).

The Peace Corps, faced with the problem of training personnel for working with culturally different groups has made many changes as a result of criticisms made by early volunteers. "We have moved away from the traditional college classroom approach and into field programs which attempt (over a fourteen week period) to re-create the conditions volunteers will be confronted with overseas" (Jack Vaughn, "The Peace Corps: New We Are Seven," Saturday Review, January 6, 1968, p.22).

A good professional training program should seek to develop an intensive training process which will involve the cooperation of Indian adults, institutions of higher education and other agencies. This training program should be designed to 1) acquaint the teacher with the theoretical background of working with culturally different and low-income pupils, 2) acquaint the teacher with the dynamics of social process, acculturation, and cross-cultural contacts, 3) make the teacher aware of the cultural and class assumptions and/or prejudices which he or she possesses, 4) thoroughly acquaint the teacher with the general history and culture of American Indians, 5) specifically acquaint the teacher with the particular local population's history, culture, and present situation, and 6) provide direct practical experience at working with minority adults and youth derived from that particular population.

It is especially important to stress that any such training program should be under the over-all direction of the local Indian community wherever feasible and should, at a minimum, involve at least co-direction by the local community. With such an approach the training program should not only serve to bring about close parent-teacher relationships and realistic knowledge on the part of new staff, but it also should serve to provide the local community with a concrete role in the exercise of power relative to the educational system.

Suggestions for Teachers and Administrators in Public Schools

A. A school serving American Indian pupils should serve as a bridge
    between these students and the adult world which they will sub-
    sequently enter. This adult world will sometimes be Anglo in
    character, but more often it will be of a mixed Anglo-Indian cul-
    ture. In any case, the school, if it is to be a bridge, must
    serve as a transitional experience and not as a sudden leap into
    a foreign set of values and practices.

    Additionally, American Indians live within the margins of a
    society which has treated them in a rather discriminatory manner
    for one hundred years, and more terribly still, has attempted
    (consciously or otherwise) to instill in the Indian a sense of
    inferiority. The school must address itself to the task of bol-
    stering the self-image of native pupils and adults in order to
    overcome the psychological effects of a century fo conquest. This
    is a doubly difficult task in view of the continuing reality of
    life in the United States, but it must be undertaken as a central
    function of any school serving native groups.

    For all of the above reasons such a school needs to develop a set
    of strategies, in close collaboration with the local Indian commun-
    ity, which will make the school truly belong to the people being
    served, rather than to the people who operate the school system.

    The following are suggestions which hopefully will help to bring
    about such a change.

    1. The school environment should have some element of American
        Indian character, subject, of course, to the desires of the
        local native community. Such character can be created by means
        of murals depicting aspects of the Indian heritage, the erec-
        tion of statues depicting outstanding leaders of Indian ances-
        try, displays of native arts and crafts, bulletin boards depicting
        brown people and their accomplishments, and by the adoption of
        a name for the school which is relevant to our indigenous past.
        The expense involved in the above will not necessarily be great,
        as adults in the local Indian community might well become in-
        volved in projects which would have the effect of making the
        school "their" school.

    2. Teachers and administrators in such a school should be familiar
        with the dialect spoken in the pupil's home and should be en-
        couraged to utilize this language wherever appropriate in order
        to enhance communication both with pupils and with parents, and,
        more especially, to help develop a positive self-image on the
        part of Indian people.

3. Imaginative administrators and teachers may wish to further
    linguistic development by using the local language as an
    early means for introducing language concepts and for develop-
    ing bi-dialectical skills.

4. If a native language or dialect of English is widely spoken
    in the area, an "English as a second language" technique may
    well prove advantageous in English instruction.

5. Where the local community is interested, an American Indian
    language might be offered along with, or in place of, European
    languages at the secondary level. The United States needs
    persons able to speak such important tongues as Quechua, Guaraní
    and Maya and even less significant languages are useful in dis-
    ciplines such as anthropology and linguistics.

6. Supplementary materials utilized in the classroom, as well as
    library resources, should include numerous Indian-oriented
    items (magazines, newspapers, books, phonograph records, films,
    et cetera), in order to provide cross-cultural experiences for
    all pupils and to provide an atmosphere relevant to the native
    pupil's heritage.

7. Every effort should be made to acquaint pupils and visiting
    parents with the rich literature now available pertaining to
    native America. Many techniques are useful, including a per-
    manent display case near the main entrance to the school, a
    paperback library operated by students or parents, a paperback
    bookstore, and an extensive use of supplementary soft-cover
    books as a part of regular classwork. Books by Indian authors
    should be given special prominence, as in a display case where
    photographs of the author can be placed next to the book being
    exhibited.

8. Curricula in the school should possess a native dimension wher-
    ever appropriate. In social science courses where the develop-
    ment of the western United States is being discussed, attention
    should be given to the Indian side of our history, and to more
    recent American Indian developments. Courses in American Indian
    history might well be offered in some schools and these courses
    should not limit their attention to United States Indian groups
    alone.

9. Courses in literature should include readings in American Indian
    literature (in translation, if necessary) and works by and
    about tribal peoples.

10. Curricula in music and "music appreciation" should give attention to all classes of Native American music, including pre-European styles and music of recent origin whether from the United States, Peru, or elsewhere in the Americas. In many schools instruction in American Indian musical forms might well replace or supplement the standard band and orchestra classes, in order to provide a mechanism for enriching contemporary music.

11. The dance would appear to be an area where many young Indians can readily contribute to the enrichment of a school's program. American Indian dance styles should be included in any dance curriculum, along with other forms of the art.

12. Arts and crafts courses should acquaint all pupils with Indian arts of the Americas and should provide a close tie-in with the various folk movements still in existence.

13. American Indian cooking should be available as a part of the school's programs in home economics wherever sufficient interest exists. Indian foods should be served in the cafeteria also.

14. Since one of the primary objectives of educators should be the linking of the school with the local adult community, it follows that American Indian adults and youth should be involved in the life of the school as resource people, supplementary teachers, teacher's aides, and special occasion speakers.

    Additionally, local advisory committees should be asked to help develop policy either for a neighborhood school or for an Indian-oriented cultural enrichment program in a district-wide or regional school. No elements of American Indian culture should be introduced into any school without the active participation of local native people in the development of the program.

15. Our American Indian cultural heritage, whenever brought into the school, should be treated as an integral and valuable part of our common legacy, and not as a bit of "exotica" to be used solely for the benefit of brown pupils. It should be stressed that the local historical heritages of the West are almost wholly Indian prior to the last century.

16. In a school composed of students from diverse cultural backgrounds every effort should be made to bring a little of each culture into the school. A part of this effort might involve incorporating each major ethnic celebration into the school routine (focusing on Chinese-Americans at Chinese New Year,

Mexican-Americans during Cinco de Mayo, Negroes during Negro History Week, American Indians during a period of local celebration as at harvest time, et cetera).

17. School personnel should receive special training in Native American culture and history and should have some background in anthropology and/or sociology. It may well be that school personnel hired for employment in schools serving Indians should have several weeks of intensive pre-service training in cross-cultural dynamics not unlike that received by Peace Corps and VISTA trainees. Such training should actively involve persons from the local community to be served.

18. A school serving an Indian community should become closely identified with the aspirations of the local community and should function, in so far as is possible, within the framework of the local culture. This may call for much reorientation on the part of middle class school personnel, whether of Indian or non-Indian ancestry. It will also call for a revamping of the curricula so that course content deals with the real world perceived daily by native children. For example, courses in United States Government should describe the manner in which political action actually takes place and not an idealized version of what might be the case in some non-existent utopia. Perhaps one appropriate manner in which to teach governmental concepts might involve training secondary level students as community organizers or community service workers.

19. School personnel who believe that it is important to examine pupils periodically in order to provide data on "ability" for future counseling or "tracking" should wish to obtain accurate information by the use of tests which are relatively unbiased. It is difficult to ascertain the potential of dialect-speaking youth by means of standard English-language tests, nor can that of low-income students be predicted on the basis of tests oriented toward middle-class paraphenalia or concepts. On the other hand, biased tests will substantially predict the formal achievement level of culturally different or low-income pupils attending biased schools. Therefore, a change in tests will accomplish little unless accompanied by changes in the school, which serve to realize and enhance the potential revealed by the new test.

20. Maximum use should be made of techniques which are designed to enhance self-concept and involve the community in the life of the school, including the use of parent teaching aides, older

pupils as tutors for younger pupils, and college students of
minority background as para-professional counselors.

21. Most American Indians are brown-skinned and, therefore,
    suffer psychologically to some degree from the common tendency
    to exalt light skin and blondeness in the United States. The
    use of periodicals, films, books, et cetera, which are of non-
    white origin should be useful in combating the above whether
    the materials are produced by Indian people or not. East
    Indian, Latin American, and Japanese items might be especially
    useful in this connection.

B. The above suggestions are basically designed to change the atmos-
   phere of the school so as to provide greater motivation for all
   concerned, as well as to impart useful knowledge. In addition,
   many curricular and methodological innovations are available which
   are expected to improve learning for all students and these new
   programs should certainly be made available to American Indian
   youngsters. It is to be suspected, however, that a school which is
   basically indifferent or hostile toward the local native culture
   will not succeed in stimulating greater learning merely by the use
   of methodological innovations unaccompanied by a change in the
   general orientation of the school.

C. Attention should be given to Native American history and culture
   in all schools, regardless of ethnic composition. Anglo-American
   young people grow up in a "never-never" land of mythology as regards
   non-whites, and it is crucial for our society's future that damaging
   myths be exposed and eliminated. We must bear in mind that the
   "white problem in America," the tendency of Anglo-Americans for
   three centuries to exploit and denigrate non-whites, is probably
   still the major hurdle blocking the advancement of brown Americans.
   White young people, growing up in a mythic world of prejudice against
   non-whites and knowing little of brown contributions, may well, as
   adults, frustrate many of the goals of educational programs directly
   involving American Indians.

   The multi-cultural reality of American life and history should be
   a part of every school's curriculum.

D. In many urban and rural settings it may be that the creation of
   "Community Education Centers" in place of age-segregated secondary,
   continuation, and adult schools will contribute to the solution of
   a number of problems. Many communities lack sufficient facilities
   for "adult education," have essentially unsatisfactory "continuation
   schools" for their most difficult students, and experience serious

discipline and motivation problems in the ordinary secondary schools.

For the above reasons, it is herein suggested that appropriate secondary schools be transformed into multi-purpose "educational centers" for the total community which they serve, after the pattern of the junior college. To eliminate the segregated "teenage" and "adult" schools, to add to the total educational resources of a community, and to improve school-community relations, the following specific changes in secondary schools are suggested:

1. Open up all classes in the regular day program to any student, regardless of age, who might benefit from the class.

2. Open up all evening "adult" classes to any student, regardless of age, and develop evening programs where none exist.

3. Combine the regular day and evening programs, along with new late afternoon and Saturday classes, into a continuous day program.

4. Provide a nursery and a pre-school so that mothers of small children may enroll for classes.

5. Provide a social lounge and center, perhaps in a partially used basement area, to be decorated by the students and kept open until 10:00 p.m.

6. Provide areas, if space is available, for sewing centers, et cetera, for adults as well as youth.

7. Utilize teenage students as much as possible in working with the nursery, pre-school, and other projects, so as to provide opportunities for the development of self-confidence and other desirable qualities.

8. Abolish all age-grading systems, so that each class consists of students capable of doing the work regardless of age.

9. Allow older teenagers to carry a partial load and still remain involved in the school's program.

10. Encourage work-experience programs.

11. Encourage the teachers, parents, adult and "regular" students to elect an advisory board to develop school policy, innovations,

and enrichment experiences.

12. Alter the curriculum and orientation of the school so as to make it fully relevant to the language, culture, and desires of the community served.

13. Conduct a series of intensive community-teacher workshops to develop a full awareness of the contributions which both groups can make, and of the character and social dynamics of the local community.

Accompanying the opening up of classes to all and their extension into the evening hours and to weekends should also be the following:

1. The development of an adequate bookstore in each school, making available a significant proportion of current educational paper-bound books and periodicals;

2. Allowing instructors to offer at least one seminar-type course each semester, perhaps on a topic of their choice, but with the approval of their faculty colleagues and based upon community relevance;

3. Allowing instructors to establish their own class schedules, using the extended day period and Saturday if so desired, subject primarily to the approval of their faculty colleagues;

4. Encouraging faculty to keep abreast of new knowledge in their fields by providing scholarships which would enable teachers to take additional subject-matter course work or pursue research-literature review interests during the non-teaching months.

In summary, it seems a shame indeed that in many urban and isolated rural areas where non-scholastics are in obvious need of the opportunity for additional secondary-level schooling, the only schools in their areas or neighborhoods capable of meeting these needs arbitrarily restrict themselves to certain kinds of potential students or segregate by age-groups and thereby diminish the educational opportunities of all concerned.

The physical facilities and most of the personnel needed for community education centers are already available. All that is needed now is a willingness to experiment and innovate.

A Note on Federal and Parochial Schools

The above principles should be equally applicable to schools under Federal and denominational jurisdiction. In addition, the community-responsive approach would require the establishment of local boards which provide parents with control over the basic programs of the school.

160

VII. GUIDE TO RESOURCES AND FURTHER READING

A. Published Sources (An asterisk indicates availability in paperback
and suitability for classroom use, usually at the secondary level).

This guide is not intended to be an exhaustive bibliography of
materials dealing with American Indians. It is, rather a selective
guide to those items which the author considers to be especially
valuable for school personnel and for classroom use.

No attempt has been made to list or analyze materials designed
primarily for elementary school classroom use. Instead the reader
is referred to Diane Olsen, Indians in Literature, A Selected
Annotated Bibliography For Children, University of Minnesota, Minneapolis, Minn. (EDRS, NCR, Company, 4936 Fairmont Avenue, Bethesda,
Maryland, 20014. Report Number: ED 014 353. Price for hard copy:
$.72)

It should be stressed that the large number of elementary-level
books about Indians are of uneven quality and should be examined by
Indian parents and community leaders prior to use in any given school.

1. Selected Works on American Indians (other than California and
                                                       Nevada)
Source material on Indians is now available in considerable
quantity. Cited below are introductory or basic works, some of
which are intended for use by secondary-level students while others
are intended for teachers. Most of the works cited herein contain
bibliographies which will guide the reader to more technical or
regionally focused sources. The periodicals mentioned will also provide guidance to more specialized resources.

Two bibliographies have been published by the American Indian Historical Society, 1451 Masonic Avenue, San Francisco, California.

Many periodicals contain articles about Indian history and culture. The reader should begin by examining G.P. Murdock's Ethnographic Bibliography of North America (latest edition available)
and then proceeding to journals such as The Indian Historian,
Ethnohistory, American Anthropologist, Ethnology, Journal of American Folklore, American Antiquity, The Masterkey, and others. Unfortunately, most of these journals are usually technical and the
non-specialist will have to be prepared to do a great deal of
digging!

*The Araucanians (Washington, D.C.: Pan American Union, Organization of
    American States, 1968). 10¢

*Astrov, Margot, ed., American Indian Prose and Poetry (New York: Capri-
    corn, 1962).

*The Aztecs (Washington D.C.: Pan American Union, Organization of American
    States, 1968). 10¢

Berry, Brewton, Almost White (New York: Macmillan, 1963).

*Chagnon, Napoleon C., Yanomamo: The Fierce People (New York: Holt,
    Rinehart & Winston, 1968).

*Collier, Donald, Indian Art of the Americas (Chicago:National History
    Museum, 1959).

*Collier, John, The Indians of the Americas (New York: New American
    Library, 1947).

Colson, Elizabeth, The Makah Indians (Minneapolis: University of
    Minnesota Press, 1953).

*Dozier, Edward P., Hano: A Tewa Indian Community in Arizona (New York:
    Holt, Rinehart & Winston, 1966).

*Driver, Harold E., ed., The Americas on the Eve of Discovery (Englewood
    Cliffs: Prentice-Hall, 1964).

Driver, Harold E., Indians of North America (Chicago: University of Chi-
    cago Press, 1961).

*Famous Indians: A Collection of Short Biographies (Washington D.C.:
    Government Printing Office, 1966). 35¢

*Faron, Louis C., The Mapuche Indians of Chile (New York: Holt, Rinehart
    & Winston, 1968).

*Filler, Louis and Allen Guttmann, eds., The Removal of the Cherokee Nation
    Manifest Destiny or National Dishonor? Problems in American
    Civilization (Boston: D.C. Heath and Company, 1962).

*Forbes, Jack D., ed., The Indian in America's Past (Englewood Cliffs;
    New Jersey: Prentice Hall, 1964).

*Gridley, Marion E., America's Indian Statues (Chicago, Illinois: Tower-
    town Press, 1966). $2.50

*Hagan, William, American Indians (Chicago: University of Chicago Press,
    1961).

Hagan, William   The Indian in American History (American Historical
    Association Service Center for Teachers of History, 1963, 26 pp.,
    50¢).

*Hoebel, E. Adamson, The Cheyennes (New York: Holt, Rinehart & Winston, 1960).

*The Incas (Washington, D.C.: Pan American Union, Organization of American States, 1968). 10¢

*Jackson, Helen Hunt, A Century of Dishonor (New York: Harper & Rowe, 1963).

Jenness, Diamond, The People of the Twilight (Chicago: University of Chicago Press, 1959).

Jennings, Jesse D. and Edward Norbeck, eds., Prehistoric Man in the New World (Chicago: University of Chicago Press, 1964).

Jones, Louis T., Aboriginal American Oratory (Los Angeles: Southwest Museum, 1964).

Kimball, Yefee and Jean Anderson, The Art of American Indian Cooking (New York: Doubleday, 1965).

Klein, Bernard and Daniel Icolari, eds., Reference Encyclopedia of the American Indian (New York: Klein, 1967).

Lothrop, Samuel K., Treasures of Ancient America (Skira International Corp., 1964).

*Lurie, Nancy O., ed., Mountain Wolf Woman, Sister of Crashing Thunder: Autobiography of a Winnebago Indian (Ann Arbor: University of Michigan Press, 1966).

MacLeod, William C., The American Indian Frontier (New York: Alfred A Knopf, 1928).

*McNickle, D'Arcy, Indian Tribes of the United States (London: Oxford University Press, 1962).

McNickle, D'Arcy, They Came Here First: The Epic of the American Indian (Philadelphia and New York: J.B. Lippincott Company, 1949).

Mathews, John Joseph, The Osages (Norman: University of Oklahoma Press, 1961).

*The Mayas (Washington D.C.; Pan American Union, Organization of American States, 1968). 10¢

*Neihardt, John G., ed., Black Elk Speaks (Lincoln; University of Nebraska Press, 1961).

Opler, Morris E., An Apache Life-Way (Cooper Square Publishers, 1966).

Oswalt, Wendell H., This Land Was Theirs (New York; John Wiley & Sons, 1966).

*Pozas, Richardo, Juan the Chamula (Berkeley: University of California Press, 1962).

*Sandoz, Mari, Cheyenne Autumn (New York: Avon, 1953).

*Sandoz, Mari, Crazy Horse (Lincoln: University of Nebraska Press, 1961).

*Simmons, Leo W., ed., Sun Chief: Autobiography of a Hopi Indian (New Haven: Yale University Press 1942).

 Spencer, Robert F. et al, The Native Americans (New York: Harper & Row, 1965).

 Squires, John L. and Robert E. McLean, American Indian Dances: Steps, Rhythms, Costumes, and Interpretation (New York: Ronald Press, 1965).

*Von Hagen, Victor, The Aztec: Man and Tribe (New York: New American Library, 1958) Von Hagen's books are written at the popular level.

    *Realm of the Incas (New York: New American Library, 1957).

    *World of the Maya (New York: New American Library, 1960).

*Washburn, Wilcomb, ed., The Indian and the White Man (New York: Doubleday, 1964).

*Wilson, Edmund, Apologies to the Iroquois (Vintage, 1966).

        Surveys of bias against Indians in American history textbooks are provided in Jack D. Forbes, "The Historian and the Indian: Racial Bias In American History," The Americas, April 1963 and Virgil J. Vogel, "The Indian in American History Textbooks," Integrated Education, May-June 1968.

2. Sources on California-Nevada History and Culture

        For additional resources relating to the Native American in any particular state or sub-region, the reader will wish to consult with commissions and agencies concerned with Indian affairs, human relations, and equal employment opportunities, with local organizations, with reference librarians in the larger libraries, and with white organizations concerned with civil liberties. The larger university libraries will usually contain some unpublished material, such as master's theses or doctoral dissertations, and may well have modest collections of documentary data in their archival or "special collections" departments. State and local historical societies and museums also usually possess material of value.

        Especially important collections of archival data are located at the Federal Records Center, San Francisco; Federal Records Center, Los Angeles; Bancroft Library, University of California, Berkeley; Huntington Library, San Marino; and the National Archives, Washington, D.C.

Books and Monographs

*Angulo, Jaime de, Indian Tales (New York: Hill and Wang, 1953).

Bailey, Paul, Wovoka, The Indian Messiah (Los Angeles: Western-lore Press, 1957).

Browne, J. Ross, The California Indians (New York: Harper Brothers, 1864).

Caughey, John, Indians of Southern California in 1852 (San Marino: Huntington Library, 1952).

Cook, Sherburne F., The Conflict Between the California Indians and White Civilization (Berkeley: University of California Press, 1943; published as a part of the Ibero-Americana series).

*Downs, James F., The Two Worlds of the Washo: Indian Tribe of California and Nevada (New York: Holt, Rinehart & Winston).

Forbes, Jack D., Nevada Indians Speak (Reno: University of Nevada Press, 1967).

Warriors of the Colorado: The Quechans and Their Neighbors (Norman: University of Oklahoma Press, 1965).

Grant, Campbell, The Rock Paintings of the Chumash (Berkeley: University of California Press, 1965).

Harner, Nellie Shaw, "History of the Pyramid Lake Indians, 1842-1959" (Unpublished master's dissertation, Department of Arts and Science, University of Nevada, 1965).

Heizer, Robert F., ed., Aboriginal California: Three Studies in Culture History (Berkeley: University of California Archaeological Research Facility, 1963).

"Civil Rights in California in the 1850's--A Case History" (The Kroeber Anthropological Society Paper, Fall 1964, no. 31).

Languages, Territories and Names of California Indian Tribes (Berkeley: University of California Press, 1966).

Notes on Some Paviotso Personalities and Material Culture (Carson City, Nevada: Nevada State Museum, 1960).

Heizer, Robert F. and John E. Mills, Four Ages of Tsurai: A Documentary History of the Indian Village of Trinidad Bay (Berkeley: University of California Press, 1952).

Heizer, Robert F. and M.A. Whipple, The California Indians: A Source Book (Berkeley: and Los Angeles: University of California Press. 1951).

Hopkins, Sarah Winnemucca, Life Among the Piutes: Their Wrongs and Claims (New York: G. P. Putnam's Sons, 1883).

"Indian Land Cessions in the United States," from the 18th Annual Report of the Bureau of American Ethnology, 1896/97. (Washington, D.C.: Government Printing Office, 1899).

"The Indians of California: Bibliography," (San Francisco: American Indian Historical Society) emphasis on the northwestern area.

James, Harry C., The Cahuilla Indians (Los Angeles: Westernlore Press, 1960).

Johnson, B. E., California's Gabrielino Indians (Los Angeles: Southwest Museum, 1962).

Kelly, Isabel T., Southern Paiute Ethnology (Provo: University of Utah Press, 1932).

Know Your Nevada Indians. (State of Nevada, Department of Education, 1966) A mimeographed, very introductory source.

Kroeber, A.L., Handbook of the Indians of California (Washington, D.C.: GPO, 1925. Smithsonian Institute, Bureau of American Ethnography, Bulletin 78).

*Kroeber, Theodora, Ishi in Two Worlds (Berkeley: University of California Press, 1961).

Ishi: Last of His Tribe (Berkeley: Parnassus Press, 1964). For Junior high school level although of interest to adults also.

*The Inland Whale : Nine Stories From California Indian Legends (Berkeley: University of California Press, 1963).

Landberg, Leif C.W., The Chumash Indians of Southern California (Los Angeles: South Museum, 1965).

Latta, F. F., Handbook of Yokut Indians, (Bakersfield Kern County Museum, 1949).

Lipps, Oscar H., The Case of the California Indians (Chemawa, Oregon: U.S. Indian School Print Shop, 1932).

Merriam, C.Hart, Studies of California Indians (Berkeley: University of California Press, 1962).

Murray, Keith A., The Modocs and Their War (Norman: University of Oklahoma Press, 1965).

Price, John Andrew,"Washo Economy," (master's thesis, University of Utah, April 1962).

Reid, Hugo, Indians of California (Berkeley: University of California Press, 1939).

Robinson, W. W., The Indians of Los Angeles, Story of the Liquida-
tion of a People (Los Angeles, 1952).

Scott, Lalla, ed., Karnee: A Paiute Narrative (Reno: University of
Nevada Press, 1966).

Underhill, Ruth M., Indians of Southern California (Ph.D., Associ-
ate Supervisor of Indian Education, Sherman Pamphlets #2.
A publication of the Education Division United States Office
of Indian Affairs. Haskell Institute Printing Department,
Lawrence, Kansas. (A very general and somewhat erroneous
introduction).

The Northern Paiute Indians of California and Nevada(United
States Department of the Interior, Bureau of Indian Affairs,
1941). Very general and containing errors.

Walker, Edwin F., Indians of Southern California (Southwest Museum
Leaflets No. 10, Southwest Museum, Highland Park, Los
Angeles, Calif. 90042).

Wheat, Margaret, Primitive Survival Arts of the Northern Paiute
(Reno: University of Nevada Press, 1968).

Periodicals and Serial Publications

The bulk of material useful for in-depth studies relating to
any particular group of California-Nevada Indians are to be found
in such publications as the University of California's Publications
in American Archaeology and Ethnology, Anthropological Records,
Publications in Linguistics, Archaeological Survey Report, and
Ibero-Americana, the series of the Nevada State Museum, the reports
of the Great Basin Anthropological Conference, the Smithsonian
Institute-Bureau of American Ethnology Bulletin and Annual Report,
the University of Utah Anthropological Papers, and various historical and anthropological quarterlies.

The following list of reports and articles is meant to be illustrative only, that is, to show the reader the range covered by
articles and types of journals.

Beals, Ralph L. "Ethnology of the Nisenan", University of California
Publications in American Archaeology and Ethnology,
v. 31, no. 6, 1933.

Brimlow, George F., "The Life of Sarah Winnemucca: The Formative
Years". Oregon Historical Quarterly, v. 53, no. 2, June 1952.

Cook, S.F., "Migration and Urbanization of the Indians of California," Human Biology, February, 1943, V.15, no.1.

"Aboriginal Population of the San Joaquin Valley", Anthropological Records 16:2 (Berkeley: University of California Press, 1955).

"Population Trends Among the California Mission Indians," Ibero-Americana: 17 (Berkeley: Univ. of California Press, 1940).

Drucker, Philip, "The Tolowa and Their Southwest Oregon Kin," University of California Publications in American Archaeology and Ethnology, v.36, no. 4, 1937.

Ellison, William H., "The Federal Indian Policy in California, 1846-1860",Mississippi Valley Historical Review v.9, 1922.

Evans, William Edward, "The Garra Uprising: Conflict Between San Diego Indians and Settlers in 1851," California Historical Society Quarterly, v.XLV, no. 4, December 1966.

Forde, C. Daryll, "Ethnography of the Yuma Indians," University of California Publications in American Archaeology and Ethno- logy, v.28, no.4.

Gifford, E.W., "The Northfork Mono," University of California Publi- cations in American Archaeology and Ethnology, v.31,no.2, 1932.

Grosscup, Gorden L., "Lovelock Northern Paiute and Culture Change," Nevada State Museum Papers no.9,(Thelma D. Calhound, editor, published in Carson City, Nevada, January 1963).

Riddell, Francis A., "Honey Lake Paiute Ethnography," Anthropological Papers, no.4 (Nevada State Museum, Carson City, Nevada, December 1960).

Kasch, Charles, "The Yokayo Rancheria," California Historical Society Quarterly, v.XXVI, no.3, September 1947.

Kelly, Isabel T., "Ethnography of the Surprise Valley Paiute," University of California Publications in American Archaeology and Ethnology, v.31, no.3, 1932.

Kroeber, A.L., "Types of Indian Cultures in California," University of California Publications in American Archaeology and Ethnology, V. 19, no.5.

Merriam, C.Hart, "Ethnographic Notes on California Indian Tribes". Compiled & edited by R.F. Heizer, Reports of the University of California Archaeological Survey, no. 68, Part I, University of California Archaeological Research Facility, Department of Anthropology, Berkeley, 1966.

Merriam, C. Hart, "Ethnological Notes on California Indian Tribes.
    II. Ethnological Notes on Northern and Southern California
    Tribes." Compiled and edited by R.F. Heizer. Reports of
    the University of California Archaeological Survey, no.68
    Part II, February 1967, University of California Archaeo-
    logical Research Facility, Department of Anthropology.

Miller, William C. ed., "The Pyramid Lake Indian War, 1860,"
    Nevada Historical Society Quarterly, v.1, no.1-2, (Nevada 1957).

Steward, J.H., "Ethnography of the Owens Valley Paiute," University of
    California Publications in American Archaeology and Ethno-
    logy, v.33, no. 3, 1933.

"The Stone and Kelsey 'Massacre' on the Shores of Clear Lake in 1849,
    the Indian Viewpoint," California Historical Society Quarterly,
    v. XI, no.3, September 1932.

Strong, William Duncan, "Aboriginal Society in Southern California,"
    University of California Publications in American Archaeology
    and Ethnology, v.27, (Berkeley: California - 1929).

Watkins, Frances E., "Charles F. Lummis and the Sequoya League,"
    Southern California Quarterly, June-September 1944, v.26,
    nos. 2 & 3.

Young, Lucy "Out of the Past: A True Indian Story,"told by Lucy young
    of Round Valley Indian Reservation to Edith V.A. Murray,
    California Historical Society Quarterly, v.XX, no.4, December
    1941.

3. Sources on Contemporary Issues

Materials for this subject are difficult to obtain, especially in book
form. But it is important that teachers and community workers keep up with
the latest trends and that contemporary materials, especially if of Indian
origin, be used in the classroom.

Books and Monographs

American Indians in California: Population, Employment, Income and
    Education. Department of Industrial Relations, Division of
    Fair Employment Practices, State of California, San Francisco,
    November 1965.

Brophy, William A. and Sophie D. Aberle, The Indian: America's
    Unfinished Business (Norman: University of Oklahoma Press,
    1966).

California Indian Education: The Report of the Statewide All-Indian
    Conference (Modesto: Ad Hoc Committee on California Indian
    Education, 1967).

Forbes, Jack D., Nevada Indians Speak (Reno: University of Nevada Press, 1967).

Progress Report to the Governor and the Legislature by the State Advisory Commission on Indian Affairs (Senate Bill No. 1007) on Indians in Rural and Reservation Areas. February 1966. (Sacramento: State Advisory Commission on Indian Affairs, 1966).

Rusco, Elmer, Minority Groups in Nevada (Reno: University of Nevada Bureau of Governmental Research, 1966).

Steiner, Stan, The New Indians (New York: Harper & Row, 1967).

Articles and Reports

Popular articles sometimes appear in such periodicals as The Humanist, The Nation, The New Leader, Ramparts, Saturday Review, Americas, and others. The Reader's Guide to Periodical Literature will serve as an initial resource for such materials.

Reports are frequently issued by such agencies as the Inter-American Indian Institute, Office of Economic Opportunity, congressional committees, state legislative committees, state commissions on Indian affairs, Canadian Department of Indian and Northern Affairs, the Bureau of Indian Affairs, the Mexican National Indian Institute, and a multitude of other public and private groups. One simply has to be alert to the kinds of agencies known to be involved in Indian affairs in the region, because virtually every such group will issue some type of report. The state college or university library nearest to you should be asked to establish a collection of such contemporary Indian materials, perhaps with your help.

Scholarly articles on contemporary Indian affairs usually appear in journals such as Human Organization, Phylon, Journal of American Indian Education, Current Anthropology, América Indígena, Boletín Indigenista, and journals concerned with economic development and cultural change.

The best source of information on current affairs stems, of course, from Indian publications. Many tribal councils mimeograph their minutes and these can sometimes be obtained by subscription. Some tribes, and many inter-tribal groups, have formal publications. Some Indian publications are listed as follows:

The American Indian, American Indian Council, Inc., 3053 16th Street, San Francisco, Calif. Published monthly; sent on request.

The American Indian: A Journal for Educators, American Indian Historical Society. The Chautauqua House, 1451 Masonic Avenue, San Francisco, Calif. 94117 (No longer published).

American Indian Bulletin, Inter-tribal Friendship House,
523 E. 14th Street, Oakland, California.

Apache Drumbeat, P.O. Box 356, San Carlos, Arizona.

Cherokee Newsletter, Finis Smith, Box 473, Tahlequah, Oklahoma,74464.

The Drum, P.O. Box 1069, Inuvik, N.W.T., Canada. $4 per year.

Early American, Ad Hoc Committee on California Indian Education,
1349 Crawford Road, Modesto, California.

The Indian Historian - Official Publication of the American Indian
Historical Society, Inc., The Chautauqua House, 1451 Masonic Avenue,
San Francisco, Calif. 94117.
Indians Illustrated, 8162 Eighth Street, Buena Park, California
90620. $5.00 per year for 12 issues. (A "must" for high schools
and colleges).

Jicarilla Chieftain, Dulce, New Mexico.

Many Smokes, P.O. Box 5895, Reno, Nevada 89503. Published quarterly.
Subscription $1.50 per year.

The NCAI Sentinel, National Congress of American Indians, 1346 Connecticut Avenue, N.W., Room 1019, Washington, D.C. 20036.

The Native Nevadan (Official Newspaper of the Inter-Tribal Council
of Nevada, Inc.), 1995 E. 2nd Street, Reno, Nevada 89503 -
Published monthly.

The Navajo Times, Window Rock, Arizona.

Navajo War on Poverty: A News Summary. Office of Navajo Economic
Opportunity, Public Information Department, P.O. Box 589, Ft. Defiance,
Arizona 86504.

Rosebud Sioux Herald, Tribal Office, Rosebud, South Dakota.

The Smoke Signal, Federated Indians of California, 2727 Santa Clara
Way, Sacramento, Calif. 95817. Subscription $2.50 per year.

Tundra Times, Box 1287, Fairbanks, Alaska 99701.

War Cry, Box 379, Pine Ridge, South Dakota 57770.

Warpath, United Native Americans Liberation News Service and National
Indian Newspaper, P.O. Box 26149, San Francisco, Calif. 94126.
$5 per year for non-Indians, $3 for Indians.

    Many of the larger tribes not listed here also have newsletters or
monthly newspapers. In addition many Indian organizations issue

reports and mimeographed materials. The leading organizations include:

Ad Hoc Committee on California Indian Education, 1349 Crawford Road Modesto, California.

Alaska Native Brotherhood, c/o Box 1287, Fairbanks, Alaska 99701.

Canadian Indian Youth Council, Box 330, Ottawa, Canada.

Coalition of American Indian Citizens, P.O. Box 944, Berkeley, Calif. 94701.

Federation of Saskatchewan Indians, Box 886, Regina, Canada.

Hopi People's Committee, P.O. Box 112, New Oraibi, Hopi Nation,via Arizona 86039.

Indian-Eskimo Association, 277 Victoria Street, Toronto, Canada.

Manitoba Indian Brotherhood, Room 204, 1181 Portage Avenue, Winnipeg 10, Canada.

National Congress of American Indians, 1346 Connecticut Avenue, N.W. Room 1019, Washington D.C. 20036.

National Indian Council, Fort Assumption, Alberta, Canada.

National Indian Youth Council,c/o United Scholarship Service, Denver, Colorado.

North American Indian Brotherhood, Box 27, Kamloops, British Columbia, Canada.

Survival of the American Indians Inc., P.O. Box 719, Tacoma, Washington.

United Native Americans, P.O. Box 26149, San Francisco, Calif. 94126.

Inter-Tribal Council of Nevada, Inc., 1995 E. 2nd street, Reno, Nevada.

Certain white-controlled organizations or white individuals also issue publications, such as the Association on American Indian Affairs, Inc., 432 Park Avenue South, New York; and The Amerindian, 1263 West Pratt Boulevard, Chicago. Many white universities also issue publications, such as The Northian published by the Society for Indian and Northern Education, University of Saskatchewan, Saskatoon, Canada; and the Journal of American Indian Education, Arizona State University, Tempe, Arizona.

Useful for keeping up with southern California events is The Indian Reporter, 3254 Orange Street, Riverside, Calif. 92501.

4. Sources on Native Indian Education

A number of bibliographies are available including one in Jack D. Forbes, Education of the Culturally Different: A Multi-Cultural Approach (Berkeley: Far West Laboratory, 1968). This latter includes references to materials relating to culture change, conquest and colonialism and their relationship to education, as well as a list of other bibliographies.

In addition to materials cited in the above source, the reader will wish to check Comparative Minority Education: A Preliminary Survey and Bibliography (to be published in 1969 by the Far West Laboratory) and the report of the Far West Laboratory's Indian Education project headed by Francis McKinley, to be issued shortly.

Additional items, worthy of special note or difficult to find in most bibliographies, include:

Anderson, James G. and Dwight Safar, The Influence of Differential Community Perceptions on the Provision of Equal Educational Opportunities (New Mexico State University Research Center, 1967).

Brown, Anthony D. A Johnson-O'Malley Educational Program for California Indians (Sacramento: State Advisory Commission on Indian Affairs, June 1967).

Bryde, John F., "Indian Educational Needs" (Denver, Colorado: Upper Midwest Regional Educational Laboratory Conference on Indian Education, February 8, 9, 1967).

Dumont, Robert V, Jr. and Murray L. Wax, ms. "The Cherokee School Society and the Intercultural Classroom."

The Education of Indian Children in Canada (Toronto, Ryerson Press, 1965).

An Experiment in Programmed Cross-Cultural Education: The Import of the Cherokee Primer for the Cherokee Community and for the Behavioral Sciences. (Carnegie Corporation Cross-Cultural Education Project of the University of Chicago).

Fennessey, James, An Exploratory Study of Non-English Speaking Homes and Academic Performance (Baltimore: John Hopkins University Center for the Study of Social Organization of Schools, 1967).

Forbes, Jack D., "An American Indian University: A Proposal for Survival," Journal of American Indian Education, January 1966.

Fuchs, Estelle, "Innovation at Rough Rock," Saturday Review, (September 16, 1967).

Gast, David K. Minority Americans in Children's Literature (reprinted from Elementary English, January 1967).

Gudschinsky, Sarah C., How To Learn an Unwritten Language, Summer Institute of Linguistics (Studies in Anthropological Method eds: George and Louise Spindler, Stanford University, 1967).

Hickman, John M. and Jack Brown, Aymara Biculturalism and Sociopsychological Adjustment in Bolivia (Cornell University, Andean Indian Community Research and Development Project, ms.)

Indian Integration in Nevada Public Schools.(Nevada State Department of Education, 1966).

Kelley, William H. Current Research on American Indian Education: A Critical Review of Selected Ongoing Studies(Bureau of Ethnic Research, University of Arizona, Tucson).

King, A. Richard, The School at Mopass (New York: Holt, Rinehart & Winston, 1967).

"A Study of Values in a Canadian School" (Microfilm, Stanford International Development Education Center, Stanford University).

Leighton, Dorothea C., and Clyde Kluckholm, Children of the People: The Navaho Individual and His Development (Cambridge: Harvard University Press, 1947).

Lund, Betty Faye, "A Survey of Comparative Achievement and Scholarship Records of California Indian Children in the Auburn Public Schools" (unpublished master's thesis. Sacramento State College, 1963).

Modiano, Nancy, "Reading Comprehension in the National Language: A Comparative Study of Bilingual and All-Spanish," doctor's thesis, New York University, 1966.

Musser, Donald K.,"An Investigation of Indian Student Drop-outs at Ukiah Union High School"(ms. 1952).

Rancharan-Crowley, Pearl, "Creole Culture: Outcast in West Indian Schools," The School Review, v. 69, 1962.

Roessel, Robert A., Jr. Handbook for Indian Education (Los Angeles: Amerindian Publishing Company, 1967).

The Treatment of Minorities in Secondary School Textbooks(Anti-Defamation League of B'nai B'rith, 515 Madison Avenue, New York 22, 1963).

Wall, Leon C., "Indian Education in Nevada, 1861-1951,"(unpublished
master's thesis, Department of Education, University of
Nevada, 1952).

Wax, Rosalie H., "The Warrior Dropouts," Trans-action, May 1967.

Whitman, Carl, Jr."Comprehensive Renovation of the Education Program,"
(mimeographed).

Wilson, Herbert, Evaluation of Social Action Education Programs:
Case Study of UNESCO Center at Patzcuaro, Mexico (Stanford
University Inter-library Loan Service, Stanford Interna-
tional Development Education Center).

Wolcott, Harvey F., A Kwakiutl Village and School (New York: Holt,
Rinehart & Winston, 1967).

B. Audio-Visual Sources

     The acquisition of audio-visual materials of appropriate quality
and relevance is always a difficult and never-ending task. Perhaps
the following suggestions will open up new avenues for the gathering
together of such aids, but it must be borne in mind that no guidebook
can take the place of imagination and perseverance on the part of school
personnel.

     The local Native American community will ultimately comprise the
best source for the greater part of audio-visual materials used in any
given school. But no matter where such materials are acquired, they
should be reviewed by representatives of the local community. Illustrations from national magazines may seem quite appropriate to middle-
class teachers but may be unacceptable to local Native American
people; or it may well be that the total context in which illustrations
or other media are used may be acceptable while the individual units are
not, or vice versa.

1. Recordings:

     The Archive of Folk Song of the Library of Congress publishes a
catalog of available recordings, entitled Folk Music. This catalog
is available from the U. S. Government Printing Office, Washington,
D.C. 20402 for 40¢. Available in the Archive of Folk Song are songs
from the Iroquois, Seneca, Mexican Indians, Chippewa, Sioux, Quechan
(Yuma), Cocopa, Yaqui, Pawnee, Northern Ute, Papago, Nootka, Quileute,
Menominee, Mandan, Hidatsa, Kiowa, Delaware, Cherokee, Choctaw, Creek,
Paiute, Washo, Ute, Bannock Shoshone, Comanche, Cheyenne, Caddo,
Wichita, Navaho, Taos, San Ildefono, Zuni and Hopi peoples. These
records may be ordered from the Library of Congress. Music Division -
Recording Laboratory, Washington, D.C. 20540.

Columbia Records, Education Department, 799 Seventh Avenue, New York 10019, also has previously issued a brochure which lists the folk records available on the "Columbia" and "Epic" labels. Interested persons should write to the above address for current information on this series.

Canyon Records, 834 North Seventh Avenue, Phoenix, Arizona, offers a selection of predominantly Navaho and Southwest Indian music. Write to the above address for the latest price lists and other information.

Folkways Records, (121 West 47th Street, New York) has an excellent selection of Native American recordings such as "Healing Songs of the American Indians', "Anthology of Brazilian Indian Music", "Indian Music of the Pacific Northwest Coast," and "Mushroom Ceremony of the Mazatec Indians of Mexico". Write to the above address for price lists and information. Similarly, write to Ethnic Folkways Records, 165 West 46th Street, New York, for information on their Native American recordings. Folkways/Scholastic Records, 50 West 44th Street, New York also has issued several recordings of Indian music.

A visit to a good record store specializing in folk music will reveal numerous other recordings of American Indian music or, if such a store is not readily available, lists of such recordings may be acquired from individual record companies or through the most current Schwann catalog on hand at most record stores.

Larger record stores, such as Sherman, Clay and Company (Record Department, 141 Kearny Street, San Francisco) and Berkeley Music House (2538 Bancroft Way, Berkeley, California), are often willing to handle mail order requests from those persons who do not have ready access to a local source of folk and ethnic recordings.

The Educator's Guide to Free Social Studies Materials lists recordings available at no charge from various kinds of agencies; however, these must be examined carefully for evidence of propaganda. Such recordings need to be reviewed carefully by appropriate persons in order to validate accuracy and perspective.

The National Audio Tape Catalog (National Education Association, 1201 16th Street, N.W. Washington, D.C. 20036) presents narratives on a wide variety of subjects concerning the Native American (e.g., American Primitive Painting, Legends of the Aztecs, the Seneca Language, and "America's First Citizens -- The American Indian Before the White Man").

2. Pictures, Posters, Arts and Crafts:

Magazines can be excellent sources of pictures for bulletin boards, along with local newspapers. Posters and illustrative material depicting current aspects of Native American life may be obtained

from the consulates of American governments as well as from air-
lines serving Central and South America. Another source of
illustrative material might be the chamber of commerce in States
where Native Americans live. Inquiries should also be made to the
New Mexico State Tourist Bureau (Capitol Building, Santa Fe, New
Mexico 87501) and to the Santa Fe Film Bureau (the Acheson, Topeka
& Santa Fe Railroad, 80 East Jackson Boulevard, Chicago, Illinois
60604) for additional free material.

United Native Americans, P.O. Box 26149, San Francisco, California 94126 offers Indian posters for sale.

State and local museums and historical societies will provide
upon request copies of photographs in their collection on Native
Americans. There is usually a small charge for this service. It
is always advisable to write first for information. Other institutions which also offer this service are:

Heye Foundation, Museum of the American Indian, 3751 Broadway, New
York, New York 10032

Still Pictures Section, National Archives, Washington,D.C. 20408

Gallup Intertribal Indian Ceremonial Association, Second and Hill
Streets, Gallup, New Mexico 87301

Southwest Museum, Los Angeles 42, California.

Useful sources for Native American arts and crafts are:

Alaska Indian Arts, Inc., Box 271, Haines, Alaska 99827

Alaska Native Arts & Crafts, Inc., Box 889, Juneau, Alaska 99801

American Indian Foundation, 26265 West River Road, Grosse Ile,
Michigan 48138

Fort McDermitt Arts & Crafts, Box 88, McDermitt, Nevada 89421

Hopi Arts & Crafts Guild, Oraibi, Arizona

Ka-Eyta, Inc., Harlem, Montana 59526

Mescalero Apache Tribe, Box 176, Mescalero, New Mexico 88340

Navajo Arts & Crafts Guild, Window Rock,Arizona

Oklahoma Cherokee Indian Arts & Crafts Center, P.O. Box 533,
Tahlequah, Oklahoma 74464

Oklahoma Indian Arts & Crafts Cooperative, Box 749, Anadarko,
Oklahoma 73005.

University and public libraries have many books containing pictures and information regarding Native Americans or can obtain them through inter-library loans. Many libraries are equipped to make photocopies of illustrations from their collections.

Naturegraph Publishers, 8339 West Dry Creek Road, Healdsburg, California 95448 have published an Indian map in color of the Pomo region. This map should be especially useful to schools in the Sonoma-Lake-Mendocino County areas, but also elsewhere in California.

The gathering tegether of an adequate supply of posters and pictures can be an excellent parent-teacher cooperative project. Involving the parents in such an endeavor will serve to activate local sources of material and will also help to insure the acceptability of the items placed on display.

3. Films and Filmstrips:

Commercial concerns are producing films and filmstrips for the school market dealing with Native American history, culture and contemporary issues. The accuracy and acceptability of these commercial products is not uniformly high, however, and they should be previewed before purchase by persons familiar with current conditions and recent research, including especially individuals from the local Native American community.

The Oakland, California schools have produced a "Resource Guide for Teaching About Contributions of Minorities to American Culture" (1966) which lists and describes some of the commercial educational films dealing with the above subjects. Readers will also wish to check with their local educational television station for information on the availability of some of the excellent television productions dealing with Native Americans.

Listed below are those organizations which offer a wide selection of films for lease or purchase on Native Americans. Catalogs of these collections may be available at local public libraries and universities or obtained by writing to these organizations directly.

Educational Motion Pictures, Audio-Visual Center, Division of University Extension, Indiana University, Bloomington, Indiana 47401

University of California Extension Media Center, 2223 Fulton Street, Berkeley, California 94720

Encyclopedia Britannica Films, Inc., 7250 MacArthur Boulevard, Oakland, California 94605.

There are also those organizations which will loan their films without charge, However, the propagandistic element in these "free" films is apt to be extremely high. Write to them for catalogs or additional information:

The Educator's Guide to Free Social Studies Materials, Educator's
Progress Service, Randolph, Wisconsin 53956

Modern Talking Pictures, 927 19th Street, N.W., Washington, D.C.
20006

The Atchison, Topeka and Santa Fe Railway Company, Public Relations
Department, 314 Railway Exchange, 80 East Jackson Boulevard,
Chicago, Illinois 60600

New Mexico Department of Development, 302 Galisteo Street, Santa Fe,
New Mexico 87501.

        The Bureau of Indian Affairs has several films which, however,
must be purchased. A film on the Washoe is available from Western
Artists Corp., 512 Calle Alamo, Santa Barbara, California 93105,
while many other films are listed in an index issued by the National Information Center for Educational Media, University of Southern
California, Los Angeles, California.

        Motion pictures produced in non-white countries, such as India
and Japan, might well be made available in assemblies so as to help
reinforce efforts at cross-cultural education and to vividly convey
a sense of the rich legacies of non-European peoples. This may be
especially important in communities lacking in theatres showing
international films.

        Guides to 16 mm. commercial films should be useful in locat-
ing suitable motion pictures and making contacts with distributors.
Useful guides include:

        Films in Review (National Board of Reviewers of Motion
Pictures, Inc., 31 Union Square, New York, $6.00 per year). Reviews
United States 35 mm. films.

        Film Reports (Film Board National Organization, 522 Fifth
Avenue, New York, monthly, free to libraries). Reviews United
States and foreign 35 mm. films.

        International Motion Picture Almanac (Quigley Publishing Co.,
1270 Sixth Avenue, New York). A guide to 35 mm. films.

        Title Guide to the Talkies, 1947-1963, by R.B. Dimmitt, 2 v.
(New York: Scarecrow Press, 1965). An annotated guide to 35 mm.
films.

        Several commercial films publish catalogues of commercial-
type movies which are available for schools on 16 mm. film. Among
these are:

Brandon International Films, Western Cinema Guild Inc.,
244 Kearny Street, San Francisco   94108.

Teaching Film Custodians, 25 West 43rd Street, New York 10036.

There are many other guides and catalogues available dealing
with "educational films" especially prepared for school audiences
and these should be obtainable in any district's audio-visual
office. Bernard Klein's Guide to American Educational Directories
(New York: McGraw-Hill, 1965) should serve as an initial source
in case such guides have not been collected locally.

CALIFORNIA-NEVADA NATIVE AMERICAN HISTORY CHART, 1539-1969

HIGHLIGHTS OF HISTORY OF INDIANS IN CALIFORNIA AND NEVADA, 1539-1969

Date	Locality	Event
1539-1769	California-Arizona	Visited by Spanish expeditions. Generally these first white contacts with the natives were peaceable,and trade goods were introduced.
1744	S. E. California	Halchidhoma of Colorado River are trading for horses. Horses came slowly to be used by California-Nevada natives, but spread rapidly after 1770's.
1769-1800	California coast	Most coastal missions & forts established. Many Indians Christianized and taken into missions to work. Indians react peaceably or with fear at first, not understanding Spanish duplicity and plans of conquest.
1775	San Diego	Mission destroyed by Kamia. First serious revolt against missions.
1776	San Francisco	Attack on San Francisco by Indians revolting against cruel treatment.
1781	Colorado River	Quechan rebel and destroy Spanish garrisons because Spanish are offensive to them. Salvador Palma (Olleyquotequicbe), his brother, Ygnacio Palma, and other Quechan leaders, as well as Francisco Xavier, a Halyikwamai, lead brave fight. Spanish are completely driven out of this area.
1782-83	Colorado River	Quechans repulse later attacks. Nationhood of Quechans preserved. Success mainly due to political unity and sophistication of these people.
1785	Los Angeles area.	Tongvas attack and almost take San Gabriel Mission. The Hapchi-vitam and a woman religious leader, Toypurina, lead the revolt.
1793-1795	San Francisco area	Indians flee mission to start revolt across bay among the Saklan and Cuchillones (Little Knives"). Charquin (Charkeen) leads the struggle. Pits dug by natives to trap attacking Spaniards on horses.
1804	Salinas Valley	Chief Guchapa of Cholan refuses to aid San Miguel Mission to secure converts. He is later arrested after fight and forced, by holding his son as hostage, to help Christianize his people.
1809-1840	Bodega Bay area	Russians come to Bodega Bay area and then found Ft. Ross. Russians are friendly with Indians and even supply them with arms against the Spaniards. The Russians leave when slaughter of sea otters brings end to their furs.
1819	Calif. coast	By this date over 40,000 Indians have died from white-brought diseases.
1822	Calif. coast	Coastal California becomes part of Mexican Republic. Conditions remain same for conquered natives at first, but seeds of new revolt brewing.
1824	Marin Co.	Hukueko put up heroic resistance against Mexicans. Leaders, such as Pomponio, Marin and Quintin, hide in woods and attack or ambush Mexicans.
1827-1839	San Joaquin Valley	Warfare and border fights and raids rage between Mexicans and natives (mainly Yokuts). Estanislao and Cipriano (ex-mission Indians) escape and lead in clever and heroic battles, often defeating Mexicans by aid of fortifications.

1834- 1847	Sonoma,	Mariano and Salvador Vallejo ruthlessly carve out empire. They enslave Indians and Salvador treats the natives with extreme cruelty. Sametoy (or Solano), Suisun leader, helps Mexicans, but leaders like Ampay of the Yolos and Saccara of the Sotoyomes (a Pomo group near Healdsburg) fight back valiantly, assisted by Miyakmas (Wappos) and Tuleyomes (south of Clear L.)
1840's- 1860's	Nevada	Slave-raids from New Mexico harm Southern Paiutes; Anglo travelers destroy food of Humboldt River Paiutes and Shoshones. Nevada Indians begin to feel direct effects of invasion after early friendly contacts with whites.
1848- 1849	California	Gold rush upsets Indian economy and many Indians seek gold to buy food. Stone-Kelsey outfit in Clear Lake area, like some other whites, enslave Indians for mining and ranching. Their cruelty causes Pomos Shuk and Xasis to execute them, bringing brutal massacre of Pomos by Anglos.
1851- 1852	Southern California	Cahuilas, Kamias, Quechans, etc., angered by great injustices, stage final revolt against Anglos, which is crushed by U. S. forces. Antonio Guarra, a Kupanga-kitom, is chief leader in this bitter fight.
1851-65	Cal. & Nev.	Treaties made with many groups, later repudiated or broken by Congress.
1860	Nevada	Northern Paiutes win victory at Pyramid Lake against white militia. As usual Indians were attacked first and Indian girls kidnapped.
1869-75	Cal. & Nev.	1st "Ghost Dance" spreads; a religious revival to bring back the good days.
1870-85	Cal. & Nev.	Sarah Winnemucca (northern Paiute) campaigns for native rights and dignity.
1872- 1873	N. E. Cali- fornia	Modoc War shows how small group of Indians holds off army. Captain Jack (Kentipoos) cleverly uses rugged lava caves for defense against attack.
1883- 1914	Mendocino Co., Calif.	Round Valley Indians attempt to burn government boarding school five times. Natives actively resist Bur. of Indian Affairs oppressive school programs.
1887- 1890	Nevada	Wovoka (northern Paiute prophet) revives the "Ghost Dance", in which Indians seek spiritual recovery and strength. Spreads mainly to Plains tribes.
1890- 1895	Western Nevada	Senator William Stewart tries to take away reservations. Northern Paiutes successfully resist Stewart and keep lands.
1904	N. Calif.	Yokayo Pomo go to court to successfully defend their land rights.
1910-11	N. Nevada	"Shoshone Mike" leads last Indian fighting in country near Elko.
1917	Lake Co.	Ethan Anderson (Pomo) wins court case to allow non-reservation Indian vote.
1918	Lake & Men. Cos.	Society of Northern California Indians organized to seek long-denied justice.
1920	California	Northern California Indians seek legislation allowing them to be paid for lost lands. This eventually results in the California Indian Claims cases.
1920-22	S. Calif.	Federation of Mission Indians resists injustices; persecuted by government.
1924	Inyo Co.	Indians win legal right to attend Calif. public schools (Piper vs. Big Pine S. D.)
1944	N. Nevada	Supreme Court rules in favor of Indian land rights at Pyramid Lake Res.
1964-69	Cal. & Nev.	Am. Indian Historical Soc. (led by Costos) fights for true Indian history.
1967-69	California	Ad Hoc Committee on Indian Education, chairmaned by David Risling (Hoopa), begins vital work to improve Indian education.
1968	N. Nevada	Stanley Smart kills deer out of season to test Indian hunting rights in court. Western Shoshones drive white hunters off their lands. Nevada Indians awake.
1968	Cal. & Nev.	United Native Americans organized in San Francisco to unite all Am. Indians.

APPENDIX:

Linguistic Classification and

Maps

LINGUISTIC CLASSIFICATION OF CALIFORNIA AND
NEVADA INDIANS

The following represents an attempt to classify the idiomalities
of California within the several divisions and branches of the seven
language families represented in the two states. This system of
classification is tentative and exploratory, because many of the
various languages have not been analyzed thoroughly by trained lin-
guists, many are known only by incomplete vocabularies, and a number
have become extinct without leaving any record.

Several points should be noted: first, the author has tried to
use a native term wherever feasible but other names are included for
comparison; second, the names of idiomalities (a group speaking a
single language or several mutually intelligible dialects) are under-
lined with a solid line; third, underlining with dashes indicates
uncertainty as to whether that particular group's idiom was intelligible to the preceding group; fourth, the numbers in brackets refer to
the map of "California Idiomality Areas;" and, finally, it is very
likely that few, if any, of these linguistic divisions meant anything
to Indian people with the exception of the idiomalities themselves and
these latter seldom possessed political significance.

I. Hokan language family

    A. Northern California branch

        1. Palaihnihan (Pit River) division

            a. Elemewi (Achomawi, Achumawi) dialects [6]
            b. Atsugewi - Apwúrokai dialects [16]

        2. Shastan division

            a. Shasta-Konomihu dialects [3]
            b. Kahutineruk (New River, Tlohomtatoi) language [9]
            c. Okwanuchu (Okwanutsu) language [7]

3. Karok division

   a.<u>Karok</u> (Karuk-v-arara) dialects [2]

4. Chimariko division

   a. <u>Chimariko</u> language [12]

B. Yana-Yahi branch

  1. Yana division

    a. <u>Yana</u> dialects [15]

  2. Yahi division

    a. <u>Yahi</u> language [18]

C. Pomoan branch

  1. <u>Shotéah</u> (Northeastern) language [84]
  2. <u>Kashia</u> (Southwestern) language [33]
  3. <u>Hámfo</u> (Southeastern) language [27]
  4. <u>Northern Pomo</u> dialects [24]
  5. <u>Central Pomo</u> dialects [25]
  6. <u>Eastern Pomo</u> language [26]
  7. <u>Weshumtatah</u> (Southern Pomo) dialects [34]

D. Washiu branch

  1. <u>Washo</u> (Washoe, Washoo) language [31]

E. Esselen branch

  1. <u>Esselen</u> language [55]

F. Iskoman branch

  1. Tepothálap division

    a. <u>Tepothálap</u> (Énnesen, Salinan) dialects [57]

  2. Stishini-Chumashan division

    a. Stishini subdivision

      1. <u>Stishini</u> (Ticho, Obispeño) language [60]

b. Chumashan subdivision

1. Kagímuswas (Akkili, Purisimeño) language [66]
2. Tsamála (Kasákompéa, Ynezeño) language [67]
3. Tsmúwich (Barbareno, Kasswáh) language [68]
4. Mishkonaká (Mishanákan, Ventureño) language [69]
5. Káshinasmú (Cuyam, Cuyama) language [61]
6. Tokya (Tecuya, Tashlipum) language [70]
7. Limú (Minawa, Mitchúmash, Santa Cruz Island) language [74]
8. Naskwe (Nicalke, Hurmal, Santa Rosa Island) language [73]
9. Wimat (Wima, Tuakam, San Miguel Island language [72]

G. Yuman branch

1. Pipai division

a. Quechan-Maricopa-Halchidhoma dialects [81]
b. Hamakhava (Mohave) language [80]

2. Ipai division

a. Cocopa-Halyikwamái-Kohuana language
b. Kamia (Ipai, Tipai, Diegueño, Migueleño, Tomaseño) dialects [82]

3. Pai division (not in California or Nevada)

a. Paipai language
b. Eastern Pai subdivision

1. Yavapai dialects
2. Walpai-Havasupai dialects

II. Penutian language family

A. Maidu-Konkow-Nisenan branch

1. Maidu dialects [17]
2. Konkow dialects [19]
3. Nisenan dialects [30]

B. Mewan-Win branch

1. Wintu-Nomlaki division

a. Wintu (Northern Wintoon) dialects [8]
b. Wintun (Nomlaki) dialects [20]

2. Patwin-Suisun division

    a. Patwin (Win, Puiwin) dialects [29]
    b. Suisun dialect or language [38]

3. Mewan division

    a. Mewuk (Miwok) dialects or languages [40 - 42]
    b. Mewko (Plains Miwok) language or dialects [39]
    c. Saklan (Bay Miwok) language [45]
    d. Hukueko-Olamentko-Tuleyome subdivision

        1. Tuleyome (Lake Miwok) language [28]
        2. Hukueko-Olamentko (Coast Miwok) group
          a. Hukueko dialects [37]
          b. Olamentko language [36]

C. Ohlonean (Costanoan) branch

1. Muwekma division

    a. Ohlone (San Francisco, Santa Cruz, Santa Clara
              San Jose) dialects [43]
    b. Huichun-Karkin (San Pablo) dialects [44]

2. Mutsun-Rumsen division

    a. Mutsun (Humontwash, San Juan Bautista) dialects [54]
    b. Rumsen (Monterey) dialects [53]
    c. Chalón (Soledad) dialects [56]

D. Yokuts branch

1. Tchoyotche division

    a. Tchoyotche* (Jatchikamne, Cholvone, Chulamni)
              language [46]

2. "Valley" division

    a. Yokots (Valley) dialects [47]
    b. Yukots (North Foothill, Chukchansi group) dialects [48]

3. "Foothill" division

    a. Mayi (Foothill) dialects [49]
    b. Palewyami (Ta-at) language [58]
    c. Toxi (Buena Vista Lake) dialects [62]

---

*The Jatchikamne-Tcholovone word for "river."

III. Lutuamian language family

    A. M̲o̲d̲o̲c̲ language [4]

IV. Yukian language family

    A. U̲k̲o̲h̲t̲-̲o̲n̲t̲i̲l̲k̲a̲ (Coast Yuki) language [23]

    B. H̲u̲c̲h̲n̲o̲'̲m̲ language [22]

    C. Y̲u̲k̲i̲ dialects [21]

    D. Miyakma ("Wappo") dialects. ⸴ 35.

V. Ritwan language family (perhaps Ritwan-Algonkian)

    A. S̲u̲l̲a̲t̲e̲l̲a̲k̲ (Wiyot) language [13]

    B. Y̲u̲r̲o̲k̲ (Yuruk) dialects [10]

VI. Tinneh (Athapaskan) language family

    A. T̲o̲l̲o̲w̲a̲ (Huss) dialects [1]

    B. Hoopa-Whilkut branch

        1. H̲o̲o̲p̲a̲-̲W̲h̲i̲l̲k̲u̲t̲-̲C̲h̲i̲l̲u̲l̲a̲ dialects [11]

    C. Nung-gah-hl branch

        1. N̲u̲n̲g̲-̲g̲a̲h̲-̲h̲l̲ (Kato, Mattole, Sinkyone, Wailaki, Nongatl, etc.)
           dialects [14]

VII. Uto-Aztecan language family

    A. Numic (Shoshonean) branch

        1. Nehmeh division

           a. N̲e̲h̲m̲e̲h̲ (Nehmuh, Northern Paiute-Bannock) language [5]
           b. N̲e̲u̲m̲a̲ (Pitanakwat, Owens Valley Paiute) language [51]
           c. N̲i̲m̲ (Mono, Monache) dialects [50]

        2. Nihmih division

           a. N̲i̲h̲m̲i̲h̲ (Shoshone-Comanche) language [52]
           b. P̲a̲n̲a̲m̲i̲n̲t̲ (Koso, Death Valley Shoshone) language [52]

        3. Nihwi division

           a. N̲i̲h̲w̲i̲ (Ute-Southern Paiute-Chemehuevi) language [65]
           b. N̲u̲-̲ʊ̲̃-̲a̲ (Kawaiisu, Tehachapi) language [63]

VII (contd)

    B. Tubatulabal branch

        1. Tubatulabal-Palagewan-Bankalachi dialects [59]

    C. Vitamic branch (Takic, "Southern California Shoshonean")

        1. Tongva (Vitam, Gabrieleño, Fernandeño) language or
                                     dialects [76]

        2. Maringayam-Kitanemuk ("Serrano")

            a. Maringayam (Serrano, Vanyume, Möhinayam) dialects [77]
            b. Kitanemuk language [71]

        3. Iviatim-kitom division

            a. Iviatim (Cahuilla, Palm Springs, Wanakik) dialects [79]
            b. Atáhum (Luiseño-Juaneño-Soboba) dialects [78]
            c. Kupanga-kitom (Cupeño) language [83]

        4. Ghalashat (Nicoleño) language [75]

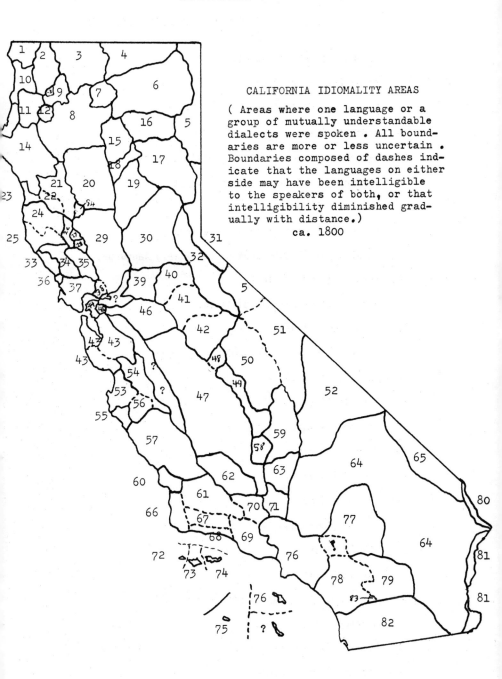

CALIFORNIA IDIOMALITY AREAS

(Areas where one language or a
group of mutually understandable
dialects were spoken . All boundaries are more or less uncertain .
Boundaries composed of dashes indicate that the languages on either
side may have been intelligible
to the speakers of both, or that
intelligibility diminished gradually with distance.)
ca. 1800

KEY TO "CALIFORNIA IDIOMALITY AREAS" MAP

1. Tolowa (or Huss) dialects.

2. Karok (Karuk) dialects.

3. Shasta-Konomihu dialects.

4. Modoc language.

5. Nehmeh (Northern Paiute-Bannock) language.

6. Elemewi (Pit River or Achomawi) dialects.

7. Okwanuchu language.

8. Wintu ("Northern Wintoon") dialects.

9. Kahutineruk (Tlohomtahoi or New River) language.

10. Yurok (Yuruk) dialects.

11. Hoopa-Whilkut-Chilula dialects.

12. Chimariko language.

13. Sulatelak (Wiyot) language.

14. Nung-gah-hl dialects.

15. Yana dialects.

16. Atsugewi-Apwurokai dialects.

17. Maidu dialects.

18. Yahi language.

19. Konkow dialects.

20. Wintun (Nomlaki) dialects.

21. Yuki dialects.

22. Huchno'm dialects.

23. Ukoht-ontilka (Coast Yuki) language.

24. Northern Pomo dialects.

25. Central Pomo dialects.

26. Eastern Pomo language.

27. Hámfo (Southeastern Pomo) language.

28. Tuleyome ("Lake Miwok") language.

29. Patwin dialects.

30. Nisenan dialects.

31. Washo (Washoe, Washoo) language.,

32. Uninhabited joint use area.

33. Kashia (Kashaya) language.

34. Weshumtatah (Southern Pomo) dialects.

35. Miyakma ("Wappo") dialects.

36. Olamentko ("Bodega Miwok") language.

37. Hukueko ("Coast Miwok") dialects.

38. Suisun language.

40. Northern Mewuk dialects.

41. Central Mewuk dialects.

42. Southern Mewuk dialects.

43. Ohlone (San Francisco, Santa Cruz, Santa Clara, San Jose)dialects.

44. Huichun-Karkin dialects.

45. Saklan language.

46. Tchoyotche (Cholovon, Chulamni) dialects.

47. Yokots ("Valley Yokuts") dialects.

48. Yukots ("North Foothill Yokuts," Chuckchansi) dialects.

49. Mayi ("Central Foothill Yokuts") dialects.

50. Nim (Mono) dialects.

51. Neuma (Pitanakwat, Owens Valley Paiute) language.

52. Panamint Shoshone (Koso, Death Valley Shoshone) language.

53. Rumsen dialects.

54. Mutsún (Humontwash) dialects.

55. Esselen language.

56. Chalón dialects.

57. Tepothálap (Énnesen, Salinan) dialects.

58. Palewyami (Ta-at) language.

59. Tubatulabal dialects.

60. Stishini (Ticho, San Luis Obispo) language.

61. Káshinasmú (Cuyama) language.

62. Toxi (Buena Vista Lake Yokuts) dialects.

63. Nu-ú-a (Kawaiisu, Tehachapi) language.

64. No permanent occupation or uncertain (note: post-1800 movements of Chemehuevi Nihwi are not reflected on this map)..

65. Nihwi (Ute - Southern Paiute - Chemehuevi) language.

66. Kagímuswas (Akkili, Purisima) language.

67. Tsamála (Kasákompéa, Santa Ynez) language.

68. Tsmúwich (Kasswáh, Santa Barbara) language.

69. Mishkonaká (Miskanákan, Ventura) language.

70. Tokya (Tecuya, Tashlipum) language.

71. Kitanemuk language.

72. Wimat (Tuakam, San Miguel) language.

73. Naskwe (Nicalke, Hurmal, Santa Rosa) language.

74. Limú (Santa Cruz) language.

75. Ghalashat (San Nicolas) language.

76. Tongva (Gabrieleño-Fernandeño) dialects.

77. Maringayam (Serrano, Vanyume) dialects.

78. Atáhum (Luiseño-Juaneño-Soboba) dialects.

79. Iviatim (Cahuilla, Palm Springs, Wanakik) dialects.

80. Hamakhava (Mohave) language.

81. Pipai (Quechan - Halchidhoma) dialects.

82. Kamia (Ipai-Tipai) dialects.

83. Kupanga-kitom   (Cupeño) language.

84. Shotéah (Northeastern Pomo) language.

[Notes: This map is based in part on the work of A.L. Kroeber, C.H.

Merriam, and R.F. Heizer, as well as upon numerous individual ethnogra-

phic and documentary sources.   It is, therefore, a synthesis of a great

amount of data and the author must accept sole blame for errors.   Many

boundaries are highly tentative, especially since the information for

the coast south of San Francisco is often based upon earlier information

than that for the interior.   The target date for the map is ca.1800,

except that some coastal groups had already been partially displaced by

that date.   Interior area boundaries are based upon a calculated guess

that conditions were largely the same in 1800 as in ca. 1850.]

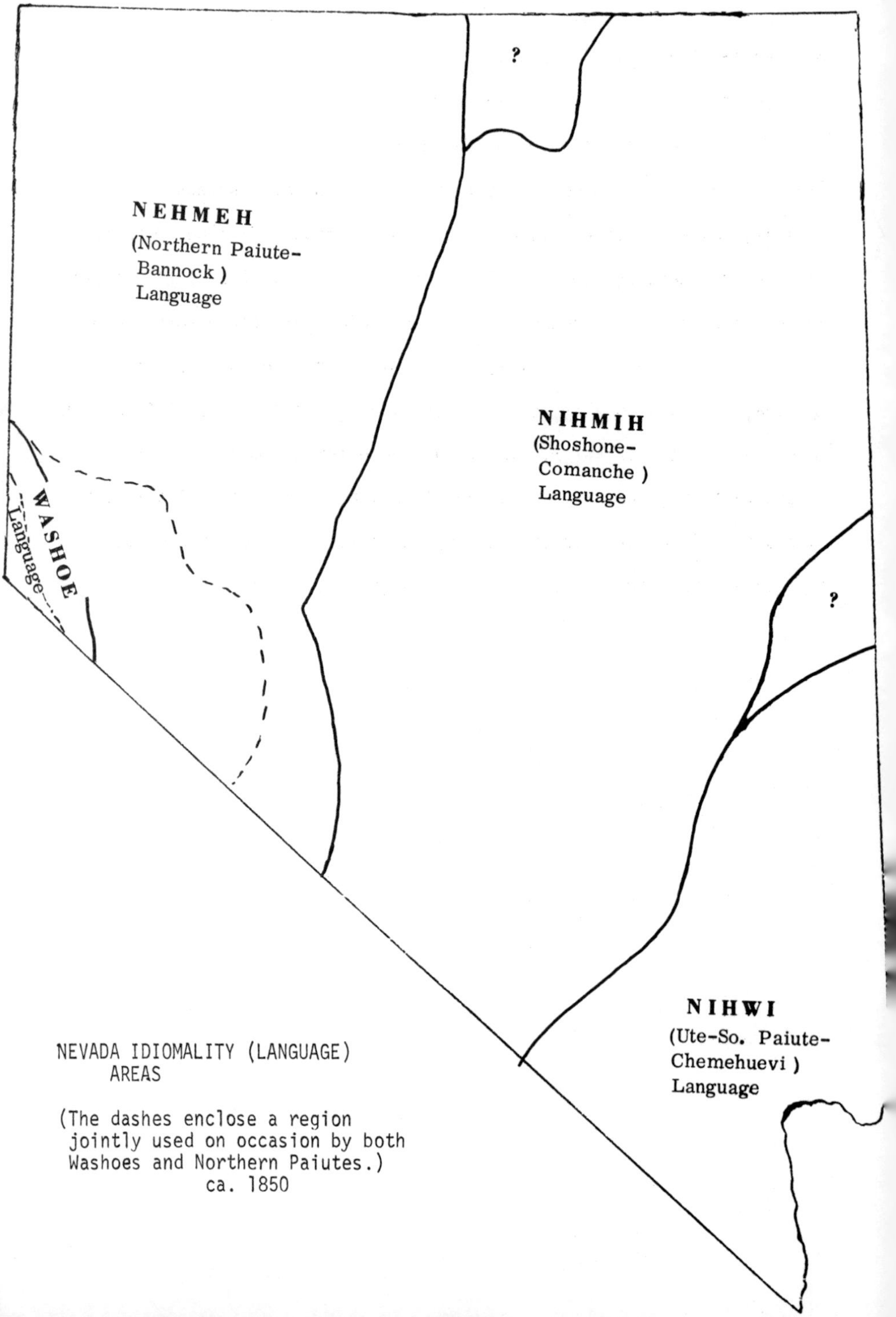

NEHMEH
(Northern Paiute-
Bannock)
Language

WASHOE
Language

NIHMIH
(Shoshone-
Comanche)
Language

?

?

NIHWI
(Ute-So. Paiute-
Chemehuevi)
Language

NEVADA IDIOMALITY (LANGUAGE)
AREAS

(The dashes enclose a region
jointly used on occasion by both
Washoes and Northern Paiutes.)
ca. 1850

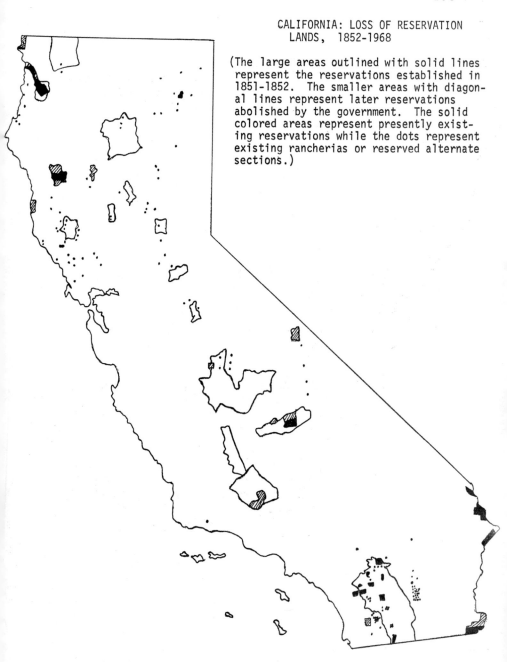

CALIFORNIA: LOSS OF RESERVATION
LANDS, 1852-1968

(The large areas outlined with solid lines
represent the reservations established in
1851-1852. The smaller areas with diagonal lines represent later reservations
abolished by the government. The solid
colored areas represent presently existing reservations while the dots represent
existing rancherias or reserved alternate
sections.)

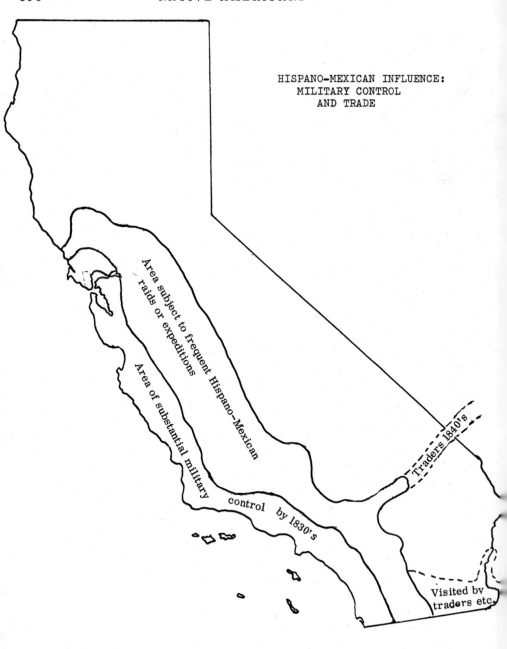

HISPANO-MEXICAN INFLUENCE:
MILITARY CONTROL
AND TRADE

Area subject to frequent Hispano-Mexican
raids or expeditions

Area of substantial military

control   by 1830's

Traders 1840's

Visited by
traders etc.

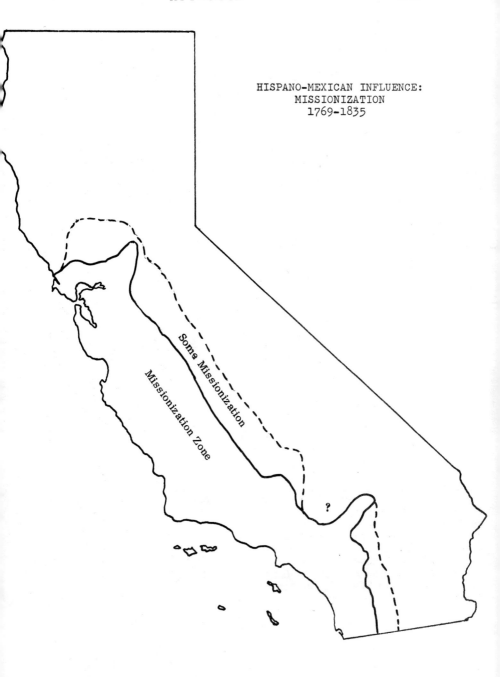

HISPANO-MEXICAN INFLUENCE:
MISSIONIZATION
1769-1835

Some Missionization

Missionization Zone

?

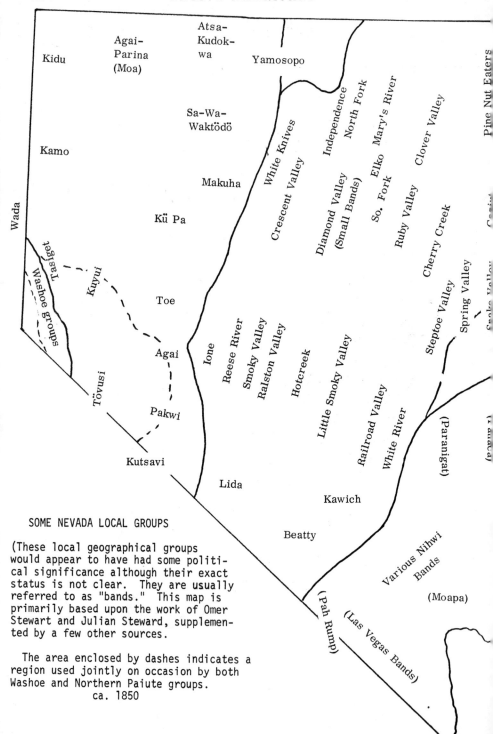

Kidu

Agai-
Parina
(Moa)

Atsa-
Kudok-
wa

Yamosopo

Pine Nut Eaters

Sa-Wa-
Waktödö

White Knives

Independence

North Fork

Mary's River

Clover Valley

Kamo

Makuha

Crescent Valley

Diamond Valley
(Small Bands)

Elko

So. Fork

Ruby Valley

Cherry Creek

Kü Pa

Wada

Tasiget

Washoe groups

Kuyui

Toe

Agai

Ione

Reese River

Smoky Valley

Ralston Valley

Hotcreek

Little Smoky Valley

Steptoe Valley

Spring Valley

Smoke Valley

(Panaca)

Tövusi

Pakwi

Railroad Valley

White River

(Paranigat)

Kutsavi

Lida

Kawich

SOME NEVADA LOCAL GROUPS

(These local geographical groups
would appear to have had some political significance although their exact
status is not clear. They are usually
referred to as "bands." This map is
primarily based upon the work of Omer
Stewart and Julian Steward, supplemented by a few other sources.

The area enclosed by dashes indicates a
region used jointly on occasion by both
Washoe and Northern Paiute groups.
                    ca. 1850

Beatty

(Pah Rump)

(Las Vegas Bands)

Various Nihwi
Bands

(Moapa)

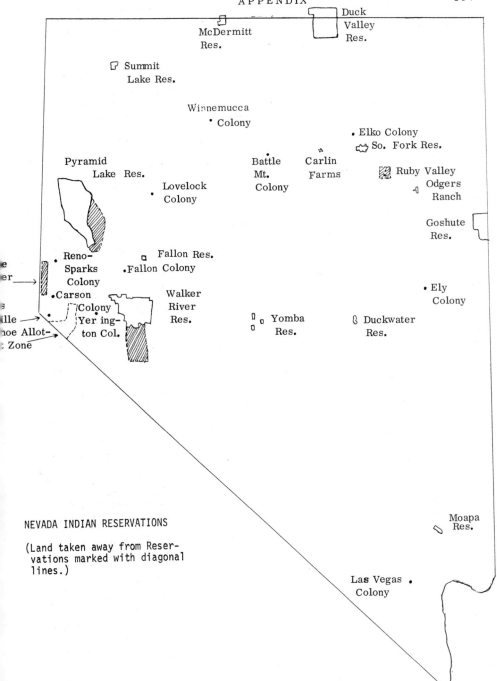

McDermitt
Res.

Duck
Valley
Res.

Summit
Lake Res.

Winnemucca
• Colony

• Elko Colony
So. Fork Res.

Pyramid
Lake Res.

Battle   Carlin
Mt.   Farms
Colony

Ruby Valley

Odgers
Ranch

Lovelock
Colony

Goshute
Res.

Reno-
Sparks
Colony
•Carson
Colony
Yer ing-
ton Col.

Fallon Res.
•Fallon Colony

Walker
River
Res.

Yomba
Res.

Duckwater
Res.

• Ely
Colony

NEVADA INDIAN RESERVATIONS

(Land taken away from Reservations marked with diagonal
lines.)

Moapa
Res.

Las Vegas •
Colony

INDEX

(NOTE: Please study carefully the map of the Indian linguistic groupings in California that is shown on page 189 of this book and the accompanying key to the meanings of the numbers shown. Also study the map of linguistic groupings and bands found in Nevada shown on page 197. Many Indian groupings not found in this index will be found on these two maps. Obviously in a book of this size not all Indian groupings in the two states can be discussed.)